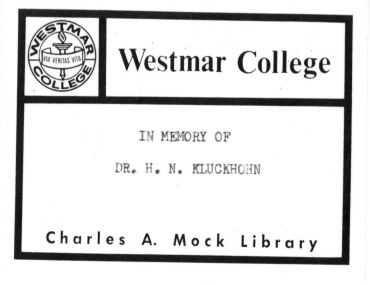

Language – The Loaded Weapon

Language – The Loaded Weapon

The use and abuse of language today

Dwight Bolinger

Longman
London and New York

To the memory of beloved Ruth

Longman Group Limited London

*Associated companies, branches and representatives
throughout the world*

*Published in the United States of America
by Longman Inc., New York*

© Longman Group Limited 1980

First published 1980

British Library Cataloguing in Publication Data

Bolinger, Dwight
   Language, the loaded weapon
   1. Sociolinguistics
   I. Title
   301.2′1   P40   80–40301

   ISBN 0–582–29107–0
   ISBN 0–582–29108–9 Pbk

Set in 10/11pt Comp/Set Times Roman
Printed in Great Britain by
McCorquodale (Newton) Ltd., Newton-le-Willows, Lancashire

Contents

Acknowledgments

My first thanks are to the person who encouraged this project when it was less than a glimmer, and who nursed it along as it grew: Peggy Drinkwater, Longman's editor for linguistics until her retirement (with the manuscript still in her hands) in 1979.

I thank the several readers who steered me away from certain quicksands: Geoffrey Leech, who read the manuscript for Longman, and William Howarth, Terence Langendoen, and James Sledd, who read it for Princeton University Press.

I thank my artist friend Shirley Ortiz for her suggestions and encouragement.

I thank all those who took the trouble to provide me with material, especially Walter M. Brasch for quotations from William Smith and Bayard Rustin; Carol N. Brown of the *Saturday Evening Post* for copies of the Curtis Code; the Miami *Herald* for material on George Smathers; Randy Riddle of KCBS San Francisco for comments on his interview with William E. Colby; and Alan Simpson for the text of his 'Liberal Education in a University'.

I thank those several scholars, too many to name, whose unpublished works were referred to and who kept me up to date on the progress of publication.

We are grateful to the following for permission to reproduce copyright material:

Harper and Row Publishers Inc for extracts from *Simple and Direct: A Rhetoric For Writers* by Jacques Barzun Copyright © 1975 by Jacques Barzun. Reprinted by permission of Harper and Row Publishers Inc; the author, Sydney W. Riser for an extract from her letter published in *Palo Alto Times* 17 November 1978 (now known as *Peninsula Times Tribune*); the author, John Simon for extracts from the Dick Cavett Show on Public Television USA 11–12 January 1978.

Preface

In this century there has been one – perhaps only one – upsurge of popular interest in how language affects our lives. It began with the publication of Alfred Korzybski's *Science and Sanity* (1933) – or, rather, with the popularizations of his work that appeared a few years later. Korzybski was a Polish-born scientist and philosopher whose interest in the continuity of culture led him to a study of the means of culture-transmission in modern society, which of course is language first of all. His laboratory was the failures of transmission, which he investigated in psychiatric patients. He was a pathologist of language; he probed the sane and insane ways of speaking and understanding, and the social ills that result from certain forms of linguistic insanity, by no means confined to psychiatric wards. He not only observed but prescribed: his system of 'General Semantics' embodied a training in linguistic hygiene.

Korzybski's best-known disciples were Stuart Chase and Samuel Hayakawa. Chase was an economist who spent two years wrestling with the formidable prose of *Science and Sanity* before bringing out his *Tyranny of Words* in 1938, a down-to-earth version of General Semantics that for a time enjoyed enormous popularity. Hayakawa's *Language in Action* (now *Language in Thought and Action*) was a Book-of-the-Month Club selection when it first appeared in 1941. Much of the excitement generated by these two books and other popularizations was due to the flood of propaganda from both sides in the Second World War, whose rumblings coincided with the appearance of Korzybski's work. The public was being lied to and knew it, and there was keen interest in ways of detecting the deceptions. In America a number of well-known figures, including Clyde Beals, W. H. Kilpatrick, Paul Douglas (later Senator from Illinois), and Robert Lynd, established an Institute of Propaganda Analysis. But the excitement soon died. By the end of 1941 the country was too busy generating propaganda to spend much time analyzing it. One of the echoes from that time is the still current use of the word *semantics* to mean verbal pettifogging – now joined by *rhetoric* in a similar sense (extended from an older unfavorable meaning, 'ostentatious language'). In the schools the ideas have been kept alive by Hayakawa's book, which has remained a favorite. Among linguistic scholars General Semantics was never highly regarded, partly because of its therapeutic claims and the fact that Korzybski became a sort of cult figure, and partly because of a shortness of vision in linguistics itself at the time.

But there was also a weakness that General Semantics shares with nearly all the writings about language as a manipulator of minds and emotions: they seldom dig below the meanings of individual words. Korzybski wanted to make everyone aware of the conflict between nature in flux and the deceptive stability of words. Labels persist: one can permanently criminalize a man or a woman by viewing the person as a unitary individual. Is George in 1981 the same George as the George of 1970, who stole a car for a joyride? The way to escape this kind of false equation is to index him: George $_{1970}$ and George $_{1981}$. Maybe he is the same, maybe not. There is no denying the importance of this kind of critique, but it sees only the bumps on the landscape. The underground streams, the buried strata, the fossils, the faults, and the veins of ore – the grammar as a whole and even the broader semantics of the words – all too often go unexamined. No slight was intended, but as the professional linguists of Korzybski's day in America were not much interested in meaning, much less therapeutics, the General Semanticists had no scientific body of information about language to draw upon. Circumstances have changed, and we are in a better position now to take up where they left off.

Though it got very little attention at the time, and none from the public, the work of two American linguists, Edward Sapir and Benjamin Lee Whorf, adopting a philosophy like that of the German linguist Wilhelm von Humboldt a century earlier, did venture into the relationships between language and thinking, on the premise that every language has a structure that must somehow influence the way its speakers view the world. Is a language that has few or no adjectives correspondingly weak in notions of detachable qualities? Is a language rich in verbs correspondingly strong in its concepts of processes as against things – which would agree better with modern physics than the noun-heavy languages of Western Europe? Whorf compared English with the language of the Hopi Indians, and believed that such differences in conceptualization exist.

Very likely they do, though linguists have hardly pursued this question beyond where Whorf left it, and some have been skeptical of the whole idea, arguing that translators have always been able to find ways of expressing even the most complex ideas in whatever language. The focus at present is on painting with a wider brush on a broader canvas. Linguists are more inclined to play down the differences between languages and look for the traits they have in common. They feel that the shared inheritance of humanity is more apt to make us think alike and use similar means of expression for all the important things. The differences, radical as they may seem, represent only the materials that particular societies have found available, handed down to them by their culture, to convey the gamut of shared human wants, interests, fears, pleasures, and concerns, with differences of no more real importance than that between the use of wood to build shelters by forest-dwellers and the use of adobe by the inhabitants of the desert. It will hardly do to assume that speakers of Chinese are telegraphic in their thinking just because a literal translation from the Chinese sounds a bit like a telegram. What happens to the rogues and victims of English happens or can happen to their counterparts in every other language in the world.

This is the assumption that underlies the pages ahead, and if it is correct, then the influences of language on thinking and behavior must be everywhere pretty much the same. The manifestations will reflect social differences more than fundamental linguistic ones. If a society lacks a complex bureaucracy, then the sort of language that bureaucrats adopt for self-identification and self-protection will not develop; but the seeds of it will be there and might perhaps be found in the incantations of a priesthood. Verbal domains that pertain to science will be absent in non-technical societies; but if there is an invasion of technology the terms and expressions will accompany it and swiftly adapt themselves to the existing linguistic structure. The marvelous thing is that every language has the CAPACITY to take the form that its users require. But it also, through its existing form, helps to shape the requirements – and that is the theme of this book.

Dwight Bolinger
Palo Alto
1980

What I think we are going to have to do is talk about language enough so that people bring language out of the closet; you know, we push it back. You can talk about a lot of other things much more comfortably than you can talk about language.

Professor Roy C. Hudson, '*Standard English: An Ambivalent Comment'* *(address at Conference on Money, Power, and Language, Hattiesburg, Miss, 16 October 1976)*

Chapter 1

Lo the shaman

The Average Citizen is of two minds about health. If a symptom can be suppressed by a pill, poultice, powder, or potion, he repairs to his medicine shelf. He will take psychic or dietary advice from quacks, have his spine adjusted by a chiropractor, go on a banana diet or on liquid protein, even get religion for its salutary benefits. But 'when symptoms persist' (as the label on the patent medicine bottle warns), or when the real thing strikes – tumor, gall-stones, heart seizure, appendicitis – nothing can stop him on his way to the nearest practitioner with a bona fide MD degree. And meanwhile he accepts, in the upper layers of his mind, the censure that the MD aims at his laxatives and liver pills even as he continues to use them. He knows a prescription from a proprietary, though he can't quite shake his belief in over-the-counter miracles (which usually come cheaper anyway).

In language there are no licensed practitioners, but the woods are full of midwives, herbalists, colonic irrigationists, bonesetters, and general-purpose witch doctors, some abysmally ignorant, others with a rich fund of practical knowledge – whom we shall lump together and call SHAMANS. They require our attention not only because they fill a lack but because they are almost the only people who make the news when language begins to cause trouble and someone must answer the cry for help. Sometimes their advice is sound. Sometimes it is worthless, but still it is sought because no one knows where else to turn. We are living in an African village and Albert Schweitzer has not arrived yet. When he comes, he will respect the shamans whose medical skills his will surpass but never entirely supplant. Meanwhile we had best prepare the way by showing that a medicine beyond verbal shamanism is an aching need. This calls for getting acquainted with the shamanite art and a typical few of its practitioners.

Verbal and herbal, the shamans have this in common: they have husbanded, toiled at, and elaborated on an inherited art. The verbal shaman is usually a writer, who has done more with his inheritance of language than use it to write letters and bills of lading. He has studied the tricks and invented a few. He has learned the words, and is impatient with people who from ignorance or mischief make up new words when old ones will serve. He has sifted out the loose parts and sanded the ill-fitting edges, to turn his language into an instrument that will do his bidding. In short, he is an expert, or at least a specialist, in the resources of his language, self-conscious about as much of it as he has consciously practiced, which includes all of those things that make up the infusion of past and present in the literary artist: a jeweler's precision with words and meanings, a delicate sense of how much is enough, and sufficient detachment to see his writing from the viewpoint of a reader or critic and most of the time avoid offending either.

The ills the shaman-artist equips himself to treat are the ones affecting not intellectual or ethical content but EXPRESSION. When he confronts the flood of speech and writing turned out by amateurs, the shaman quickly concludes that:

First, the craft is not being learned. Johnny can't read. Applicants are turned away from jobs because they can't write an intelligible or even a legible letter. Schools are graduating 'functional illiterates'. SAT (Scholastical Aptitude Test) scores are falling, and unless we get 'back to basics' and do something about the sloppy teaching of English, the next generation will not be able to spell its name.

Second, the medium of the craft is in peril. The language is being corrupted. As one more optimistic shaman puts it, even as he dismisses the danger of imminent collapse, 'a great language does not fold; instead it slowly rots'.

The shaman's answer is that of the faith healer – to take the revivalist trail. But why does the public flock to him? Because having helped to inspire the fear of the devil, he offers redemption. Because good language, as much as a good appearance – good clothes and good health – is one of the things that open the doors to advancement in our middle class world. The person bent on moving up – into a better job, into a higher circle – is afraid of making mistakes that will betray his origin. He needs someone who can catalog mistakes and prescribe remedies. Not a whole education in a new kind of behavior, for that would be too hard for the busy employers and other wardens of higher status to judge. Rather, a list of SPECIFIC mistakes that can be avoided if you are alert to them and machine-scored if you are not. This suits the shaman to a T. He graduates himself as an authority in spelling, punctuation, grammar, and style. He compiles dictionaries and writes manuals of correct usage, with common errors listed from Acronym to Zeugma. He is the Emily and Elizabeth Post of linguistic etiquette.

But – slow down a minute. Surely, this is an exaggeration? There must be more objective standards than that, if shamans as a class are not to expose themselves as downright quacks. Indeed there are, and in Britain at least the revivalist tone is muted and we find such respected scholar-shamans as H. W. Fowler and Sir Ernest Gowers, who give the kind of advice that no budding writer can afford to do without. In America, the evangelical background supports greater extremes. Sins are quickly spotted and remedies as quickly prescribed. More people are on the make, so there is no lack of pupils eager to be shown the light.

Revivalism comes in waves, and we are on the crest of one now – why, in Chapter 6. For the moment, to understand shamanism in its magical form, we must turn to the American species, and pass a few of its specimens in review.

Shamans W, X, Y, and Z are living and thriving practitioners of the art. So is Aristides, whose cape of pseudonymy renders the cloak of anonymity superfluous. Here is a brief look at their professions and their chief concerns:

W is a film and drama critic with a popular magazine, who till 1980 ran a regular column on language. For him, the worst thing happening to English is the condoning of non-standard speech used by particular social or ethnic groups. People who take it seriously he believes are guilty of 'a benighted and despicable catering to mass ignorance'. Speaking of the expressions *I be*, *you be*, *he be* in the English of Black Americans, he writes,

> [T]hese may indeed be comprehensible, but they go against all accepted classical and modern grammars and are the product not of a language with roots in tradition but of ignorance of how language works.

Perhaps this seems like a fair judgment, but a linguist would counter that every language and every dialect has a tradition – language by definition IS a tradition, for otherwise we could not understand one another – and would add that ignorance of how language works has no more to do with the fact that it works than ignorance of digestion causes dyspepsia. And he would say that it is not only possible but highly revealing to describe the use of *be* in Black English – it makes a distinction that standard English lacks.[1]

W is frank about his patrician tastes:

> [A]bove all, language is not just a matter of communication. It is a way of expressing one's fastidiousness, elegance, and imaginative-ness; it is also a way of displaying one's control over a medium, just as a fine horseman displays his horsemanship by the way he sits in the saddle and handles his horse.

No one would quarrel with imaginativeness, which is not the property of any class or dialect. But fastidiousness and elegance are for fastidious and elegant occasions; certainly these happen, but (a linguist would say) skill in them comes after skill in getting one's message across.

In common with most other shamans, W is quickly aroused when he hears such things as *he don't* for *he doesn't*, *different than* for *different from*, and pronouns without proper antecedents.

X is a well-known newsman who works for a radio and television network. He too has strong feelings about language, but they are directed mostly at marshmallow prose. He despises the triteness of politics and diplomacy (*eyeball to eyeball*, *adversary relationship*, *ongoing dialog, these United States*), the clichés of journalism (*ailing* premier, *left-leaning dictator, posh headquarters, globe-trotting diplomat*), the general pushing of empty words (confidence *factor*, play *situation*, head wind *components*), and the inflated language of advertisers and social scientists (*pre-owned car, consistent growth pattern, pursuant days, interdisciplinary process approach*). He worries a bit, too, about such things as *hopefully, to impact,* and *comprised of* for *composed of,* but less so than W, who regards inflated language as less reprehensible than misusing *lay* for *lie.*

Y is a dictionary editor, writer of a syndicated column on language, and co-author of a book on usage. His book is dedicated to a poet and playwright from whom he quotes the following declaration of the shaman's calling and faith:

> As a poet, there is only one political duty and that is to defend one's language from corruption. And that is particularly serious now. It is being corrupted. When it is corrupted, people lose faith in what they hear, and that leads to violence.

Y has been one of the leaders in the crusade against the Merriam Webster *Third New International Dictionary,* which dared to stop calling itself the Supreme Authority (as its predecessors had done) and made an honest effort to set down the words of the English language without asking for pedigrees. Though Y counsels tolerance, at least in speech, toward many things that other shamans can't abide, the entries in his book show the kinds of questions he deems important: Is a singular verb all right with *data* (The data *has* been collected)? Is *more perfect* acceptable? Should the *a* be allowed in *kind of a*? Must one avoid *due to* for *because of*? Is *their* all right to refer to *everyone* (*Everyone* should take *their* seats)? All are questions that have to do with whether the individual tiles can pass inspection, not with how the mosaic is put together or what it means.

Z is a consultant on language with one of the national press associations, and is the author of a popular book on reading and another on style. He is probably the most influential shaman in America, with clients in journalism, education, and government. His best contribution has been persuading writers to avoid pomposity and wordiness, and explaining how. But when he settles down to making a compendium of do's and don't's, his advice sounds very much like that of his fellow-shamans: *all of* should be reduced to *all* (this would give us *Will you settle for part of it? – No, I want all it*),[2] *in* should be avoided in the sense of *into* (which would force us to say *Don't run into here with those muddy shoes*), *which* should be changed to *that* in relative clauses wherever possible (*the house which he bought, the house that he bought*), and so on.

Aristides is a magazine writer who leaves his own name behind as ritual shamans ceremonially leave their bodies. He deserves a place here mainly because he expresses in one sentence the confusion between form and substance that besets all shamans: 'Bad language has, of course, always been with us: language meant to obscure, to deceive, to defraud.' This comes in the context of censuring a supplement to the Merriam *Third* for its continued hospitality toward lowbrow and middlebrow usage. It confuses two kinds of badness: language meant to obscure, deceive, and defraud is not usually 'bad' language of the sort condemned by Aristides – such things as *lifestyle, putting it all together, citizen input*. Rather it is most often the language of those 'who couch their nefarious thoughts in the very sort of eloquence Aristides probably admires'.[3]

For all his sensitivity to correctness and his good advice in some particulars, the shaman fails us by not grasping the whole problem and by oversimplifying the part he does grasp. What are we trying to save the English-speaking world from – mistakes in grammar and individual word choice, speech or writing that fails through ineptness to communicate its intent, speech or writing used as a refuge FROM communication, or the kinds of language (or non-language) designed, like the Barnum and Bailey sign *This Way to the Egress*, to lead the circus-goers out of the tent when they would rather stay and look around some more? Only the last two questions have an ethical side, and the shaman speaks almost exclusively of the first two (sometimes of the third, but usually in terms of the second), yet he regards his judgments as ethical ones.

Shamanism is at its best in dealing with the problems of effective communication; in this, shamans and linguists can join forces (see Chapter 14). But the average shaman pays more attention to the ill-chosen word and the grammatical error, and looks for quickie remedies to deal with them. If students can learn to write well by studying manuals of errors then the arduous person-to-person tutoring of hand and mind will be unnecessary, classes can go from ten to fifty, no programs will be needed to retrain semi-literate teachers who serve as models for language even when they do not teach it, and tax monies can be released for other purposes. And would-be self-improvers among adults need only keep one eye on the checklist to produce an acceptable composition.

It is in the nature of language for any set list of errors to be trivial. No two shamans agree on what ought to be listed. In a survey of opinions on usage set forth in nineteen dictionaries and usage books, Thomas J. Creswell described the task as 'the orderly documentation of chaos'; except for very small sets of items in just a few of the books, there was no consistency at all.[4] Besides, for every abuse that is listed a dozen more already exist and more appear every day, while others cure themselves. Making the right choices, like protecting freedom, demands eternal vigilance. Every new challenge puts all the resources of the communicator to the test, and most solutions belong to the occasion.

The list is trivial by being a list, and the typical entry is trivial in itself. Most verbal shamans are as uninformed about linguistic structure as their herbal counterparts are about anatomy and physiology. Here is a sentence from Shaman X:

> Some of the most impassioned letters [inspired by his book] have come from people who were not born in the United States, who worked hard to learn English and to use it well, and who were puzzled and pained by the language's decline.

The *language's* decline? Take the sentence *The important thing is the soup's consistency,* try replacing *soup* with *porridge, mush,* or *toast,* and see if you like the result. The scapegoat-hunter, pursuing his quarry over the crags of Jargoslurvia, has not been taught to listen for grinding sibilants with the possessive, where they are unnecessary; *of* is always available. That is a matter of structure, not of simple word-choice. So is the system of modal auxiliaries in English, now undergoing a wholesale reorganization. *May* and *might* are being redefined, the past is taking over the functions of the pluperfect in unreal conditions (*If I knew it I would have waited* instead of *If I had known it I would have waited*) – right under the shaman's nose.

The symptoms may even be a sign of health rather than illness. Take the last-ditch stand of another shaman against 'misplaced *only*': 'To me,' he says, 'it remains nastily and obviously wrong. To say *He only died a week ago* is . . . to suggest that all sorts of things more important could have happened to him; the rule is simple – that *only* stands immediately before the word or phrase that it modifies.' Shaman Y recognizes that this cause is hopeless, and embraces 'misplaced *only*' as 'a perfectly acceptable part of the American idiom'. But 'idiom' has nothing to do with it. Both canonizer and exorcist assume that word order is the only way of showing what goes with what. They overlook intonation: *He only died a WEEK ago* leaves no doubt that *only* goes primarily with *week.* The language is more subtle even than that – by giving freedom of movement to *only,* it enables the word to do double duty. Y gives as one of his reasons for acceptance the 'fussily over-precise' effect of saying *I want only orange juice,* failing to notice that it is not the overprecise language that is objectionable but the overprecise demand. The sentence *I only want orange juice* not only limits the choice to orange juice but tones down the demand – 'That is the extent of my want, you don't need to give me anything else.' To understand language, one must see things in their relationships. *Only* has to be compared with other 'misplacings' – the word *just,* for example: *I just want ten* is awkward when *just* follows *want,* and *I just want to see* becomes almost impossible as *I want just to see.*

More than linguistically trivial, list and entries alike are trivial in a practical sense. The same number of muggers would leap out of the dark if everyone conformed overnight to every prescriptive rule ever written. The lightweight shaman is just right enough in small matters to convince the ignorant that he is right in large ones. There ARE words and phrases whose very existence symptomatizes, for a time, something out of joint in our society. But there are just as many fully respectable words and constructions that are used daily to 'obscure, deceive, and defraud'. It is important to identify them – the concealed weapons as well as those worn on the hip – and to examine how some people use them to get the better of others.

Even so, what is trivial linguistically and practically may be elevated to importance socially. Some people are more disturbed by a fork placed on the wrong side of the plate than by a fork tines-up on the seat of a chair; and all of us are liable at times to be distracted by violations of the code that have been heavily advertised. Here the shaman performs a service – a bit after the fashion of a fireman who makes himself necessary by setting a fire (since the shamans are among the advertisers),[5] but still a service. There is an etiquette of giving the right signals at the right time to the right person. Some signals offend because they miscue. Others offend because they offend – if we know that our hearer or reader dislikes an expression such as *hadn't ought*, courtesy may demand that we avoid it, as we avoid loud conversation and black cigars in the vicinity of sensitive people. The editor who threatens his reporters with extinction if they insist on writing *transpire* for *happen* or describing everything agreeable as *exciting* is doing what he is paid to do. The harm comes in promoting local preferences into a universal code of ethics. Besides, most ills of the language are not noticed until it is too late to do anything about them. We have no techniques of early detection before they metastasize. And when they do, they are mostly rendered harmless by the body's protective mechanisms. Aristides objects to *putting it all together* because the expression is vague; but *putting things straight* is just as vague, and would not have triggered his mental alarms because he is used to it. As one of the wiser shamans has observed, 'In usage I accept what I have come to accept and reject what I don't accept. It is that subjective.' Rejections become a matter of tradition – many of the same 'errors' that shamans pursue today were already on the condemned list published by George Campbell in 1776, which leads the editor of *American Speech*, John Algeo, to wonder 'whether to rejoice over the fidelity of our concerns after two hundred years or to lament that we seem to have made so little progress toward a more immaculate state of the language'.[6]

Shamans should get together with linguists, but BRINGING them together will not be easy. One reason is that there exists as yet no branch of linguistics that quite compares with medicine as an applied field. Many investigative sciences converge on the treatment of disease – neurology, pharmacology, biology, radiology, psychology – and medical practice, with its enormous advances in our century, draws from all of them. Linguistics is an amalgam of sciences – phonology (the study of speech sound), morphology (the study of word forms and their parts), syntax (the study of arrangement), plus more recent specializations whose names testify to a greater involvement with society: sociolinguistics, psycholinguistics, developmental linguistics (the study of child language) – but a synthesis like that of medicine is yet to come. For now, we can only try to persuade the shaman that there exist the makings of a better medicine than the one he dispenses.

A more serious impediment to cooperation is that professional linguists have for a long time been in trouble with the shamans. At first this was because they were too academic, too lifeless and dry-as-dust. They got this reputation because for a century they studied literary texts not for the message or quality of style but as evidence – of etymologies, grammatical forms, and historical change. Now they are criticized because they are not academic enough. Linguistics has outgrown philology – the study of texts – and one of its discoveries is the incredible diversity and ingenuity of language everywhere that have caused many linguists to repudiate value judgments about anyone's form of speech (see Chapter 6) – this, for the shaman, amounts to a value judgment in itself: ignorant Hottentots are being credited with the same linguistic subtlety as educated Europeans. (Not the same philosophical or metaphysical subtlety, necessarily, for that resides in how language is USED, not in how it is constituted.) The change began when linguists started to look at languages distant from their own and realized how bigoted they had been about the superiority of the peoples and cultures of Western Europe. Fieldwork became the rule, in South America, Africa, the Western Pacific, and in the byways of their own lands – in the United States, for example, on Indian reservations. After anthropology and the study of languages remote in space and structure, came sociology and the study of dialects – or VARIETIES, as they are called by those who would rather avoid the suggestion of quaintness or inferiority.

All of this was an antidote to smugness. Today's linguist is suspicious of any form of authoritarianism. As a scientist he recognizes it as an inevitable reaction to change – self-protection, actually, on the part of older users of the language; but he denies the rationalizations, the claims that logic, correctness, and elegance inhere in the shallow layers of language where the shaman takes his stand. Logic and elegance are desirable, but they are cognitive skills that have little or nothing to do with whether one says *He doesn't know any better* or *He don't know no better*.

Naturally such upstart 'permissiveness' has not endeared linguists to shamans. Worst offended have been the shaman-educators, for they have felt betrayed by the linguists down the hall. Most linguists are in the colleges, for lack of steady employment elsewhere, and they tend to be friendly with non-literary types such as mathematicians, computer specialists, psychologists, and logicians, well-known users of impenetrable jargon, not noted for their tact. Linguists gave themselves a reputation some years ago that they have not been able to live down. It is epitomized in the title of a book published in 1950 by Robert A. Hall, Jr, *Leave Your Language Alone* (a very useful volume, later prudently renamed *Linguistics and Your Language*).[7] The resulting stereotype was that of a person steeped in linguistese, opinionated, anti-humanitarian, and a meddler in serious matters that do not concern him, especially the teaching of English (or French or German – pick any language with a literary tradition). The linguist, as far as the shaman-educator is concerned, is a person for whom 'anything goes', who has influenced the makers of dictionaries to adopt their policy of 'open admissions' and coaxed the government, with his pretense of being scientific, into spending millions on revisions in language arts teaching that have led to lower and lower rates of literacy. (Linguists don't really have this much power, and most of the guilt is by association.) Linguistic writing, much of it, does nothing to dispel the illusion, even for those who know their way in the field. But in this, linguistics is no different from the other social sciences, where sounding impressive too often passes for deep thought.

Somehow the two camps must be brought to council, given the peace pipe, and told to learn from each other. Beyond good manners, effective and honest communication calls for skills that no avoiding of catalogued errors – no program of avoidance at all – can begin to touch. The sharing of thoughts, feelings, and aspirations is all that makes human relationships possible, and nothing that can be learned from the study of language is so remote as to bear no relationship to it.

So in the pages ahead we take the linguist's view, to learn what we can about the nature of language. After that we bring the shaman back, and invite him to pick what he needs. And finally invite society to do the same.

Chapter 2

The nonverbal womb

What has made humanity the most dreadfully successful species of animal on earth? Simply that human beings learned how to carry their environment with them. When the climate was no longer warm, clothing kept out the cold. In the absence of natural caves for shelter, artificial ones were contrived of walls and roofs, or of stretched skins. When game was hard to find, animals were bred domestically. When legs did not serve to pass over a sea, floating craft supported them. To keep HIS environment hospitable to him, man has made THE environment his own, modifying it to the point that a city-bred child rarely sees anything that has not been arranged at least partly by human hands.

We know now that the blessing of a man-made and man-molded environment can also be a curse. When there is no more of nature to conquer, when everything in the world bears the stamp of human interference, the human needs that were supplied by air, water, earth, and the organisms that feed on them, each with its own requirements for existence or stability, can no longer be satisfied. The re-made environment turns hostile.

But that is a theme for another day. It touches the story of this book in one way: how the vast enterprise of turning our world into a machine that spins for human comfort was made possible by man's capacity for symbolism, interwoven with every thought and object but compacted with all the power of man's intellectuality in the computer-like program that we call language.

Every act that every human adult performs communicates. Within hours of birth, a human infant is already responding to the rhythms of the mother's speech, in 'a dance-like sharing of microbody motion'.[1] Even involuntary acts communicate. They are symptoms. And they are modified in significant ways – a sneeze may be unavoidable, but the manner of it betrays attitudes of hygiene, courtesy, or self-restraint. When the act exists BECAUSE it communicates, it becomes symbolic – a handshake for friendship or frankness, a bow for deference or submission, an affected sob to evoke sympathy or pity. And when the symbol ceases to look or sound like what it symbolizes, it becomes a sign. Language is our most complex system of signs – an intricate structure of words and relationships that interpenetrates our world so thoroughly that nothing 'out there' can be disentangled from it. To understand language as in large part the mirror of the world and the world as in large part the creature of language we must look at how this marvelous instrument is put together and how it works.

The common-sense view is that language is a collection of words. The educated common-sense view is that it also contains rules for putting words together – a dictionary lists the words, a grammar states the rules. This impression comes from our formal schooling which emphasizes 'letters' – it is so important to learn to read and write that listening to a live voice in a live setting hardly seems a proper way to study language. But building a description by starting with words and grammar is moving in the wrong direction, from inside out; for true understanding one must go from the outside in. Language is the most intensified part, but still only the inner part, of an enveloping scheme of communicative behavior.

Eye contact, head movements, gestures with the arms and hands, posture, facial expression, distance from another speaker, noises such as clearing the throat, loudness and softness, high pitch and low pitch, the real or pretended quaver that accompanies emotion – all communicate singly, together, and in concert with language. The live voice, insists the Hungarian linguist Ivan Fónagy, is a world apart from the printed page.[2] Every spoken word or phrase conveys meanings that are not present in the words: anger, affection, inquiry, displeasure, reassurance, uncertainty, restraint, haughtiness, submission, authority – 'moods' and 'emotions' which have to be signaled and detected if people are to know how to deal with one another. Even many of our 'out of control' signals are largely controlled, systematized, and ritualized – utterances such as *oops, ouch, wow, a-a-ah, oh-oh, yipes, whee* pretend to be expressions of our inner states, but are fully managed to keep the proper adjustments between the speaker's behavior and the hearer's expectations within a particular setting. We do not say *ouch* to accompany the sensation of pain, but immediately afterward, to imply 'that went too far' or 'this has gone far enough' (we'd better look out next time, your price is too high, go easy with that dental drill, etc).[3] Some nonverbal messages are so necessary to language that they must be included in descriptions of it. Loudness or a sudden change in pitch is called ACCENT when used to make part of a sentence stand out;

> JOHN
> did it.

It is our FEELING for the importance of John that causes us to highlight his name in this sentence; but without the highlighting the special meaning would be lost – it was John, not someone else, who did it. Similarly, the undulations of pitch are called INTONATION when they assist in interpreting the grammar of a sentence. When one is 'through' speaking, the normal thing is to relax, and untensing the vocal cords is part of the relaxation; but the effect is that the pitch goes down – and falling pitch thus becomes one of the signals for the end of a sentence. Contrariwise, a question that awaits an answer is something that tends to key us up – and one of the signals of asking is a high or rising pitch. Here are some other more or less automatic or unconscious acts that help to package our words and sentences:

It is normal to	*Therefore*
inhale rapidly, or clear the throat, before starting to speak	rapid inhalation or clearing the throat = 'I am about to speak'
leave the mouth open for wonderment	mouth open = question
raise the eyebrows for surprise	raised eyebrows = surprised or expectant question
establish eye contact for appeal	eye contact = request
bow the head in submission	bowing of the head and/or a 'bowing' (falling-rising) pitch = courtesy
make an aggressive move with head or fist to assert oneself	a downward jabbling motion of the head and/or a thump of the fist = assertion, emphasis

Without actually hearing what a speaker is saying, one can tell the points of greatest emphasis by observing the thrust of the jaw or the karate cut (ending in mid-air) or the thump of the fist (if a solid object is handy).

```
          NOT    MIT          HAVE
I will         per     him to be
                               like that!
```

These 'natural' acts may be codified differently in different societies, but usually some direct meaning can be associated with them. Other acts may be equally important as accompaniments of language, though not tied closely to particular things in grammar. An undulating movement of the head often simply imitates the undulations of pitch. In the following, notice how easy it is to make your head do what the pitch does – and how hard to make it do the opposite:

```
    Don't
        be
            d!
        SA
```

Or take finger-wagging and head-shaking: if English had as clear and formal a way of marking warnings as it has of marking questions (*Did he go?* opposed to *He went*), those gestures would fit the grammar of warnings as tightly as raised eyebrows and open mouth now fit the grammar of questions. The right gesture relieves the grammar of having to distinguish warnings from statements (*I wouldn't do that* can be either, depending on gesture).

To see how important the unspoken acts are to the spoken ones, the reader may test the 'mood' of the following (in caps) by observing the rise and fall of pitch, the bright or solemn expression of the face, the eye focus of the speaker (is it on the hearer or not?), and the motion of the head (toward the hearer or not?). The expressions appear to 'mean the same', but do they, actually? (It is possible to say anything stony-faced; the idea here is to notice the LIKELY differences, exaggerating them if necessary.)

1a IT HAS NO PURPOSE.
1b IT DOESN'T HAVE ANY PURPOSE.
2a She said she would buy it and SHE BOUGHT IT.
2b She said she would buy it and BUY IT SHE DID.

(Suggestion: Is it easier to say the *a* sentences or the *b* sentences with raised eyebrows? with lowered intonation? Which is easier to say with head bobbing affirmatively, 2*a* or 2*b*? What is the effect of the extra syllables in 1*b* and 2*b* on the opportunities for extra accents?)

An act of language is like a skilled acrobatic rider controlling a high-strung, partly-tamed horse. When the mount does the rider's bidding, the two are a centaur – it is almost impossible to tell them apart. When the horse has his way, the rider may be thrown – if a look or a gesture or a body movement contradicts what a speaker says, the listener knows better than to believe the words. (Or to believe the gesture either if another gesture contradicts it: 'Applauding with a sarcastic grin on one's face is not the same thing as applauding with a cheer.')[4]

It would simplify matters – for the linguist who describes language – if one could think of the communicative resources beyond language as a reservoir from which devices are drawn and incorporated in language at its convenience. In reality, language is part of an all-encompassing system – it overlaps other parts of the system and is overlapped by them. Music is a subsystem as tightly integrated as language, and yet the two draw upon each other or share mutual traits in countless ways. One such way is the use of musical steady pitches to convey one of the messages that music regularly carries: 'This is something that can be repeated, something familiar, something everyone knows' (we listen many times to a familiar tune but grow bored or impatient if a fact we already know is repeated even once). Compare the following – the underlining marks pitches that are held steady for an appreciable amount of time:

How was I supposed to know? – I told you so.

I guess it's no good after all. – I told you so!

In the first, the gliding pitches are characteristic of answers to questions. In the second, the sustained pitches, especially the one on the last word, are used for relaying what is supposed to be known already. Children's taunting chants have the same sustention in addition to a steady beat – they are INTONED

                    a
  Susie   tat-tle
        is   tale!

So do adults' recitals of series of things to which they might add *you know:*

  I got up at <u>six,</u> I did the<u>laundry,</u> I got <u>breakfast,</u> I

  posted my<u>mail,</u>(you know, all the rigmarole I usually do) and then . . .

If this were spoken with an upglide,

                     ;x,
                    i
  I got up at ^s I did the laundry...

it would imply that the activities had something new or unexpected about them.[5]

Not only do all the schemes of music, movement, and language draw upon one another, but they are organized together in the grander schemes that represent the drama of life, the rituals that distinguish one culture from another and are the province of the anthropologist. They are the substance of our socialization, the web in which we are caught which constrains us to act in certain ways and makes our behavior more or less predictable – and social living possible. Or impossible for a few: the autistic child, for example, who cannot coordinate, either with each other or with the movements of his own body, the signals that come from external movement and sound – a withdrawn and lonely outsider to the complex social dance that makes human society seem rather like a hive of bees.[6] One's feeling of awkwardness when confronted with speakers of another language is only a part of the more general discomfort felt in the presence of attitudes, expressions, poses, gestures, approaches and withdrawals, inhalations and exhalations, with meanings different from those of one's own people, place, and time.

If spoken language is even today nurtured in a non-verbal womb of tones, stances, and movements which – unlike speech – are to some degree the common property of all animal life, one naturally wonders what this means for the past of language and for the possible sharing of communication with other species, particularly those closest in their evolution to human beings.

We are fairly sure now that the vocal apparatus that makes human speech possible is a relatively late development – perhaps one of the consequences of our upright posture. If, as seems likely, human or humanoid intelligence had developed far enough at an earlier period to imply the presence of a rather highly structured communication (which in turn became a factor in raising intelligence), then it would appear that human beings were 'talking' to one another without voices long before voices became articulate.[7] The obvious candidate as vehicle would have been gesture. The physical equipment was there, with highly mobile arms, wrists, hands, and facial muscles – and the tradition of using them actually comes down to us from the past, unbroken, even if somewhat crowded to one side. Gesture is still our first line of retreat when we try to make a speaker of another language understand us, and among the plains Indians it was a highly formalized system. Most importantly, the sign language of the deaf – in the US, *Ameslan*, or American Sign Language – turns out to be almost as rich in its resources as any spoken language – in fact, to differ significantly only in that its medium is visible rather than audible. It is not far-fetched to imagine, as many linguists now do, that in the ancient past there existed a gesture language that was more than an obbligato to speech – a developed system that was the primary means of communication, which then gradually shifted to speech as the vocal organs acquired a shape to make it possible, under the pressure of convenience and necessity: the hands were thereby freed for other labor and communicators no longer needed to be visible to one another. With a more stable food supply, a meal could be eaten quickly in a protected place and the mouth was free the rest of the time for talking.

As for what we may share with our primate cousins, the claims for language-like behavior as an exclusively human ability have been in steady retreat since the beginning of the 1970s. The chimpanzees Washoe, Moja, Tatu, and Dar have learned to use numerous simple signs and combinations of signs – with strong indications that many of the combinations are original 'sentences' – to communicate in Ameslan with their human native signers (deaf or the children of deaf parents) under the guidance of the psychologists Allen and Beatrice Gardner.[8] A young gorilla, Koko, has been similarly trained,[9] and a project with a baby orang-utan was begun in 1978. To keep language and all it implies an exclusively human preserve – if the optimistic view of these experiments is accepted – those for whom absolute human uniqueness is important have had to accept a constantly shrinking definition. First, it was conceded that the chimps might learn a few signs, but would never be able to transfer them to new meanings. After Washoe disproved that assumption, it was allowed that she was a clever ape but of course would never be able to put two signs together to form a complex sign. That hurdle too was passed, and then it was argued that while a chimp might communicate in sentences about the here and now, the past and future (language DISPLACEMENT) would still be beyond reach. That barrier too appears to have fallen. But a more conservative – perhaps too conservative – interpretation of the experiments disputes the apes' originality and views them as more cunning than intelligent – possibly they pick up subtle cues from their trainers (as the famous horse Clever Hans did) which suggest some desired request or response that is then given by imitation.[10] Still, the critics themselves concede that 'Even if apes can only learn a couple of hundred words and can use them only to communicate simple wants, their achievement is staggering. Twenty years ago we thought all they could do was hoot'.[11] Whatever their achievements in sign language, the apes will never be able to talk – or, rather, the experiment of teaching more than rudimentary sounds would not be worth the effort – not necessarily for lack of mental ability but of physical equipment, which is like the human inability to fly unaided because of the lack of wings.

The significance of language as an experience we share with other creatures should not be viewed as a denigration of humanity but as an exaltation of life. It manifests the highest form of intelligence because it is a form that gives shape to intelligence. Its attainment has taken millions of years of step-by-step advancement and painful selection, and in that sense it is unique. But it can never be separated from its past.

Chapter 3

Signs and symbols

Only a few years ago, little was known about the parts of the communicative network that are not properly linguistic – kinesics (communicative movement) and proxemics (the meaningful use of space) are new fields. But the structure of language has aroused man's curiosity for all recorded time. The reason? – because it is not obvious. Meeting a stranger, one can make a fair guess at the meanings of his gestures and facial expressions – much of this is biologically determined anyway, and some of it is shared by other species (a chimpanzee begs, rejects, comforts, and shows emotion in much the same way as a human being). Not much to stir the imagination here. But the codification of language creates a sort of mystery where guessing is of little use. Encounters between speakers of different languages have always been a sharp reminder that any two of them 'have different words for the same thing'. It is hard to explain this, but not hard to talk about it – a word can be looked at as a word, especially if it is the name of an object. Rules of grammar are harder to lay hold of, but Sanskrit had its grammarians many centuries BC, and the classical grammars of Greek and Latin have influenced all such studies since.

The codification is hard to penetrate because of its high degree of arbitrariness. There is nothing in the sound of the word *tree* that hints at its meaning. The arbitrariness goes still deeper: words are not the result of free-form speaking – like freehand drawing – but are put together from a limited set of sound units unique to every language. Words are 'digitized', like the faces that children draw by tracing lines through numbered points on a graph. Different faces can be evoked by tracing through different numbers – not exactly high art, but in language it doesn't matter so long as no two faces are the same. Language manages with comparatively few 'numbers' because it is allowed to repeat and use them in different orders. *Boy* and *girl* are distinguished by having different units, but repetitions and reorderings are what distinguish *dodo* from *do* (musical note), *redder* from *red*, and *mash* from *sham*. In writing, of course, letters take the place of distinctive sounds, and most writing systems relate letters to sounds rather closely. Writing thus connects with speech, and children who already know words by ear can learn to read and write them without having to memorize a completely separate system. (The separation is extreme in Chinese.)

The arbitrary units of communication can be of any kind – pebbles, chips, notches, sounds, letters, picture signs. Spelling in most languages is so conventionalized – a heaven of authority for the shaman – that doubts are easily settled by referring to a dictionary. But identifying the individual sounds requires a rather delicate analysis, and linguists sometimes disagree. All the same there is general agreement that every language has a limited number of phonemes, or distinctive sounds, any one of which may vary to some extent depending on neighboring sounds, speed of talking, and speech level (for example, a platform lecture versus a relaxed conversation). English has some 35 phonemes, about twice as many consonants as vowels. The vowels alone, for example, are what distinguish the words *seed, Sid, sade* ('to weary'), *said, sad, sod, sawed, sud, sowed, sood* (a variant of *soot*), and *sued.* Probably most Americans no longer distinguish between the vowels in *sod* and *sawed, popper* and *pauper, Otto* and *auto* – these speakers have simply lost a phoneme, and listeners look to the context to tell which word is meant. They do this much of the time anyway – it is hard work to listen with both ears, and half listening combined with half guessing will usually get us by (obviously *He was buried in a popper's grave* makes no sense, so the speaker must have meant *pauper's*).

The important thing is that in the two main systems – speech and writing – there are arbitrary units that when combined according to certain rules will represent all the thousands of words that make up the physical bulk of a language. Every complexly coded system requires such units. In the language of the deaf they are gestures, manifested by such things as hand configuration, direction of movement, and position relative to the body.

All this makes language sound very logical, as if it had started as a sort of contract in which speakers agreed to let certain sounds stand for certain things – just as two geometrists today have no trouble agreeing on some such proposition as 'Let *d* stand for the distance between point *P* and point *P'*; if we had to haggle over matters of this kind, logic and mathematics would be impossible. But language is not all that conventional and matter of fact. The logic of language carries us to the middle of the stream and drops us there. Arbitrary and conventional is a fitting description of distinctive sounds, less so of words, even less of sentences, and beyond that scarcely fits at all. The larger the scope, the looser and less arbitrary the structure. By digitizing the bottom layer into a tight system of signs, human communicators stumbled on a way to open the upper layers to more and more creative symbolism.

The difference between a sign and a symbol, says the anthropologist Victor Turner, is that 'in symbols there is always some kind of likeness (metaphoric/metonymic) . . .; in signs there need be no likeness'.[1] A sign is arbitrary, a symbol is not. Metaphoric symbols resemble what they symbolize – a line on paper for a street, a burning in effigy for a cremation alive, the sound *bow-wow* for the barking of a dog. A metonymic symbol is related to what it symbolizes not by resemblance but by contact – some kind of indirect association. *The pen is mightier than the sword* uses *pen* for 'writing' and *sword* for 'warfare'. *That happened before Pearl Harbor* uses *Pearl Harbor* for a date. Most signs were originally symbols, becoming signs as the original relationships began to fade. The letter *A*, from Greek *alpha* which was in turn from the Semitic *aleph*, originally represented the head of an ox; but as a letter of the alphabet it lost the useless metaphor.

The smaller the unit, the greater the arbitrariness, as a rule. The upward expansion of freedom – the transition from 'mere signs' to almost-pure symbols – can be seen by starting at the bottom and asking what remnants of symbolism are left in the otherwise arbitrary distinctive sounds. Some linguists feel that everything was symbolic, once on a time – the phonemes have evolved from meaningful sounds. In small and subtle ways, some of them still are, and to that extent are ICONIC; that is, their physical form resembles, and by that resemblance suggests, something in nature (or in our natures). Suppose you were asked to use *dreamt* in one of the following passages and *dreamed* in the other. How would you choose?

Visions came and went. Idly I ——, and as I lay
   dreaming I saw her face again.
Last night I —– I was back home in Michigan.

If you preferred *dreamed* in the first and *dreamt* in the second, you were probably responding to the sound symbolism of the longer vowel and longer consonant in *dreamed* as a way of suggesting the slowly moving action, and the shorter vowel and shorter consonant in *dreamt* to suggest the completed action. Speakers seem to react similarly to pairs like *spilled-spilt* (*The water gradually spilled out of the pitcher; She stumbled and spilt the milk all over the floor*), *burned-burnt*, and *smelled-smelt*.[2] Another kind of symbolism or iconism that crops up in languages all over the world is the association of the high vowels (pronounced with a small mouth-opening) with smallness, nearness, and sharpness. English has contrasting pairs like *chip-chop, keen-dull, this-that, here-there, near-far*, and for 'extra smallness' often uses *teeny* and *leetle* instead of *tiny* and *little*.

If it is a bit hard to recognize iconism at the bottom level of distinctive sounds, no one has any trouble hearing it in words. All languages have a vocabulary of onomatopoeia – words such as *bark, meow, howl, murmur, rumble, thunder, scream, wail, moan, sigh, grunt, hum*. They are not perfect copies – our speech apparatus has its limitations – and are rarely the same from language to language. One may even need to know the meaning of the word in order to associate it with the sound at all (how much does *bang* resemble the report of a gun?), but even a slight resemblance gives one the feeling of rightness between sound and sense. As for things outside the domain of sound, the voice can imitate only indirectly. We say *It was a l-o-n-g, l-o-n-g way*, a long sound for a long

road. There is a family of words, including *crash, mash, bash, lash, slash,*
gnash, and *splash,* where the *-ash* part suggests the noise of the action.
Since actions that make a noise like this tend to be sudden, riming words
like *dash* and *rash* have a sort of borrowed suggestiveness – as does *hash*
(the edible kind).

Abundant as symbolic words are, the great majority of words are still
only signs, or would appear so to any speaker of another language. But
at the level of sentences, symbolism makes a quantum jump. When two
persons perform an act together, the sentence that reports it contains the
same togetherness – the two persons are mentioned side by side (*Jane*
and Mary Lou paid the bill). When one act precedes and another follows,
the normal sentence reports them in the same order (*John came in and sat*
down, not *John sat down and came in*) – this can be reversed, but then
usually needs a special word such as *before* or *after* (*Before John sat down*
he came in). Sentences can be arranged for symbolic effects – for
example, building up to a climax. If things or qualities are associated,
the arrangement in the sentence usually shows the association (adjective
next to the noun it modifies, subject close to the verb it governs). The
part of a sentence that relates most closely to what has gone before (the
topic, as it is called) usually comes first: *Tell him WHAT YOU DID.* –
WHAT I DID doesn't concern him. Reversing this gives *It doesn't concern*
him what I did, with *what I did* marked with a low pitch to show that it is a
displaced topic.

Beyond the sentence, symbolism is the rule. Almost any two
languages will tell a story in the same order, sentence by sentence,
though internally the sentences may differ greatly. It seems that the
closer we get to the organization of thought – in paragraphs and
discourses – the more alike we all are. It is the accidents of history that
have given us the incommensurate sounds and words that make
communication difficult from language to language.

But what iconism there is in the lower levels is the more powerful as it
passes unnoticed. People are reasonably alert when they hear and
produce sentences – a proposition such as *Jones committed a felony* can
be spotted as something meant to influence our opinion, and countered
if it is untrue. There is no test of truth when the followers of Sun Myung
Moon are called *Moonies* – a name that trades on the sound symbolism
tied to the disparaging gesture of lip-protrusion (the *oo* sound), as in
loon, goon, coon, ghoul, fool, and a host of other *oo* words including of
course *moonstruck* and the verb *to moon* itself. In fact, in the last analysis
the sound symbolism of a language does not depend on outside ties at all
but is self-generating. The word *slunk,* as in *They had slunk,* is about as
arbitrary as a word can be in terms of its meaning, but the words it rimes
with – *stunk, clunk, skunk, drunk, funk, flunk, junk, punk, plunk* – mostly
refer to something unpleasant or awkward, and many speakers will
avoid the tense that requires it. (The more so, the less it is used – *slink* is
not as frequent as *sink,* and it is hard to avoid *sunk.*) A word gets
contaminated. The adjective *catty* takes its edge not only from

'resembling a cat' but from having a sound like that of *cutting* and *sarcastic*. The word *bombast* originally meant cotton wool used as stuffing, hence turgid language; but now it connects with *bombing* and *blasting* – an indignant caller on a California talk show opined that *He should be writing and bombasting Sacramento* – presumably bombarding with bombast. Few who use an expression such as *It sapped his strength* would think of 'undermine' as the sense of the verb – sapping sounds like draining the sap from something. Every word in the language becomes imbued with its meaning, and that meaning rubs off on other words that sound like it, especially if there is already some degree of similarity in meaning or use. The need to make sense – to have a word sound as if it means what it says – may cause hearers to misinterpret, or, rather, to REinterpret, what they hear.

One form of this is called folk etymology. The first syllable of *hybrid* sounds like *high*, but the second syllable, with its shwa [ə] sound, is meaningless as part of any *high-* compound. Many speakers accordingly convert it to *bred*, yielding *high-bred* – hybrid plants and animals are generally those bred up to a high degree of yield or perfection. Such relationships are a mysterious and unexplored domain. We have no conception of the interconnections that influence us in our associations of words and meanings. Why is the verb *to tug* used for emotions while its synonyms are not? We say *It tugs at my heart*, but not *It pulls* or *draws at my heart*. There is the same intimacy about *tug* that we sense in *hug* and in *snug as a bug in a rug*. Have these words formed some kind of associative network? Does it account for the success of the verb *to bug* in *It bugs me*, which means 'to bother in an intimate way'?

Poets intuit these things. As one critic writes, 'Language . . . is unavoidably dual, simultaneously referring to something external to itself and projecting its inherent power to signify.'[3] When signs become symbolic, language has to that extent created its own reality.

Meanings that a word hints at are found in other words. But hinting at must be distinguished from pointing to. Only in the frankly imitative words like *buzz* and *lisp* do hint and pointing coincide. The rest of the time, iconism in words is important in everyday communication only because it is insidious. Attitudes can be unconsciously influenced by it – as happens with persons whose names are their misfortune: *Professor Hogg, Senator Hickenlooper. Monk* is not enhanced by *monkey* nor *flat* 'apartment' by *flat* 'dull'. But iconism is entropy. All words TEND to become symbolic, yet if they were allowed to go all the way, communication would be impossible. Language is primarily a system of signs, and it is because that is what we rightly expect that we are caught off guard when their supposedly chiseled edges turn out to be rather badly weathered by chafing against other signs. The first principle of the basic units of any signaling system is CONTRAST.

Language is the same in this respect as telegraphy, genetic codes, and mathematics. In language the basic units are distinctive sounds and words. For ordinary communication they must be KEPT distinctive –

that is, as free as possible from irrelevant hints and contaminations – because they are the units over which the speaker or writer has almost no control. The words we use are the words that are THERE; we can only choose from them, rarely invent them, and if they are not clean to begin with, the precision – not to mention the honesty – of our messages will suffer. For scientists the 'loading' of meaning is a special problem: they are often compelled to make up new words (not necessarily for new things) or to redefine old ones in order not to be misunderstood. The problem is less acute with phrases and sentences because there the speaker or writer is more fully on his own. We may have to choose from the available stock of words, but we can put them together more or less as we please.

So, since languages are practical instruments as well as raw material for poets, they resist – which is to say their users resist – any blurring of contrast. The tendency in the long run is to go to the opposite extreme – to give ANY difference in meaning, however slight, a MAXIMUM difference in form. A dog and a wolf are both canine, but the word *wolf* is as different from *dog* as *dog* is from *cat*. The practical reason is simply that we can associate 'dog' and 'wolf' in our minds if we need to – the resemblance between them does not require any resemblance in their names; but if the names were similar and in an emergency we misunderstood one for the other, we might be in trouble. (This is why the taxonomies – the scientific names for plants and animals, for example – where similar forms get similar names, are not the rule in ordinary speech.) The hunger for contrast is one reason why sets of word forms have such a hard time becoming regular. Take a pattern of adjectives like this one:

malign   malignant
benign   benignant

Tumors are not *malign* and *benign*, or *malignant* and *benignant*, with the same ending in both, as would seem logical. Instead, a physician calls one *benign* and the other *malignant* – and is less likely to be misunderstood. The word *flammable*, which the *Century Dictionary* marked 'obsolete' in 1914, was revived a decade or two later and now replaces *inflammable* – a dangerous word because its *in*-prefix is too much like the *in*- of *inactive* or *indecent*, suggesting that something quick to ignite might be the opposite. The vocabulary of every language is so vast that there is no way to eliminate all such hazards in the short run. Imagine what can happen if you are teaching someone to drive, and you come to a corner and he asks *Left*? and you say *Right*! meaning 'That's correct'.

Our memories are so roomy that it is easier to cross-index forms in our minds – '*starboard* and *port* are companion terms to refer to the sides of a ship' – than to be continually on guard against misunderstandings caused by like meanings attached to like-sounding forms (*starboard, larboard*).

So it comes about that we are most often aware of iconism when it leads to a FAILURE of contrast – when the speaker permits what a word 'really means' (its arbitrary value) to be influenced by what its appearance says it 'ought to mean'. One typical mistake of this kind is the malapropism – the use of one form for another that vaguely resembles it in form and meaning. The columnist Peter Weaver wrote *Professional bill collectors are having a heyday*, confusing *heyday* with *field day*; the two are faintly related in the common notion of 'prosperity'. *Heyday* itself may have developed in a similar way from an exclamation *heyda* 'hey there!' used to express exaltation and later applied to a TIME of excitement, causing the *-da* part to be identified with *day*. The novelist Colleen McCullough on a radio talk show said *Australia is a more homogenous society*, confusing *homogenous* ('having the same origin') with *homogeneous* ('having uniform parts') – and enough people have done this so that dictionaries now give both meanings to *homogenous*. When John Dean wrote *A pallor hung over conversations* he confused *pallor* with *pall* – both words suggest an ill state of affairs. Here are three more to work out (note 4 has the probable answers);

> At the discrimination of the police chief.
> The fighting which has ravished Lebanon.
> I don't appreciate people who try to foster their views off on me.[4]

The weight of the whole language – all that we have learned and remember of it – bears in upon us at any such moment of hesitation in our choice of words. Meanings, complexes of meaning, forms, and complexes of forms swarm about us; influences may come from a dozen directions, and even the most skilled self-observer cannot trace them all back. A person who intends to say *shake roof* is on the point of saying *shag roof*. A shake roof is rather shaggy in appearance. *Shag* and *shake* sound alike. So do *shake roof* and *shag rug*. Both *shake roof* and *shag rug* are household appurtenances. Our colors run together, and it is a constant struggle to keep a neat palette with each hue in its place.

Naturally we struggle hardest where we are most aware of the risks. The change from *inflammable* to *flammable* was deliberate, promoted by someone aware of the risks of fire. Where contamination gets out of hand is in the more elusive realm of attitudes and emotions – echoes of sound and sense that we half-hear yet respond to subliminally.

To sum up: Symbols are 'natural', non-arbitrary representations IN language (more generally, in any communication system) of things OUTSIDE. Signs are arbitrary representations, purely distinctive and contrastive.

But what is 'natural'? Many birds and animals are named for the sound they produce: *chickadee, cuckoo, peetweet, towhee, cricket, howler*. One who learns the name also learns the connection with the sound, as a rule. But howler monkeys are sometimes quiet and peetweets do not always go *peetweet*. The connection between the object and its sound is intermittent, as much so as the connection between the object and its name. For the child – the learner – how things are called is just another side to how things sound. The fact that the noise comes not from the thing but from the mouth of another human being complicates the symbolizing process a bit but does not really change it. What counts is predictability. The *m-m-m-m* of a bee in flight and the word *bee* are equally imbued with beeness. A child will play with the word to make it sound like a buzz or a hum. If the sound of *bee* is not in the insect to begin with, we speakers of English put it there to extract it later whenever we want to refer to bees, just as surely as we extract any 'natural' sound or look or feel to refer to an associated thing. The distinction between the arbitrary and the suggestive is ultimately groundless. There is always something of the arbitrary, because all that can truly stand for a thing is the thing itself. And there is always something of the suggestive, because our minds accept all predictable ties on the same footing. Arbitrariness is the illusion of the outsider who approaches a culture without knowing its inner bonds. This is why sound symbolism in language is self-generating. And why the name of a thing has such a powerful hold on our conception of it.

Sign and *symbol* refer to the extremes of a scale, and with that understanding it is safe to go on using them.

Chapter 4

Above the word

Sounds, words, and grammar are the three great layers – more like the layers of atmosphere than layers of cake, for it is impossible to cut cleanly between them. One of the earliest two-word expressions that most English-speaking children learn is *all gone*. But it is hardly two words for the child. Rather it is a two-syllable unit with a unitary meaning, something like 'disappeared' – it is learned early because of the fascination of things vanishing from sight and then reappearing. A child is not equipped either semantically or phonetically to split up the utterances that come flooding from adults. If there is a phrase with parts hard to hear separately that squares with a meaning that is hard to analyze, the two will be matched one to one. Later, as more expressions using *all* are learned (*all wet, all done, all over, all well again*), the *all* part will acquire a face of its own; the child now approaches the skill of an adult and begins to improvise – *all the cats, all rinsed, all your money*. Earlier there will have been many false starts, like that of the four-year-old chattering on the telephone who was admonished by her father to 'get off the telephone' and responded with *Don't inter me rup*, treating *interrupt* as she had learned to treat *push up, hold up*, and *wake up*. (If enough children make an odd division like this, it may become permanent. Children invented *a whole nother* for *another whole*.)

Even after the child learns to unglue them, the old phrases linger on. *All gone* yields *all* and *gone* without surrendering its own identity. This blurs the line between words and phrases. In fact, some items that we consider words are seldom or never encountered alone. The word *shore* sounds odd in an exchange like

She's gone for the weekend. – Where to? – The shore.

It is more comfortable to say *lakeshore* or *seashore*. And even if there were no chance of ambiguity it would be awkward to say *She has a shore cottage – a lakeshore cottage* is better. The word *sleight* for most of us probably never occurs outside *sleight of hand*. Similarly *walks in from*

*The asterisk means that the form it accompanies is (1) nonexistent, (2) incorrect, or (3) inappropriate. A question mark placed before an example means 'doubtful'.

all walks of life. Words that are pinned this way to one or a few set phrases are like the smaller elements called affixes, which are rarely if ever pulled loose – the *in-* of *inept*, the *-kin* of *lambkin* – and which differ from words in that they cannot usually be attached at will (English admits *lambkin*, *babykins*, *catkin*, but not **fingerkin*, **girlkin*; instead of **ringkin* and **princekin* we say *ringlet* and *princeling*). Many phrases that we feel could logically be broken up still carry hidden meanings that pass unnoticed until someone misuses them. *Half a dozen* and *a half dozen* ought to mean the same, yet only the first is usual in an approximate sense: *I've told you already half a dozen times.* Whole constructions may be involved – even sentences. Sometimes they carry unexpected meanings and then are called idioms. The request *Leave me alone* means 'Don't bother me', not necessarily 'I want to be by myself'. People are often surprised when they realize what something they have been saying all their lives 'really means'. Hearing an exchange like this,

> I'd like to speak to Professor Smithers. – I'm sorry, he's tied up for the moment; could you come back a little later?

few would picture the professor secured with ropes. Sometimes the way we pronounce an expression reveals that it is operating as a unit and not part by part. The common phrase *and so on* has just one accent, on *so*; if it were still felt as the equivalent of *and SO ONward* that it once was, there would be two (the same is true of *and SO forth* versus *and SO FORTH*).

While some elements lose their independence, others regain it. Countering the word combinations that become so tightly cemented that speakers toss them off like single words are the parts of words that break free and enter into new combinations. No native speaker would have any trouble understanding this: *I had just finished shingling my roof when a tornado hit and de-shingled it for me.* The affix *de-* never occurs by itself – that is true of affixes by definition (the exception proves the rule: *They discussed it pro and con*). Yet speakers are free to coin words, up to a point, and when they do it is obvious that the verbal atom is as much alive as the verbal molecule. Most likely *de-shingle* will never be entered in a dictionary – though *de-bug* has made the grade and probably looked just as unpromising the first time someone said it. (The missing factor is cultural – there is more de-bugging of gardens than de-shingling of roofs.) Words keep getting coined; there is always a first time.

The typical word is LEARNED and REMEMBERED; its first use is an INVENTION – it is COINED out of its elements, and to survive it must hold together as a unit. The typical assemblage above the word is thrown together; it is not retained in memory as a unit but passes from the scene as soon as it has fulfilled its momentary purpose. If someone says *Today's workaholic is tomorrow's alcoholic*, the phrase *today's work-aholic*, even though it is a grammatical unit (it is the subject of the sentence), will not be stored in long-term memory as a unit; but its component *workaholic* enters the permanent storeroom despite the fact that it too is made up of smaller parts (*work* + *-holic*).

The storeroom where words and idioms are kept is not like the hackneyed closet from which everything comes tumbling out when the door is opened, but is a rather orderly place with separate shelves for the separate purposes that words serve – words that name things, words that describe qualities or assign quantities, words that embody actions and processes taking place in time, words that point, affirm, deny, conjoin, and relate, words that tell how other words are to be understood. We go there like a good secretary, knowing where everything is because we have a sense of the arrangement, not because we read the labels on the shelves. But the grammarian is tonguetied without his labels: noun, adjective, verb, adverb, conjunction, pronoun. These serve pretty well everywhere, though languages differ in the ones they favor. For example, not all languages have adjectives – some use verbs and nouns instead. (English does this too, but not regularly: *Geraldine excels in tennis = Geraldine is excellent in tennis*; *It is a city environment = It is an urban environment.*) Nouns can be used instead of adverbs (*She works a lot = She works hard*). Verbs can replace comparative adjectives (*Bede exceeds Ambrose in strength = Bede is stronger than Ambrose*). The fact that different resources are used in different proportions only underscores the availability of pretty much the same resources everywhere.

More than grammatical categories, the 'parts of speech' are broad semantic ranges. Grammarians who fancy themselves scientific like to make fun of schoolteachers who say that nouns are 'names of things' – how foolish that is, they say, when nouns include words like *cyclone* and *collision*, which are actions, and *anger* and *inspiration*, which are emotions, and *democracy* and *inferiority*, which are abstractions. But they forget that language is creative – an interpretation of nature, not a reflection. *Cyclone* is the name of a thing because it treats an event AS IF it were a thing. The quality of the noun is that it captures a concept on the wing and holds it still for inspection. Nouns name things because children learn the solid world first, and go on to solidify mentally whatever they think or talk about.

The parts of speech are syntactic as well as verbal because they mark the way words are used in sentences. A noun can do only certain things – like being a subject or an object (A *favor* deserves a *favor*). But nounness is also part of the word's meaning – *sparrow* is a noun, and is singular, and refers to a kind of bird. The comparative stability of the word, its relatively permanent investment in meaning, is what sets it apart from the higher impromptu assemblies.

Above the word, what memory holds is patterns of combination. Syntax is a putting together according to conventions that often have the look of traffic rules. Within a sentence, two words of the same class or of different classes stand in a certain relationship, signaled by which comes first or by the presence of a signpost word or a mark on the word itself. In the sentences *They gave the bird the rat* and *They gave the rat the bird* a rule of English holds that when two objects occur side by side, the first is indirect (naming a recipient or beneficiary) and the second is direct. But in place of the rule of position we can substitute the word *to*, which to some extent frees us from the constraint of order:

> They gave to all their friends a nice remembrance of the occasion.
> They gave a nice remembrance of the occasion to all their friends.

(Only a fairly long sentence makes a good illustration because the word order is not entirely free even with *to* – we would not say **They gave to their friends a remembrance.*) What this dual possibility opens up can be seen in answers to questions:

> Who got the rat? –
> > They gave the rat to the BIRD.
> > ?They gave the BIRD the rat.
>
> What did they give to the bird? –
> > They gave the bird the RAT.
> > (?) They gave the RAT to the bird.

The better answer is the one that puts the emphatic element – the replacement for the question word (*who, what*) – at the end. In this case a more or less arbitrary rule makes possible a psychological iconism: what comes last remains most vivid in the mind.[1]

A similar traffic rule distinguishes the sentences *John saw Mary* and *Mary saw John* – object and subject have different positions relative to the verb. Some languages (Latin, for example) make this distinction by adding an inflection on one or both nouns to mark their status, leaving the word order free for other purposes. Inflections, positions, and signpost words are the mainstay of syntax. The word *by* in English is used to point out the agent of an action – typically, as in the first example, in the 'passive voice':

> The play was written *by* Shaw.

> For every advance *by* them there was a retreat *by* their foes.

In the 'active voice' the agent is normally just the grammatical subject of the sentence: *Shaw wrote the play*. So one way of expressing a rule for forming the passive is to set up a switching mechanism that transforms the active to the passive by turning the sentence around and adding a couple of words:

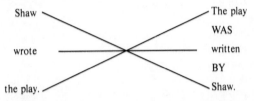

As before, the arrangement made possible by the passive voice enables us to put the emphasis in the most effective place: *It appeared at first that Bacon had written it, but later evidence showed that it was written by SHAKESPEARE*. It would be anticlimactic here to say *showed that*

SHAKESPEARE wrote it. But the most useful – and dangerous – function of the passive is to enable the speaker to keep silent about who performs the action: *The cars are loaded here* says nothing about who does it – which is fine if who does it is not important, but misleading if it is, unless something else fills us in.[2]

English is rich in its uses of arrangement to signal meanings. Here are four examples:

1 When modifiers are grouped next to a noun without a comma between them the one closest to the noun is the 'inner' modifier: *modern popular music* means 'popular music that is modern'; *popular modern music* means 'modern music that is popular'.

2 When a modifier goes before a noun, it characterizes the noun, says something about the way the noun 'really is'. When it follows, the 'really is' quality is neutralized. *The corner house* is the house that belongs on the corner; *the house on the corner* could be one in the process of being moved, perhaps parked there overnight. *The people ready were picked up* refers to a temporary state of readiness; *The ready people were picked up* sounds strange because it implies that 'being ready' is something you have with you as part of your nature, not just a temporary condition. Sometimes the same adjective can be used both ways: *the only handy tool* and *the only tool handy*.

3 When the verb, or part of it (but not an adverb, as in *well might they, so did I*), precedes the subject, the effect is to make the sentence hypothetical rather than factual. Most grammars associate this only with questions of the type *Had they seen John?* But such yes–no questions are really hypotheses that the speaker puts forward for confirmation. Other hypotheses use the same inversion: *Had they seen John, they would have known he was there.* These we call 'conditions' – and just as with indirect objects, there is another way of saying them, likewise by adding a word, this time *if*: *If they had seen John, they would have known he was there.* (The connection with questions shows up in another way – the same word *if* is also used to introduce indirect questions: *I wondered if they had seen John.*)

4 When two elements are otherwise free to be arranged either AB or BA, the tendency is for the one that follows to restrict the one that precedes, so long as the intonation remains the same. English reveals this most strikingly when whole phrases allow the AB–BA orders:

I'll have breakfast   as soon as the bus gets to Anaheim.
As soon as the bus gets to Anaheim   I'll have breakfast.

The first answers the question *When will you have breakfast?* The second answers the question *What will you do when the bus gets to Anaheim?* But this left-right restriction is found with smaller freely moving elements as well, especially adverbs in relation to their verbs:

Slowly she crept down the hall.
She crept down the hall slowly.

It is clear that the second describes the action in a way that the first does not. When the adverb comes first, it often ties to something outside the sentence proper:

> Kindly tell me why.
> Tell me why kindly.

– the first is 'Be kind enough to tell me why'. With some adverbs this tendency creates striking differences in meaning:

> She simply writes. ('All she does is write.')
> She writes simply.

Fairly, *plainly*, *positively*, and *clearly* are other examples. Adverb position illustrates how hard it is to say positively what goes with what in a sentence. In the pair

> You cruelly hurt her. (OK You hurt her cruelly.)
> *You terribly hurt her. (OK You hurt her terribly.)

the first is possible because *cruelly* modifies *you* as much as it modifies *hurt* – it stands between *you* and *hurt* and faces both ways. *Terribly* makes less sense taken with *you*, and therefore is placed after the verb. Up to a point, the sentence is a pot in which words are mixed and entangle themselves with all the neighboring words – children enjoy experimenting with such combinations. But then patterns begin to freeze, making relationships more explicit and meanings more precise.

The rules of order have an arbitrary look but hark back to natural choices that speakers once made and later turned into habits. As one linguist puts it, 'Syntax is frozen discourse.'[3] The most obvious example is the tendency – which some languages convert into a rule, at least in the 'main' types of sentences – to express subjects before objects: *The cannibals ate the missionaries*, not *The missionaries ate the cannibals*. (In a sample of sixty-three languages from around the globe, sixty showed the subject typically before the object.)[4] The reason may well be that the initiator of an action has to start functioning before any effect begins to be seen or felt in the object. Doing this most of the time for a good reason seems reason enough to do it as a matter of course and then you don't have to think about it – unless something special shocks you into doing the opposite: *The missionaries the cannibals ate, but the choirboys were eaten by the crocodiles* – 'As for the missionaries, the cannibals ate them.' Here *missionaries* has become the TOPIC, and there are even stronger reasons for having topics first than for having subjects first – they announce what is being talked about, and generally connect with what has gone before.

A more subtle example of frozen discourse is the rule in English that every declarative sentence must have an expressed subject. *It's raining* is the grammarians' pet example. The *it* is a 'dummy word' – all the real information is packed in *raining*, and *it* merely fills the slot of that required subject. Or so most grammarians claim. But this *it* is the same *it*

as the one in *It's unsafe down here*, 'This down-here situation is unsafe' –
it refers to any 'situation' that is obvious in the context, and nothing can
be more obvious than the weather. (Even with the weather we specify
sometimes, as when we ask a question like *Is it raining out?* – 'Is the
outside situation one of rain?') The *it* does not tell us anything we don't
already know, but it is not a 'dummy' – unless one also insists that *her* is
a dummy in *Jenny stuck out her tongue*, since it is unlikely that she will
stick out someone else's. The *it*, and the required possessive in *stick out
one's tongue*, do figure in rules of syntax, but they started out meaning
something, and still do.

As sentences grow more complex in their intra- and interrelationships, other controls besides word order are needed. (English is
more generous than most other languages in the load it allows word
order to carry.) It is not always necessary to specify the relationship –
sometimes the facts speak for themselves:

    It was raining. I stayed home.
    I stayed home. It was raining.

Whichever way we say this, any sensible person knows that the staying
home is *because of* the rain. Other times the hearer would be at a loss:

    Mary has investments. She is rich.
    Mary is rich. She has investments.

Now there is no way to tell (without more context) whether she has
investments because she is rich or is rich because she has investments. By
adding a word such as *because* or *since*, or using a dependent structure
with *-ing*, the speaker can clarify:

    Since Mary has investments, she is rich.
    Since she is rich, Mary has investments.
    Having investments, Mary is rich.
    Being rich, Mary has investments.

Languages have a variety of signpost words – 'function words' is the
usual term – which specify the relationships between sentences and
between clauses of the same sentence. ('Same sentence' is often a matter
of taste, of the speaker's – or writer's – sense of how closely connected
two ideas are. *I ate it, but I didn't like it* differs from *I ate it. But I didn't
like it*. The latter expresses the second idea as a kind of afterthought –
perhaps the speaker holds it back for dramatic effect.) English has *and*,
but, *still*, *however*, *nevertheless*, *besides*, *instead*, *afterward*, *yet*, and a
dozen or so more function words that connect two relatively
independent ideas. It also has function words that hitch a dependent
idea to an independent one, as in

    Don't leave *till* I get back.
    I don't know *why* he said it.
    Anybody is crazy *who* says that.

Other words of this class include *after, when, before, while, which, wherever*. And there are function words that substitute for other words, enabling a speaker to avoid repeating himself:

> Was Jill there? – I think *so*. (I think *that she was there*.)
> Jack stands six-three in his stocking feet. – Gosh, I didn't know he was *that* tall (*six feet three inches* tall).
> The voter turnout was 93 per cent. *It* (*the voter turnout*) was truly impressive.

Other substitute words are *he, she, they, this, his, such*. A different kind of substitute word has its identification at a later point – the interrogatives are typical:

> *What* will you send? – I think I'll send *roses*.
> *How* can they lower it? – They can lower it *with a rope*.

The function words differ from 'content words' (such as most nouns, adjectives, and verbs) in the nature of their meaning: it is primarily relational. In *Do you see that?* the word *that* relates to visible reality. In *He says you did it but I don't believe that* the same word *that* relates to an idea in the sentence. Function words are also rather special in being a 'closed set' – unlike other classes, they rarely acquire a new member. One fairly recent addition is a new use of the old word *plus* to mean 'in addition to which': *Jerry is willing, plus he knows the country and its people*.

The relational devices such as word order and function words are explicit ways of linking ideas. A word such as *because* makes an outright claim of a causal relationship between one idea and another. But sentences can be collapsed in ways that hide the relationships, making them difficult to detect and often slipping their claims past our guard. Even the most ordinary constructions sometimes do this: *That dumb sheriff had me up on charges* takes it for granted that the hearer will accept the implied claim 'That sheriff is dumb.' *Dumb sheriff* looks like the same noun-phrase construction, consisting of an adjective and a noun, whether it occurs in *that dumb sheriff* or in *a dumb sheriff* (as in *A dumb sheriff is a rarity*); but there is a difference, which becomes visible when the relationship of the adjective to the noun is made explicit:

> That sheriff, who is dumb, had me up on charges.
> A sheriff who is dumb is a rarity.

In the first, the commas show that the adjective is not a limiting adjective; an independent claim has been made in the guise of a simple adjective: 'That sheriff is dumb.' The claim may wear an even thicker disguise. There is a class of words known as epithets which are really nouns plus adjectives masquerading as pure nouns. Instead of *foolish person* we have *fool*; instead of *stupid person* we have *idiot*; instead of *rattletrap car* we have (or had – these terms are often ephemeral) the noun *heap*. In the sentence *That cur bit me* we have in effect *That dog*, *which is a cur, bit me*. For the less devious sentence *That dog bit me* it is of course possible to substitute *That animal, which is canine, bit me*, but now the included adjective in 'canine animal' classifies the noun in a way that is true by definition, without adding a further claim.

The swallowing up of sentences by sentences – logophagy, we might call it – takes many forms. One of the most interesting is that of a class of sentences which when ful., stated are seen to be comments on what is being said – often comments that are essential to conveying points of view or biases. When the translators of *Papillon* wrote *From the sun's position, it was now two in the afternoon*, they did not mean that it was two o'clock from the position; actually they omitted a verb: *From the sun's position I judged* (or *one could tell*) that it was two in the afternoon.[5] In an exchange like this one,

It's not going to last. – I don't think it is going to last either.

the word *either* makes sense only if we assume that the first speaker was not being categorical about his prediction but really meant to say *I don't think it's going to last* – the *either* ties the second *I don't think* to the absent earlier *I don't think*. A special case is the 'floating adverb' in sentences like *It frankly didn't matter*, which has evidently been cut down from *I say frankly that it didn't matter*; but as so often happens with footloose adverbs, this one comes to be vaguely felt as the modifier of what actually is there, and it reinforces the 'not mattering'.

By this process entire sentences become encapsulated in a single word. When someone says *He was fatally shot*, the intention is not to describe the manner of the shooting, as one expects of an adverb (*He was cleverly shot*), but to imply 'He was shot and he died as a result'. The word *reliably* in *He was reliably reported to be drunk at the time* does not refer to a manner of reporting but condenses a whole additional sentence: *and I believe the report*.

The process by which larger segments get buried this way seems to be a kind of perverse shorthand. The first step may be quite logical, as with the omission in

I want to report that some jewels have been stolen.
I want to report some jewels stolen.

But then a more familiar structure – in this case modifier-before-noun – gobbles up the less familiar one, and we get

I want to report some stolen jewels.

which makes no sense, except that we understand it perfectly.

A logician will find still more buried implications. Take a pair of sentences like

A man spoke to me.
A man has his pride.

In the first, *a man* presupposes the existence of such a person: 'There was a man, and he spoke to me'. In the second we have a hypothesis: 'If there is an *x* such that *x* is a man, then *x* will have his pride.' The notion of existence or being is regularly assumed when a thing is named, and sometimes gives odd results: *Highways and county roads were blocked by high water and no travel was advised*, goes a newspaper report, intending 'it was advised *that there be* no travel'. The subtle implication of existence on the strength of a name is something that will occupy us later.

Not all the grammatical features of a sentence have to do with the way it is pieced together – explicitly with things like function words, implicitly by taking a short-cut. There are elements that are neither signposts nor traffic rules, but meaningful bits in their own right, though without the relative independence of words. One neat little pair with opposing senses is that of the suffix *-ing* and the *to* of the infinitive. Much of the time they seem to be interchangeable, or just to depend in some arbitrary way on another verb in the sentence:

> I like playing golf.
> I like to play golf.
> They kept on complaining, *They kept on to complain.
> They continued to complain.

Yet there is a difference. The infinitive leans toward the unreal or hypothetical, the *-ing* toward the concrete and real:

> To hesitate would be fatal, and they will regret it.
> *To hesitate had been fatal, and they regretted it.
> Hesitating had been fatal, and they regretted it.

The first sentence speaks of something that is only a possibility, and the infinitive is normal; the second and third speak of a known fact, and only the *-ing* gets by. Another situation is with *remember* and *recall*: *recall* looks back on something that has actually happened, whereas *remember* invokes something to be done:

> She remembered to speak to him.
> She recalled speaking to him, *She recalled to speak to him.

(*Remember* can be used both ways, with the contrast in meaning: *She remembered speaking to him.*) So it turns out that *It's no good worrying* and *It's no good to worry* differ ever so slightly. *It's no good worrying* is advice one is apt to give someone worrying now; *It's no good to worry* hypothesizes about worry in general.

English uses more function words like *to* than inflections like *-ing*. Some other inflections are the plural endings on nouns (*girl*, *girls*), verb endings (*walk*, *walked*), and the endings for comparative and superlative (*new*, *newer*, *newest*). The last of these has its own function word, *than*, which couples the two halves of a comparison: *Bill is wider than Joe is tall*. There is no practical difference between inflections and function words – for example, *more* can and often must be used instead of *-er* (*more established*, *establisheder), and when we want to compare equality rather than inequality, we use the word *as*: *Bill is as tall as Joe.*

The last chapter referred to the expansion of freedom as one goes up the ladder from distinctive sounds through words to phrases and sentences. Sentences seem almost infinitely free by comparison with words, yet they are themselves infinitely more compact and rule-bound than anything farther up the scale. Nevertheless there is organization even there. When a writer breaks up a discourse into paragraphs, he implies a degree of cohesion among the sentences – or ideas – that make up each one. In some languages there are fairly definite markers of paragraph organization. In Ica, an Indian language spoken in Colombia, the individual who holds the stage in a narrative paragraph is introduced in the first sentence or two and marked with the suffix *-ri*. That individual is understood to be the subject of all the following sentences except those that may be marked with another suffix, *-se*.[6] So each time the *-ri* appears, the listener knows that a new paragraph has begun.[7] In English, the best cue for the ear is pause combined with intonation. The spoken paragraph is rather like an exaggerated sentence. Most sentences which are statements go down in pitch – the end is a relaxation point, as was noted earlier. The end of a paragraph is a bigger relaxation point and the pitch tends to go down farther and the pause tends to be longer on the final sentence than on any of the others. The beginning, too, especially that of a narrative paragraph, often has a typical intonational shape that implies something like 'unquestioned fact'. It differs from what occurs later in the paragraph, where the speaker may be answering questions previously raised, using a typical question-answering intonation. At the beginning no question has been asked and none can be answered. Example:

Once there was a little girl whose name was Guin

The oth er children made fun of her and called her Guin evere. ny.

The 'unquestioned fact' intonation starts high and moves steadily downward. The 'question-answering' intonation has higher pitches toward the end than toward the beginning. The first sentence establishes a topic – the child and her name. Once the name is given, the speaker is free to pretend that the audience is wondering – what about that name? – and proceeds to answer the unspoken question.

To sum up, language reveals itself as a cycle of cycles, a contained and containing universe, an expansion of concentric spheres surrounding and partially absorbing one another. At the center are the most rigid shapes of all, both in form and in their almost-deadness of meaning, the distinctive sounds. Encompassing that is the sphere of words and word-parts such as affixes, rigid in form but not quite rigid in meaning – a new breed of dog can be called *a dog* if it is LIKE known dogs: metaphor works tirelessly to bend meanings and sometimes break them. Out from that is the sphere of phrases and sentences, often pulled centerward by idioms, but in general rigid only in its patterns of arrangement. Here are meanings freely built, more or less original concoctions of words which may be as unpredictable in their effects as the green that one gets by mixing blue and yellow. Beyond the sentence is the paragraph and beyond that the discourse, or the chapter and the book, with only the loosest constraints of form and virtually none of meaning.

It is probably no accident that the total picture resembles the way living organisms are put together, or even the constitution of matter. In both systems, the smaller the unit, the more arbitrary the behavior. In both, the hierarchy has no obvious limit. Organisms build communities and communities societies; molecules accrete and the accretions make worlds and worlds gravitate. If language is to be the human mechanism for dealing with nature, then it must in some way be a simulacrum of nature and of life. A crude comparison goes like this: Nature has things, language has words that code meanings corresponding to things. Nature has events that bring things into relationships, language has words that bring those thing-meanings into corresponding meaning-relationships. Say that among nature's phenomena are a *snag*, a particular lad called *Casper*, and a particular action known as *tripping*. Also an occasion that brings the three together. The report comes out *A snag tripped Casper*. Somewhere between the event and the sentence is a mental picture. The speaker who sees the event and remembers the picture will encode the sentence as it appears here; but a hearer needs only the sentence in order to reconstitute the picture in his mind. The relationships between the outside world and our verbal translations of it are not necessarily point-by-point – the snag precedes Casper in the sentence, though both are present in the event at the same time. But the correspondence is close enough for us to assemble things mentally by using assemblies of words. This enables us not only to picture the physical world but to control it, for we can simulate changes before making them – which is to say that we THINK OF a result and then go about achieving it. Computer simulations are only mechanical extensions of this verbal power, which manipulates signs and symbols as a prelude to manipulating things.

The world picture is distorted by being seen through human eyes. It is not only that our vision is limited to the narrow band of electromagnetic radiation known as light, but that even the things in full view are observed not so much for what they are as for what they mean to us – something to get around, something to eat, something to fear. Worse still for our freedom to reach beyond ourselves, the verbal codifications are not of our making – with a few trivial exceptions – but are part of the tradition of our society. They come to us like an assembly-line battery, already charged with meaning. Imagine yourself a spectator at this little scene in a Bakweri village in Africa, described by Edwin Ardener:[8] 'A crowd howl at an old man hiding under a bed. Dismantled sheets of rusty corrugated iron lie in the vicinity.' You try to guess the motives of the crowd: the old man is an official who has cheated the villagers; or a lunatic who has attempted to commit a murder; or a cornered spy from another village; or a peeping Tom caught in the peep. The corrugated iron obviously comes from the roof, so the old man must have tried to shut himself in and the sheets had to be torn away to reach him. All these hypotheses make sense in terms of your experience and background. But they miss the mark. The truth is that the old man is being persecuted because he is a zombie master, a controller of the living dead who work for him by killing children and forcing their spirits into slavery. He has been identified by his tin roof – a sign of being a little better off than his poverty-stricken neighbors, and hence as having a supernatural source of income. 'Corrugated iron' is – or was – a pregnant term in Bakweri.

The verbal codifications represent the things that people, in society, have found worth noting and talking about. The storeroom is indeed vast and its powers of representation are enormous. But it is not perfect. Some of its imperfections, and our imperfect uses of even the best it offers, pose dangers.

Chapter 5

Appointment in Babylon

In the story of Genesis, after the great flood the nations of mankind settled in the plain of Shinar and began to build a tower, 'to make themselves a name, lest they be scattered abroad upon the face of the whole earth'. But the tower was to reach to heaven, and the Almighty, with His omnipotence in doubt, came down to inspect the works. He was not deceived in what was giving these Lilliputians the power to challenge Him. 'Behold,' He said, presumably to Himself, 'the people is one and they have all one language; and this they begin to do; and now nothing will be restrained from them, which they have imagined to do.' So, to curb their enterprise, He confounded their language.

Linguists may not take the myth of Babel seriously, but they have to take seriously the multiplicity of languages on earth, and try to account for it, just as social scientists have to account for its consequences – the lack of communication and disruption of cooperation that the myth symbolizes so well. The languages spoken today still number in the thousands, all but their own one – or two, or a handful – unintelligible to most speakers. How did this come about, if humankind at one time spoke a single primordial language, or at least fewer languages than today?

The germ of confusion was the very quality of language that conferred its magic: the reduction of symbols to signs. Why should the symbolic and self-evident have turned arbitrary? What was the reason for the divorce between meaning and form, that caused a consonant sound, for example, with a meaning of its own, to become a mere counter in a code of signs?

If it had not happened, human language would have stopped evolving at about the point where natural chimpanzee communication seems to be today, with relatively simple gestures standing in a one-to-one relationship with what they signify. But this could not continue as the needs of communication multiplied. The human signaling apparatus, whether gestural or vocal, can manage only a limited number of easily discriminated symbolic movements, and the demands were bound to overload it eventually. Besides, the symbolism itself could not avoid being thinned out. It is easy to gesture the motion of a hammer to signify 'hammer', but how does one gesture the idea of 'dark'? Or, if the apparatus used was the vocal one, which can convey the notion of 'loud' easily enough, how does one convey that of 'old'? Even calling on both gesture and sound at once, there comes a time when the limit is reached, or when extending it is too great an effort of discrimination and memory. The farther a metaphor is extended the more it approaches a sign – if the symbol for 'friend' was a clasping of the arms, that gesture was already some distance from an actual hug, and using it metaphorically for 'kindness' would have stretched it beyond one's ability to detect any real resemblance with the thing signified. The ground was prepared for a leap into arbitrariness. The smallest units could no longer be in a one-to-one relationship with a meaning, but had to be recycled as meaningless sub-units available for arbitrary combinations making new meaningful units at a higher level. Where formerly A stood for one thing and B for another, now A and B still might have that privilege but in addition could be combined as AB and BA or doubled as AA or BB or doubled and recombined, and so on to infinity. A small number of distinctive units was enough to yield a limitless number of new signs.

Of course this in itself would not lead to Babel, since everybody could have kept the same set of signs. What did the mischief was the loss of symbolism. The effect of metaphors further metaphorized and of signs put together out of already bleached-out distinctive units (becoming phonemes in the process) was the loss of a natural curb on change: if a word is no longer required to bear any physical resemblance to what it signifies, it can 'just as well' be something other than it is. All that is needed is acceptance by the community. This does not mean any necessary loss of vividness, as we have seen – a dog is just as brightly represented by *dog* as by *bowwow*, if the connection is established early in the learning period of childhood. But it does permit small changes to take place and accumulate from one generation to the next. As long as the community remains intact, the changes will be imperceptible, since everyone will adopt or at least understand the new forms. But if it splits up, change may take different directions in the divided halves, and eventually the members of one will not understand those of the other.

Language is carried by sound, and the most corrosive change is in the distinctive sounds – phonetic change. It has two main causes and takes two main forms. One cause is the effort that children in all societies must make to master the phonemes of their language. It is not an easy task, and some sounds are harder to learn than others – one of the hardest is that of a trilled or tapped *r*, and several of the languages of Europe which formerly had it have replaced it with other sounds (or even lost it altogether in some environments – the '*r*-less' pronunciation of *park*, *short*, etc, for example, that one hears in much of Britain and in parts of the East and South in the United States). Or a phoneme may be easy enough alone but hard in combination: multiple consonants and multiple vowels are harder than alternating vowels and consonants, so we hear *ellum* for elm and *nucular* for *nuclear*.

The other cause is language contact. It may be violent, as when one tribe invades another and imposes its language, which the speakers of the former language are able to acquire only imperfectly yet, if they are numerous enough, may then pass, along with some of the imperfections they have introduced, to the children of the dominant group (Anglo-Saxon nursemaids in Britain after the Norman invasion, Black nursemaids in the South of the United States). Or it may be a 'pidgin', a makeshift that is worked out for trade purposes and then may be used so often that children learn it more and more as a native language, thereby 'creolizing' it.

As for the two FORMS of change, one involves changes of but not in the phonemes. They are merely switched around. Many speakers of English seem to feel that it is more distinguished to say *eyether* than *eether*. Both sounds are normal to the language; only a single word is affected. Some speakers make *ration* sound like *ray*, others like *rash*. Again, both sounds are common in many other words (*nation, station; passion, fashion*).

The other form of change is more sweeping and involves the phonemes themselves. The change from a trilled or tapped *r* to the kind of *r* that English has in *ring, irritate*, etc is an example. (Scots English has kept the 'burr'.) Instead of transforming one sound into another (by altering its place or manner of articulation, as with *r*), a language may pick up a new phoneme, or lose an old one. Loss usually occurs where it is least noticed – it may not be a very vigorous sound to begin with, hence easy for a child to overlook; or it may affect only a very few words; or it may be too much like some other sound, so that the two merge. A sound that is not very vigorous is that of *h*. In Castilian Spanish it has been lost entirely; in English it has been lost from the pronoun *hit* (still heard in the Ozarks), now pronounced *it*, and many speakers have lost it in all the *wh*- words: *where, why, which*, etc. A sound that is too much like another sound is the vowel of *taught, caught, caller*, which as we have seen Americans are coming more and more to pronounce the same as *tot, cot*, and *collar*. The gain of a new sound may come from within or without, the latter by 'borrowing'. In Old English the sounds of *f* and *v* were only variants of a single phoneme (relics of this still exist, as in *wife-wives, loaf-loaves*), just as the *t* of *bat* and the *t* of *batter* are a single phoneme today, in spite of their difference in sound for many speakers; there were no words in which the contrast between *f* and *v* mattered. But then, along with other influences, French words began to come in which made the distinction, and the two English sounds were graduated from the status of mere variants to that of separate phonemes. A gain from within may come from speakers' being compelled to rely on a difference like the *f-v* one because of a loss elsewhere. Formerly the final *g* of words like *sing, bang, dung, gong* was actually pronounced (as it still is in some Midland dialects in Britain and in New York City); at that time it had the same effect on the *n* that *k* has in *bank, punk, tinker*, and potentially in *Dunkirk* and *sun-kissed* – that is, the *n* was 'velarized', brought close to the pronunciation of the *g*. Then the *g* was dropped. But by this time it was no longer needed, which partly explains why it was dropped – the KIND of *n* that would occur before a *g* was already there and sufficed to distinguish *sing* from *sin*, *bang* from *ban*, *dung* from *dun*, *gong* from *gone*. A new phoneme, the velar nasal, was born.

In the last century or so a curious new force of change has come on the scene, which is now the strongest disturber of the peace in most literate societies. It is 'spelling pronunciation', and is most potent in languages with spelling systems that match the sounds of the language closely enough to invite guesswork, but not closely enough to ensure accuracy. English is the showpiece. Many words are met for the first time in print, and speakers venture to say them without ever having heard them before. The *gyn-* of *gynecology* is the same as the *-gyn-* of *misogynist*, and was pronounced the same, as in *gin*. But the letter *y* made it look like *guy*, and nowadays the gynecologists themselves have forgotten how to pronounce the name of their profession, by the old standards. (To call them 'ignorant' of course is to pass a judgment that no linguistic scientist is entitled to make. But the temptation is very strong.) A whole class of words may be affected. Many more words spelled with *o* are pronounced like *bottle*, *spot*, *hot*, *modern*, *hostile*, *hobble*, etc than like *son*, *come*, *done*, and *money*. These four (and a few others) preserve that sound of *o* because they are so common – children hear them long before they learn to read. But less familiar words are guessed at, and as a result the *o*'s of such words as *constable*, *pommel*, even *sponge* and *frontier*, have come or are coming to be pronounced with the *o* of *pot*. *Grovel* no longer rimes with *shovel*. (Where the spelling was changed, the old pronunciation has been kept, as in *tunnel* and *funnel* for old *tonnel*, *fonil*.) A generation that rarely listens to a sermon is beginning to pronounce the word *pulpit* as if it were related to *pulp*. The hold that a spelling has on our minds can be gauged by the tendency to transfer a spelling pronunciation even to a foreign language. Native speakers of English who are students of Spanish often have difficulty pronouncing a word such as *presidente*, persisting in saying the *z* sound of the English *s* even though English has the correct sound in *precedent*.

Where languages grow most unlike one another as they drift apart is in the shapes of their words. Change affects words more drastically than it does phonemes. For a phoneme to change its nature implies a change in a host of words containing it, but for a word to lose a phoneme or gain or transpose one implies no necessary change in any phoneme. This happens constantly and sometimes imperceptibly, and the small changes accumulate till a word eventually takes on a shape that would have been unrecognizable to speakers of earlier generations. Many Americans now say *canidate* for *candidate* – the *n* and the *d* are similar enough for one to absorb the other. (Compare *take it for granite*, a common mispronunciation of *take it for granted*.) A natural further step – one that has occurred again and again – is the loss of an unstressed vowel next to a stressed one; this, if it occurs here, will yield **candate*.

Many speakers already use the shwa vowel (like that in the second syllable of *bonnet*) in the last syllable of *candidate*, so the result would be *cand[ə]t. If the *nd* yielded *n* before, it could do so again, producing *can[ə]t. A loss of the unstressed shwa would finally give *cant*, a phonologically legitimate descendant of *candidate*, but scarcely a recognizable one. People sometimes get tired of long words and force a change like this in one leap by abbreviation: *pen* for *penitentiary*, *pram* for *perambulator*.

Such radical alterations of words over time are the rule, and are the natural result cf the separation of form and meaning. Words are the elements of the code that stand most directly for segments of reality in all its range and variety. The vastness has a twofold effect. First, as we have seen, it destroys the possibility of a natural resemblance between the form and what it signifies – once arbitrariness takes over, 'anything goes'; a word can change without becoming any less appropriate to what it stands for – *cant* is as good a word (some would say better) for a political aspirant as *candidate*. Second, the larger the vocabulary of a language – the more choices we have from our memory store – the more the crowding in the storeroom presses one word on another. The relations among words begin to interfere with the relations between words and reality. A word may pick up a meaning from its context. This has happened with the English word *rather*, which by association with *would* has virtually become a verb – a child says *What would you rather me do?* Originally *would* alone expressed the wish: *I would* (it is my wish) *rather* (instead of something else) *you stayed*. *Rather* in its new and old functions can be seen in the repetition of the word in the following, from a newspaper medical column: 'Unless the condition is very serious I believe most doctors would *rather* have a feverish child play quietly out of bed *rather* than put up a constant fight in bed.'[1] But most interference between words is caused by similar meanings. The commonest instances are blends, where a new word comes from the fusion of two or more old ones. This is really a kind of malapropism. When something is *protuberant* it *protrudes*, and one is tempted to say *protruberant*. (The *American Scholar* succumbed, Spring 1961, page 233.) *Portentous* sounds like *pretentious*, there is a vague association of meaning, and the suffix *-tious* is more substantial and possibly more frequent than simple *-ous*, so we begin to get *portentious*. *Glob* is probably a blend of *gob* and *blob*. Like a swarm of bees, the swarm of words becomes self-governing, with internal forces as strong as external ones.

Above the level of the word, changes are fewer and slower. Yet they do occur, especially under conditions similar to those that caused the change in *rather*. When the burden of a total meaning is shared by a succession of words, the load may shift. This happens especially with verbs that stand together when one comes to be felt as a mere satellite of the other. The future tense in English is a cross between *will* or *shall* and other verbs, and a whole class of 'auxiliaries' behaves much like *will*: *can*, *could*, *may*, *might*, *should*. They form a class apart in that they are not inflected: *I may*, *you may*, but not **she mays*. (Though they were inflected within recent memory: *I may, thou mayest*.) As time goes on, other verbs drift imperceptibly into the auxiliary class. An example is *go* in *Will you go see who's there?* Of the forms of this verb, only *go* itself can be used in this sense; *went*, *goes*, and *gone* are forbidden (**He went see who was there*). The verb *get* is like an auxiliary in *get going*, *get moving*. Similarly *keep*: *He kept telling me* is shorthand for *He told me and told me and told me and*. . . . Its connection with the *keep* of *Keep your money* is obvious, but it has been specialized.

Changes like these occur in all languages at all times. Often two different languages stumble in the same direction – which is just to say that human propensities are the same everywhere. For example, the formation of the perfect tenses by using the verb for 'have' occurred in both Germanic and Romance languages. The process is obvious. If *I have a letter written*, it must be that *I have written a letter*. So we get a new tense in which a past action (*written*) is made relevant to the present (*have*). In a similar way, 'have' has provided identical expressions of obligation in English and Spanish: if *I have a letter to write*, clearly *I have to write a letter* (*Tengo una carta que escribir, Tengo que escribir una carta*).

But it is more usual for somewhat different devices to be adopted, or for the same devices to be used in slightly different ways, and the wedge between any two formerly related languages is driven deeper. For language to grow, form had to be divorced from meaning. But the price was high. The forms became so various that nations could not converse, and within nations the smaller diversities were cause for misunderstanding.

The divorce between meaning and form has been called DUALITY. As one linguist puts it, 'Duality freed concept and symbol from each other to the extent that change could now modify either one without affecting the other.'[2] The devastation of form is obvious, and some of its inroads have been examined in this chapter. It is the object of most linguists' historical investigations, and is the evil spirit that the shaman would cast out, for he regards change as corruption.

But few have looked at the other side for what it truly is: the effects that MEANING has undergone by being cut loose from form. It is not quite true that change modifies one without affecting the other. The friction on both sides is not due just to their independence but to their lingering connections. The problem is not separation but slippage. The unhappy couple have been divorced, but continue to live under the same roof – the thatched roof of the human head. Every day they have to settle their quarrels anew. A further look at this domestic scene – from the side of meaning – will come in Chapter 7.

Chapter 6

Stigma, status, and standard

When an American hears an Englishman say *They do you a very adequate hearing-aid on the National Health*,[1] and finally manages an interpretation, 'You can get a pretty good hearing aid from the National Health Service', he is puzzled at first, but respectful. These people have a strange way of turning a phrase, he thinks, but once you get the hang of it, it's OK. When the same American hears a Hawaiian say *This kind car better* or a Black child say *Some of them be big and some of them be small*, though he has no trouble understanding either sentence, he makes a mental note of the grammar.

On the other hand our American is delighted with the attractive French lady's remark to her companion, as he passes them and favors her with a stare, *Pour qui se prend-il?*,[2] uttered with a returning stare. He understands no French.

In all these instances there floats, along with the meanings of the words, the answer to a hidden question: WHO is doing the talking?

Since everyone knows that people of different backgrounds speak differently, why this selective appreciation? Perhaps there is something in the millennia of exogamy that makes a foreign accent in someone of the opposite sex attractive. But even without the spur of biology we are often more forgiving toward someone who is harder to understand. Why?

In part it is sheer provincialism. Another American is supposed to be 'one of us'. He drives an American car, eats hamburgers, watches Saturday football on TV, and mows the lawn on Sunday. So he ought to TALK like us. A foreigner is not to be blamed for lack of opportunities to learn English; our fellow citizen has been offered grace and refused it.

This resentment of others' rejection of our kind of talk is found in speech communities everywhere. The linguist Eunice Victoria Pike tells of going with a companion from one Mazatec-speaking village in Mexico, Chalco, to another, San Marcos, after having already learned some Mazatec. In the second village a family of teenage girls took on the responsibility of teaching them to 'talk right'. They naturally made mistakes by transferring English grammar and meanings to Mazatec, and many of those the girls let pass. But 'they shouted us down when we used a phrase peculiar to Chalco speech'.[3]

Attitudes toward a form of speech are hardly other than attitudes toward the speakers. Inferior people speak in inferior ways. Naturally. And the differences that mark their speech tend to be stigmatized. They are mostly trivial, as a rule, but are enough to activate a prejudice. They may be the only obvious signs of social status. You have an old friend in London, a successful plumbing contractor who now owns his own business. He looks and dresses like anyone else. You ask him to lunch at a posh restaurant. Even with your un-British accent you have no trouble getting what you want, but the waiter does not disguise his distaste at having to serve the broad Cockney demands of your friend.

Sometimes all varieties of a language except one are stigmatized to a certain degree. This happens in highly stratified societies and may bring on official attempts not only to teach the standard variety in the schools but to protect it by law. A 1975 French law applied the penalties of fraud (80 to 160 francs for the first offense, 90 to 5,600 for later offenses) to the use – by the 'media' – of forbidden terms in the language, which are those borrowings (mainly from English) for which a supposedly adequate equivalent already exists.[4] Such drastic steps betray an undercurrent of chauvinism – laws against a form of language are usually aimed at political entities at home or abroad that are assumed to be wielding too much influence. But domestic social pressures, with their own inlay of politics, are generally more powerful. In Britain the standard – and until recently the sign of social position and the key to social advancement – has been a variety of Southern English called Received Pronunciation. As the name implies, the earmarks of RP are not in grammar or in choice of words but in the sounds. A mispronounced vowel is more serious than an *ain't* or a *he don't*.

In America the stigma is more selective, and therefore, sometimes, more tenacious. The dialects that were transplanted from Britain were not so different from one another that they were ever a great hindrance to communication, but a number of regional standards – for example those centered on Boston, New York, and Charleston – were nevertheless established as a result of varying patterns of immigration from Britain, and others crystallized with the expansion westward. People living near the confluence of the three great rivers were not apt to be much influenced by the speech of New York, but were too close not to be influenced by that of St Louis. The relative openness of American political life and the prestige of high office has led to the acceptance of many styles of pronunciation, most recently the clipped New England-isms of John F. Kennedy, the Texan drawl of Lyndon Johnson, and the lower Georgian dialect of Jimmy Carter. In a popular television show during the Carter administration, a character representing a State Department official spoke conspicuously like a Georgian. When the New Yorker next to him called attention to it, he replied, 'We don't have an accent any more. You do.'[5]

The social groups whose speech is looked down upon can be stratified in any direction. There is the vertical stratum of homosexual speech, or the slang of teenagers of all classes. Horizontal strata embrace the established poor as well as recent immigrants, including those who migrate from one part of the country to another. Count a person's prejudices toward others – Jews, Mexicans, Indians, landlubbers, farmers, clergy, Oklahomans, rock artists – and you have a measure of the forms of speech that will arouse his suspicion or his resentment, or serve as the butt of his humor.

The negative attitudes lurk undetected till a social upheaval forces them to the surface. In America the most flagrant case is that of Black English. No other form of stigmatized speech in history has been discussed, written about, deplored, and justified as much as this. It deserves our attention as a classic of bedevilment.

In the beginning, the linguistic plight of the Negro slave was deliberate policy. In *A New Voyage to Guinea*, 1744, William Smith spoke of the dangers of having a shipload of captives all speaking the same language – they were sometimes able to overpower the crew. 'But the safest Way,' he wrote, 'is to trade with the different Nations, on either Side of the River, and having some of every Sort on board, there will be no more likelihood of their succeeding than of finishing the Tower of Babel.'[6] There is evidence that at least some of the mixed tribesmen were able to communicate by means of a pidgin English that incorporated elements of Portuguese and African languages, but the main benefit of this, according to one theory, was to serve as a nucleus of a common creole in the New World, which absorbed more and more from English as contacts with whites increased – especially among Blacks employed as domestics rather than as field hands. Pockets of a creole remain; it survives in the Gullah dialect of the Sea Islands of Georgia and South Carolina, protected by its isolation. And traces, possibly creole in origin (though some authorities deny this), are found in Black speech everywhere, especially among children who learn it from other children. Whatever their source, these traces – most in pronunciation but some in grammar – are enough to make Black English easy to identify and a ready target. Here are three of the most noticeable grammatical traits:

Ommission of the copula *is*: *You out the game.*

Dropping of the present-tense inflection *-s*: *He fast in everything he do.*[7]

Use of *be* to mean 'repeated occurrence', as in the example cited earlier: *Some of them be big.*

This use of *be* is often cited as evidence of semantic finesse in Black English. It is a distinction that the standard has difficulty making: *He workin'* means that he is busy right now; *He be workin'* means he has a steady job.[8] As for *He John* for *He is John*, the absence of the copula is no loss – other languages, including Russian, do without it, and even standard English omits it in expressions like *George here? I can't believe it!*

A comparison of two dialects is always misleading when one is taken as a standard. A few lines up is a reference to 'omission of the copula *is*' in Black English. Does Black English omit it, or does standard English add it? The temptation is to single out certain features in the standard and to judge the other dialect deficient if it lacks them. If there is a radical failure to mesh, then one may simply overlook what is truly a rich array of communicative resources in the downgraded dialect. Black culture in some ways is more different from mainstream American culture than, say, Scottish or Irish culture is. The differences in the means and manner of communication are no doubt correspondingly great, perhaps more so in the nonverbal than in the verbal – with most white observers simply blind to them. One place where this comes to view is in school testing:

> The older Black students have often learned to value wit as a means of self-protection and identity-projection, to parry questions with witty responses. The assessors' attempts to solicit information, then, may be met with responses in the form of counter-questions, or statements to the effect that 'you aren't for real'. A favorite manipulative activity of this sort may be 'running a game' on the tester, delivering messages in some form of in-group language knowing full well that those who do not share the cultural orientation of the 'hip' world will be unable to decode the messages. Too often whites unable to decipher these messages conclude that Black students are unable to assert command of the appropriate English varieties and brand them as 'linguistically deficient'.[9]

Black English in this respect is a form of secret language, promoting solidarity and intra-communication while excluding outsiders – a common phenomenon all over the world. (EVERY language is a secret language when it is used to exclude people who do not understand it. Some forms of speech – such as Pig Latin – are specially designed to serve that way.)

Dialects clash not only in their forms but also in what their speakers may regard as appropriate settings for different kinds of discourse. Take questions. In the average urban white household, parents like to quiz their children about this and that. Black families are more reticent:

> Questions seldom are encountered between adults and children, because there simply is little verbal interchange between the generations. When questions ARE asked, they generally arise from Mamma seeking quick information because of some failure in the smooth operation of the household. Thus, direct querying from adults to children tends to be associated, by Black children, with prospective threat in some accusation of wrongdoing.[10]

Counterbalancing the deemphasis of verbal interchanges is the increased reliance on nonverbal behavior or a greater interweaving of verbal and nonverbal. Most white Americans and white Britishers are uncomfortable with a high level of gesture or bodily communication, and inept at interpreting it. So, when Black children in the average mixed classroom unbend to the point of showing interest, their manners 'are interpreted as restlessness, inattentiveness, and sometimes hostility'.[11] Black culture is one to which sitting still in an audience while someone performs, and applauding in set ways at approved intervals, seems very strange.

In all respects – as far as it is possible to measure something as complex as a culture's whole means of expression – Black English is as good a working instrument for communication as any; but it has two faults: it is different, and it is spoken by Blacks.

Next to Black English, the most widespread stigmatized dialect in America is the Spanglish of the Southwest, spoken by the largest ethnic group in the country with a non-English background. Its users are in a linguistic no-man's-land: their speech is despised by English-speakers and Spanish-speakers alike. Among the dominant English-speaking majority, it is attitudes-as-usual: Spanglish is 'sloppy speech'; its speakers are not intelligent enough to learn a correct language.

Of course, Spanglish is learned as any language is learned – by the logical processes of abduction, deduction, and induction from the speech that children hear. No child is TAUGHT a language, except to the extent that elders – as a form of possibly instinctive play – model their speech: slowing it down, exaggerating the intonation, making sentences short, and mixing it with a richness of gestures, facial expressions, and clues from the context. On both sides, English and Spanish, Chicano children do their best with the means they have. Their Spanish, by comparison with that of speakers who have had the advantage of cultural continuity in a Spanish-speaking country, is full of grossly incorrect forms. Their English likewise. Yet when looked at in its own terms, each – and the blend between them – reveals the same organizing principles that characterize human linguistic ingenuity everywhere.

This does not exempt Chicano speech from being downgraded or its speakers from being judged as linguistically deprived – the 'deficit theory', as it is called. The children are classed as handicapped. A child who mispronounces English because of a Spanish background is given the kind of speech therapy designed for those who have something wrong with their physical equipment for speaking. In its crudest form this same theory charitably explains that the Black child is unable to pronounce correctly because of his thick lips. Other problems with language are put down to mental deficiencies, and the child – Black, Chicano, Navaho, Portuguese – ends up in a class for the mentally retarded. Everything is done, of course, to improve the lot of these unfortunates, except to understand the real cause of their plight. In one series of tests conducted by the California Department of Education a mere shift from the English to the Spanish version of the Wechsler Intelligence Scale resulted in an average mean gain in IQ of 13.15 points, for pupils who had earlier been put in classes for the 'educable mentally retarded'.[12]

A misdiagnosed deficiency becomes self-fulfilling. The children are retarded because the schools help to retard them. A common experience is that the IQ of Black children declines with age. (Since intelligence is supposedly native, it should remain the same, and tests are normed accordingly.) In one pair of tests, Black children were given questions specifically designed to eliminate cultural bias. The predicted drop in IQ still occurred between grades three and six.[13] Among the things that contribute to this depressing effect may be the unconscious attitude of the teacher, who, on hearing 'poor English', EXPECTS the child to do badly.[14]

Not all is submission on the part of minority speakers. It is not easy to give up one's heritage, of which language is the most intimate part. Revolutions have been fought over less, and language has been the rallying cry for resistance everywhere in the world – a Catalonia that opposed Franco in Spain, a Belgium where language riots unseated the government in 1968, a Quebec that in 1979 was threatening to secede from Canada, a Brittany that backs up its demands for autonomy by teaching Breton in defiance of French law and bombing French installations within its territory.[15] The speakers of a dialect that is dispersed through an area all of which is controlled by a dominant culture are not able to operate from a secure geographical base, but there are other ways of surmounting the barriers. The United States in the 1960s and 1970s saw the surge of minority groups – Blacks and Chicanos especially – pressing for better education, for jobs and recognition. Concessions and painful adjustments had to be made in the schools; standards of performance were changed – 'lowered' in terms of middle-class norms – and a high school certificate or a college diploma no longer guaranteed that its bearer would have certain linguistic or mathematical skills. At the same time, the problems of social adjustment compelled the schools to make room for instruction in other things besides language and mathematics, such as mechanical arts, environmentalism, consumerism, and sex education. The result was a partial breakdown in the schools' operation as a transmission belt – or at least reinforcer – of middle-class norms. In 1900 – the approximate base line of the shaman's nostalgia – one could reasonably demand the standard language in high school or college because it was mostly standard-speakers who were enrolled there: they had learned it at home, and needed only a trim, not a new hair-style.[16] And they were the ones who taught the next generation from grade school up. Today not a few teachers are themselves uncertain of their usage, and are hardly in a position to insist on more than a handful of formalities, where correctness is concerned.

Worse, there are newly confident elements that refuse to wear neckties and avoid double negatives while still demanding a share in middle class benefits. If test scores are interpreted to mean that Black or

Chicano candidates are not entitled to be admitted to the freshman class of a university, many of those rejected claim it is not they who are at fault but the scores. The minority protest is one more threat to middle class order. 'Language is a class weapon,' writes the British journalist Henry Fairlie, 'and the triumph of the middle class in the past few centuries has made our language a middle-class instrument. This is why the aristocrats and the underprivileged protest.'[17] One such protest, from a Black educator: 'Language conventions in America bees based on a preoccupation with what is correct English, not what is dynamic, not what is vivid, not what is truthful, but simply what is correct.'[18] As the middle-class educator, publicist, or politician looks at the declining test scores and hears the accents he does not understand, he condemns as frills the courses that crowd the three R's and calls for a return to the basics.

But a return to a strictly enforced standard becomes more and more difficult as the gap between generations widens. It was thought for a time that the rate of linguistic change stayed more or less the same, and statistical techniques were developed to determine how many hundreds or thousands of years ago two languages diverged, measuring the numbers and amounts of difference between them against a constant scale. Now we are fairly sure that change speeds up at some times, slows down at others. In American society and to some degree in other societies the effect of two generations of television-viewing is beginning to be felt. Radio began the process, but television has brought a range of dialects into the average home that would never have been heard in the first half of this century. And it is cumulative – the more the bonds are loosened, the greater the freedom to speak before the camera in the same tone and idiom as with friends. In one sense this leads toward uniformity as speakers unconsciously imitate one another across the old boundaries – predictions that British and Americans would no longer understand each other by the end of the twentieth century have not only been disproved but turned upside down: the two varieties of English have drawn closer together. But in another sense – the generational one – there is greater diversity. Children are bound to speak more differently from their parents than they would have if their models had been only the members of their own older generation and their friends and neighbors. The different parts of the English-speaking world converge even as their amalgam pulls away from each of the separate local standards and semi-standards. As part of the general loosening up, usages that were fairly widespread but had been held in check by some traditional regulation begin to occur freely. (A trivial example is the use of the word *kids* for 'children', which in the 1960s and 1970s began to crowd *children* out of its position as a generic. Of course it had been used for a long time, but always with a degree of affection or humor. Now it appears a new generation of speakers has drawn the inference, from hearing it so frequently, that it is the neutral term.)

One is always wise after the fact where linguistic change is concerned.

Fifty years from now it will be possible to judge whether the second half of the twentieth century was a time of speeding up. We can only say at the moment that it seems to be, and remark the difficulty that this poses to maintaining a more or less literary standard. The first two of the three-R basics are reading and writing, whose medium inevitably lags behind speech – and a speech more and more liberated by audio and video devices tends more and more to sheer off from the anchor of writing. Television and its congeners have begun to reverse the process that started with the invention of the printing press. Before Gutenberg, information was by word of mouth; even afterward, for several centuries, the press served a very limited and mostly scholarly public. But with the popular revolutions of the eighteenth and nineteenth centuries, the press came into its own – the DAILY press in particular, as the channel of universal information. This in turn gave the schools the heavy assignment of universal literacy. Reading and writing were no longer educational luxuries but necessities, and as they were increasingly integrated with speaking skills, speech was more and more affected by them. The conservatism of writing put a brake on some forms of linguistic change and speeded up others (most notoriously, spelling pronunciations – see page 41). By mid-twentieth century the process had reached its peak with literacy not only spread across the whole population but pushed to higher levels as graduates of secondary schools began to throng the colleges. It is ironic that at the very point of almost achieving the ideal, the immediate practical need for literacy has begun to decline (though our lives will depend on it for the foreseeable future, and without it we lose our history). The 'declining literacy scores' deplored by educators and editors reflect the television watershed: 'Who needs to read?' Shirley Brice Heath reports one of her students asking, 'I can learn all I need to know by keeping my ears and eyes open.'[19] A generation of youth will learn what it needs to know and not much more.

So the schools are caught in a double confusion. On the one hand, the language is being destabilized on the literary side – the standard loses its grip as fewer and fewer learn to read and write well. On the other hand, there is as yet no REstabilization of speech. Heath describes an earlier period in our history:

> Stump meetings, the lyceum movement, debating clubs, and literary societies give evidence of the . . . emphasis on talk for exchange of information. Conversation across various sectors of society was highly valued for the immediate review and challenge of ideas it offered.[20]

The lyceums in the first half of the nineteenth century and the Chautauqua in the latter half were among the great diffusers of oral culture, and the skills they represented were cultivated in the schools, where DICTION was as much a part of learning English as reading and writing. But with the triumph of literacy, oral delivery has been neglected – there is less debating, the reciting of poetry is no longer part of the general culture, and a class in oratory would probably have to be canceled for lack of students. Speaking skills are not taught for themselves nor for what they have in common with writing: clarity, eloquence, logical organization, standards of correctness. Speech goes its own way, and speakers drift farther than ever from a literary standard. Shamans and traditionalists of all camps sense the general subversion, and it panics them.

If the average middle class white schoolchild is out of touch with the literary standard, the minority child is doubly so. There is a colloquial standard to learn on the playground and a literary standard to learn in class. To satisfy all communicative needs, both standards have to be learned, and the burden is a heavy one, for all that it may be eased by remedial and bilingual classes. The desired uniformity could be achieved by adopting the forms used by the underprivileged, but it never is – they are the ones who must demote their own language and learn a new one, replacing the threads that join their minds and their feelings to reality – like the operation of reconnecting the flesh and nerves of a severed limb. The task is hardest for those most distant from the standard and those whose exclusion for other reasons – such as color – has imbued them with feelings of defiant loyalty to their inheritance.

Nevertheless a society needs a standard and a fairly uniform one, whether it wells up from below or is imposed from above. The alternative can easily be worse. How vital a single mode of communication can be is seen in countries divided by language where, until the division is healed, government is impossible. If one of the rival languages is made official, speakers of the others complain of favoritism. If together they have enough political power, they may be able to prevent the enforcement of a native standard. This has happened in various countries since the Second World War, chiefly former British colonies with inherited English-speaking bureaucracies. In Nigeria, the number of indigenous languages, possibly running into the hundreds, 'makes it impracticable to adopt any one of them as the national language. English therefore by its neutrality recommends itself as the only choice available for adoption as a national language. No one ethnic group can feel cheated through its use as it naturally would if the language of another ethnic group were adopted.'[21] In India, English is still the language that trains the armed forces, examines students in the universities, conducts foreign affairs, and opens the way to a business career.[22] In Nigeria even the nursery schools are taught in English. Though English is hardly a native language to any of them, the Indian – like the Nigerian, the Malayan, the Ghanaian, the Ceylonese, and the Filipino – accepts the burden for its practical benefits. Maintaining a standard in a country like England or America where most speakers already command a variety of the same language comes cheap by comparison. To what extent this promotes economic power would be hard to estimate, but the two are certainly not unrelated.

But what makes it easy also raises the question of its necessity. If all speak a language universally understood in spite of its dialectal variation, why standardize any one of the dialects? The answer seems to be that people expect it. Communication is interfered with by many things besides unintelligibility. Mere DISTRACTION is a hindrance – if manner of expression draws attention away from content, a listener may lose the thread; listeners come in all degrees of sympathy, and many expect to be coddled. Unintelligibility too exists in degrees: a train of thought is easily derailed by a message that comes clear only after a second or third hearing or reading. A standard that embodies SOME precepts is desirable, and works best when the precepts are self-enforcing, that is, when speakers impose them in the act of communicating, by showing annoyance, incomprehension, or amusement when they are violated. The permissivist is apt to forget this, and to be as unreasonable in objecting to a good rule as the purist is in trying to enforce a bad one. An example is the rule for avoiding dangling modifiers:

> You remember your Wonderful English Teacher – everyone had one – the one who hated bad language and loved grammar. And loved even more making fun of bad grammar. Like this sentence:
>
> Lincoln wrote the Gettysburg Address while riding on a train on the back of an envelope.
>
> 'You see what that means?' says the Wonderful English Teacher: 'The train is on the envelope—'
>
> We do not, usually, see that without one or two rereadings of the sentence. But we learn to. And we learn to alter that sentence so as not to confuse all those people who don't know that a train is bigger than an envelope. And we learn a great many more important solutions for which there are no problems.[23]

The Wonderful English Teacher is too good a disciple of the shaman not to be wrong a good part of the time, but this happens to be one solution for which there IS a problem. Of course people know that a train is bigger than an envelope – but that sentence suggests the opposite (especially in writing), which makes it funny, which is distracting – and distractions are best avoided. Most readers are well aware that murder victims, once dead, are incapable of further action; nevertheless – and THEREFORE – their thoughts are apt to wander from what the writer intends when they read a sentence like the following, with its dangling participle: *Then all three victims were shot execution style with a large-caliber weapon before cleaning out a safe and fleeing.*[24]

There will be a prestige variety so long as speakers and writers must take account of the needs and desires of hearers and readers. And if producing messages and receiving and decoding them are psychologically opposed operations, as some linguists think,[25] then that accountability will always be with us. Speakers naturally prefer to sing their half of the duet with no more effort than necessary – to use the words and constructions that come first to mind, to speak at low volume, to slur the sounds. Hearers just as naturally want comprehension to require no more effort than necessary – to be favored with background information, unambiguous sentences, and reasonably crisp articulation. The speaker or writer of course is the one who has to make most of the concessions, especially if he has an audience of more than one and most especially if the audience is remote in space or time. This explains why a prestige variety is so needed in writing. There is no feedback. The audience may run in the thousands, with a demonry of misunderstandings waiting to pounce on every ambiguity. The lessons in what works best, learned by trial and error, can be put together in a sort of code, and taught. This is rhetoric, in the original meaning of the term. It is by definition conservative, because innovations do not spread immediately or evenly, and may threaten communication if they are admitted too soon. Though he probably offered it on esthetic rather than practical grounds, John Ciardi's advice deserves a hearing: 'It will not do to resist uncompromisingly. Yet those who care have a duty to resist. Changes that occur against such resistance are tested changes. The language is better for them – and for the resistance.'[26] The PRESTIGE STANDARD is better for them, but if a standard is needed, then what is good for the standard is good for the language.

Though speaking is not the same as writing, there is a standard there too, and since the motives are the same – to do as you would be done by if you were the reader or hearer – the two standards often coincide. With speaking, the consideration that must be shown is not only intelligibility and avoidance of distraction but regard for status. Societies differ in the signs of deference they expect, but there is always some degree of formality when one speaks to a stranger, an employer, a clergyman, or someone of rank. In some languages the forms of courtesy are rigidly stylized. In English they tend to be added on rather than manifested in the grammatical structure – as they are for example in the verb forms of Romance and Germanic languages that distinguish a more distant *vous* from a more intimate *tu* in the endings of the verb (as English once did with its *thou mayest, you may*). In one area the verb still retains a courtesy marker, the use of the past to soften a request: a clerk in a store may ask deferentially *Was there something you were looking for?* rather than *Is there something you're looking for?* Elsewhere, courtesy is shown in English mostly by choice of words (addressing someone as *sir* or *madam* rather than *you there*) and tone of voice – especially in intonation, by toning down the accents. Of the following, the first, with its accent on *leave* at a lowered pitch, is more restrained:

```
         it              Leave
   Leave                    it
         there.                there.
```

Other indicators of relationship between speakers – intimacy, for example, or condescension – are just as important to know but less important to teach. The child grows up with intimate forms of speech, but requires the deferential forms in later contact with the world.

A hearer or reader sensitive to these marks of consideration is apt not to be cooperative if they are disregarded. No matter how democratic the society, they will always exist in some form. Americans in this century have tended to overlook them because of long indoctrination in the ethic of equality, which in its extreme form even denied that social classes existed in the United States. (It was still a new idea in the nineteenth century, when numerous manuals of good conduct explained for the benefit of men, women, or children how to speak and behave with persons of a different age, sex, or class.)[27] Many young people of the 1960s went further and scorned courteous behaviour as insincere, sometimes going out of their way to use profane language (at the University of California in Berkeley it was the 'Free Speech Movement' – FSM, dubbed Filthy Speech Movement by their opponents). Rules of respect, condescension, intimacy, and avoidance – what to say where and to whom – are learned along with the rest of language. One may break some of them, on whatever pretext (to 'show that I don't have to kowtow to those people', 'to let this humble person know that I respect him as much as I do an aristocrat'), but they are there to be observed for the most part, and to the extent that the standard is explained and taught, they have to be made explicit. No one wants to break all of them all the time – a conversation that did would probably stall before it got started.

This leaves us with a dilemma. If the shaman's scapegoat rules are off the mark, must we still observe them to avoid offending him? It all depends. The fact is that we humor some of his prejudices as a matter of course – the ones that have been so insisted on that everyone's eye is caught when they occur, to the confusion of the message. One example is *ain't*; the proscription against it was unreasonable, yet most people avoid the word or use it to be consciously funny. Another is the double negative, as in *They don't have no money*, which goes back to Chaucer and beyond and is the rule in many languages. It is common today, and is avoided or not depending on the speaker and the audience. If rules are to be broken, it is better done from knowledge than from ignorance, even when ignorance ultimately decides the issue.

So standards are inevitable – and their champions are eternal. William Caxton wrote in 1490, 'For in these dayes, every man that is in ony reputacyen in his contre will utter his commynycacyon and maters in such termes that few men shall understonde them.' And Thomas Sheridan in 1780: 'Some of our most celebrated writers . . . have been guilty of great solecisms, inaccuracies, and even grammatical impro- prieties, in many places of their most finished works.'[28] And Charles Morgan in 1948: 'The area of experience which cannot be described in the ordinary language of cultivated men extends year by year. . . . In part the loss of communication is due to loss of craftsmanship in language, to the belief that if some abandon rules sometimes (as all artists do), all may abandon rules all the time.'[29] When language changes it always seems to be going to the dogs, because we are more aware of the discomforts, of the inconvenience to our habits, than we are of the benefits. We are distressed by the loss of a distinction (*disinterested* is ruined because of confusion with *uninterested*, *gay* is ruined by homosexual associations), by a shift in pronunciation that puts a greater burden on inferring meaning from context (*popper* and *pauper*), by a reflection of new attitudes that make our courtesy formulas obsolete. But human ingenuity and intelligence, plus what may amount to an instinct for symbolism, comes to the rescue. Today's amenities are not yesterday's, and the language must keep pace. When one distinction is lost, another is gained – occasionally even through the unwitting efforts of the shaman. Insistence on *well* rather than *good* in such contexts as *Shake it well* (*good*) has created a semantic split related to the adjective-adverb distinction but extending beyond it: *good* has become emotionally charged, *well* is colorless. *He treats me good* expresses more appreciation than *He treats me well*, and *She scolded him, but good* can hardly be expressed with *well* at all. Years of railing against *sure* in sentences like *He sure must want it* have specialized the word to imply that the hearer will agree (*He surely must want it* is indifferent – it can be used to counter disagreement). Anything that creates linguistic debris is an invitation to recycle. More new meanings find expression this way than by almost any other process. Language could not live without it. Errors and slippages are like the mutants in biology – from them are made the selections essential to survival. This is happening before our eyes with the *each other* construction. It was plural (*They all took each other's classes*)[30] but now is becoming indifferent to number (*Everyone took each other's classes* instead of *Everyone took everyone else's classes*); any kind of reciprocal action may soon be allowed (examples where this has already happened: *Every policeman will be able to communicate with each other*; *Banks now move money between each other electronically*).

The durability of standards and their defenders probably reflects, somewhere inside us, hatched no doubt by the lesson we learned as children that some things are said and others not, a deep craving for authority. There are cultures in which people 'characteristically prefer to hear a political speech or an expository lecture or a recitation of poetry in H [higher level] even though it may be less intelligible to them than it would be in L [lower level]'.[31] The same is true of our own subcultures. Many devout people have objected to each new version of the Bible, and when a decree of Pope Paul in 1963 introduced the vernacular languages to the Roman Catholic ritual, it kindled a reaction that still smolders; in 1976 Archbishop Marcel Lefebre was forbidden to celebrate Mass after he refused to give up the Tridentine Latin service – but he celebrated it anyway, with the support of French traditionalists. Just the way something SOUNDS is important to many people; language is a mainstay of ritual, being itself the High Church ritual of communicative behavior.

Even the populations that might seem to benefit most from a relaxation of authority often reject it. At the very time some educators and many linguists were trying to understand Black English and draw out the stigma, others, even including the officials of the National Association for the Advancement of Colored People, were denouncing the move: 'Black parents throughout this nation should rise up in unanimous condemnation of this insidious conspiracy to cripple their children permanently,' said an editorial in the NAACP journal in 1971[32] – an understandable reaction on the part of those who see ability to use the standard fluently as the only way to get ahead. And when schools that lack the resources in money, teachers, and materials to do the job properly try to meet the needs of their minorities by offering special instruction in non-standard languages and dialects, they may disrupt other programs and do more harm than good.

As long as precepts are inevitable, they had better be made sensible. Lost causes should be abandoned. Useful changes should be recognized for what they are worth, even if they force the older among us to adapt ourselves to new conditions. The standard should accommodate a reasonably wide variation. Above all, the public and its policy-makers have a right to demand accurate information in this field as they demand it in those of health, public safety, and the cost of living. We need to be able to point to the rule-givers and say, 'We know you are a necessary evil, but we know enough about language to recognize the charlatans among you.' Authority is fine when not made of whole cloth and trimmed with lunatic fringe.

Chapter 7

We reduced the size because we didn't want to increase the price

This chapter is about the nature of THINGS. About entities and pseudo-entities. About reality, and the sorcery of words.

On 29 May 1976 the female employees at Carter's Semiconductors in Ipoh, Malaysia left their workbenches and ran from the factory, terrified and shrieking that they had been molested by a ten-foot ghost without a head. The worried management called in a witch doctor who proceeded to sprinkle rice and water around the factory and sacrificed a goat to appease the spirits of the dead. The workers went back to their jobs and the ghost back to its limbo. Ghosts in Malaysia are a restless lot. Every so often one will show up at a school and frighten the daylights out of the pupils. There are clinical-minded people who claim that the youngsters are just hysterical from overwork, but that of course is pure speculation.

Papua New Guineans believe themselves composed of body and spirit, and that the spirit is able to leave the body and does so during dreams. One must not wake a sleeping person too abruptly, or the spirit may not have time to get back in. If it leaves the body during waking hours, the result is the sensation of fear: they say, 'His spirit went away.'[1]

All over the Middle East and around the Mediterranean the Evil Eye spies out its victims and follows them when they migrate to other lands. It pursues the Yemenite Jews, for example, to New York City, focusing its malevolence on the Oldtimers and the Orthodox. Children are the most vulnerable, and adults have rituals to protect them. If a child is too precocious, a parent can avert the consequences with an incantation such as 'Poverty to your enemy' or 'Let me sacrifice my liver for yours'.[2]

In October of 1976 a Suffern, New York lawyer, Warren Berbit, described a manifestation: 'Shaped like two enormous upside-down soup bowls, the objects hovered in the sky just over a dip in the Ramapo mountain range. The red-orange rays of the setting sun glinted from their silvery metallic bodies. One remained motionless above the horizon while the other slipped gradually and silently from a vertical position to a horizontal one.'[3] It is not recorded whether Berbit was alarmed over a possibility announced a year earlier by Robert D. Barry, Director of the Twentieth Century UFO Bureau, that the UFOs might have been piloted by two of Lucifer's fallen angels.[4] Other claims of sightings between these dates brought an angry letter from a reader who decried the UFO 'con artists' and called for realism in communication with the beyond: 'One radio contact could yield the greatest social and philosophical benefits to our civilization since the discovery of fire.'[5] The National Aeronautics and Space Administration, in its linguistic sophistication, continues its efforts to communicate with intelligent beings in outer space. In 1976 the *Encyclopaedia Britannica* published in its *Book of the Year* a four-page special report by Lawrence K. Lustig on 'Science and Superstition: An Age of Unreason'.

Near Allahabad, India, a seven-year-old boy, to tease his mother, touches a servant – an Untouchable – and is rushed to the washbasin to be scrubbed free of the *impurity*. A few days later he drinks a glass of ceremonially *pure* water from the river Ganges, and in three weeks is dead of typhoid fever.

In 1886, in *Santa Clara County vs Southern Pacific Railroad*, the United States Supreme Court decreed that corporations were *persons*, and extended the protection of the Fourteenth Amendment to their life and liberty (and property, of course). One result, commented the *Britannica*, was that corporations 'developed a personality'.[6]

In 1975, thirty thousand pilgrims thronged Bogotá, Colombia, for the First World Congress of Sorcery.

'By habit,' wrote Jeremy Bentham in 1815, 'wherever a man sees a NAME, he is led to figure to himself a corresponding object, of the reality of which the NAME is accepted by him, as it were of course, in the character of a CERTIFICATE. From this delusion, endless is the confusion, the error, the dissension, the hostility, that has been derived.'[7]

This is the meaning side of the Babylonian separation. Formal Babel was created by the unchecked growth of forms cut loose from symbolic ties and left to travel their own ways toward the confusion of tongues. Or toward the FURTHER confusion if more than one symbolic language existed before the mythical Babel. In any case, meaning too was set adrift, and began to cling to any bit of flotsam within reach: this was semantic Babel. In the long ago, when meanings were conveyed by look-alike forms, to symbolize something nonexistent was limited to fanciful juxtapositions – physically or pictorially – of odd parts: a god with a horse's body and a lion's head, a tree sprouting hands or an arm sprouting leaves. Once resemblance was no longer required, no curb was left on the verbal imagination – a name could stand for anything, or for nothing; for something definite enough to stub one's toe on, or too vague to describe; for two things together seen as one; for a visible effect and an invisible cause. This is not to say that all ghosts and UFOs depended on words in the first place. There are thoughts and images that have no embodiment – the seer undoubtedly sees SOMETHING, but is it what he thinks he sees? Once he names and reports it, Bentham's axiom comes into play: the name certifies the reality.

We call this REIFICATION, the materializing of abstractions. It rests, like everything else in language, on the child's experiences while learning. First come words that are visibly and tangibly attached to objects. Then words with pictures or figurines, with verification later – the first soldier is a toy soldier, the first giraffe an illustration in a storybook. Finally words with no immediate counterpart, but by then so much has already been confirmed – real soldiers in a parade, real giraffes in a zoo – that confirmation is expected in all serious discourse, and words are accepted with suspended judgment. As long as there are no indications to the contrary, a word is a ticket to a meaning; and for most of us the threshold of indications to the contrary is very high. Gullibility is another name for misplacing the burden of proof. The believer is not required to establish his belief, but the skeptic is required to prove his doubt. Clairvoyance and astrology are happy to stop with 'but it could be true' or 'for all we know' or to quote Hamlet on all the things in heaven and earth that are not dreamt of in our philosophy. Santa Claus lives. Witches come out on Hallowe'en. Specters walk in the rain forest.

Not all this is deception or self-delusion. It is an essential mechanism of language to assemble by name what is toilsome or impossible to assemble by hand. A two-year-old child applies the word *door* to the act of opening or closing a door, a handbag, a toy teapot, a box, the flap on an envelope, and to removing the wrapper from a piece of candy. All these acts have been 'seen' as one. Every general term and every abstraction is an elaboration of this, and is matched by reality with its often indeterminate borders. In fact, both practically and philosophically our reality often turns out not to be very real. Practically it may be in the process of becoming real – what is an invention before it is invented? Philosophically we know that nothing is quite the same when viewed in a different light – the fabled blind men describing an elephant could only describe the parts, and to describe the whole would have required an inductive theory. Faced with a reality that has only a tentative relationship with the names of things as we know them, we are not too skeptical of dreams and visions.

The fallacy of a logical language, with words drained of passion and syntax pretending to represent the true articulation of events, resembles the fantasy that any form of human communication, as it has emerged through millions of years of human evolution, could mesh sufficiently with the form of signals from outer space to enable us to communicate with unearthly beings. As if we had not enough trouble already merely translating from one earthly language to another – and teaching our closest anthropoid relatives OUR sign language in order to communicate with us! In the Second World War the Japanese struggled to decipher a code that utterly baffled their cryptographers. The Americans had slyly recruited Indians to relay their dispatches in Navaho. Understand messages from another planet? It is begging the question just to ask it. What is understanding? What is a message?

Still, clever people have for centuries tried to devise a logical, neutral language, transcending national tongues, free of irregularities, and corresponding point by point with the real world. The nearest this has come to success is with Esperanto, devised in the 1880s by a Russian physician, Ludwig Zamenhof. It has had a limited usefulness in Western Europe because it embodies common features of Western European languages and is easy to learn – for Western Europeans; it is of less use to a Vietnamese or a Guaraní. Neither Esperanto nor any other such invention will ever be a language in the full sense till it is learned and absorbed by children as their first language. And when that happens, its neutrality will be attacked by all the old inherited contradictions, foremost of which is the conflict of interests between hearers and speakers: 'You want to speak with least effort, so you speak sloppily; I want to hear with least effort, so I listen with half an ear.' The ancient round of making a mess of things and cleaning up the mess starts over again, with its consequences of near-chaos alternating with last-minute rescue.

It is not as if fresh starts were never made. There are both 'natural' and 'artificial' examples of them. The natural ones are the pidgins – trade languages that were compromises of two or more natural languages with most of the formal difficulties stripped away and a highly concrete vocabulary, whose use in particular areas became so intense that children began to learn them, and in the process turned them into natural languages – 'creoles'. Probably every language spoken in the world today is at least to some extent a creole, an offspring of contact and conflict.

The relatively artificial examples include the sign languages for the deaf, which have been partly worked out by design but once adopted have taken on the characteristics of a natural language (except, of course, for being manual rather than oral). Also included is the artificial adoption of dead languages for nationalistic purposes. The official language of Israel is Hebrew, whose status, prior to its adoption there, resembled that of Latin in Europe. Once again, exposed to the needs of live people and to the hazards of being learned by infants, this language too has begun to evolve away from the paradigms that the schools and synagogues had shaped for it. It is always possible to have special languages for special purposes – logical language for logical discourse, artistic language for art, mathematical language for computation; yet even these could probably not exist without some natural language through which they can be elaborated. The multi-purpose language that all human beings require for the ordinary business of living can evolve in just one direction: toward being, in its faults and virtues, like every other natural language on earth.

And that includes the part of our human condition that fuses language and reality and bares our minds to deception.

Every language abounds in words for pseudo-entities. In English, many testify to ancient beliefs preserved in myth and folklore – *goblin, woodnymph, satyr, griffin, unicorn, Zeus, Gorgon, elixir.* Others are creations, mostly literary: *Utopia, Brobdingnag, Erewhon, Lothario, jayhawk*. Real or unreal depending on one's faith are the entities of religion: *Trinity, heaven, purgatory, devil, resurrection, millennium, transsubstantiation*. There is a verb that goes with these entities: *believe in* – not the acceptance of what is thought to be true expressed by simple *believe*, as in *I believe the story* or *I believe you*, but the prior suspension of doubt – faith rather than credence: *I believe in you, in life after death, in the Virgin Birth*.

In a sense the entities of history are pseudo-entities; they are known by hearsay. The evidence for them tends to be persuasive and overcomes our doubts. But the habit of accepting the reality of a Julius Caesar – who offers no proof to our senses – makes us more willing to accept a Cyclops. Memory is hard to distinguish from imagination.

But more numerous than words for things imaginary, otherworldly, or past and gone are words that incorporate a certain amount of undisputed reality but lay claim to more. They are found in great abundance in societies with proliferating goods and services which must be labeled, priced, advertised, regulated, and otherwise dealt with as if they were natural phenomena; these are reified, and so are their social effects. Tradesmen have always made *profits*. It was not till profit-making became unconscionable that people began to speak of *profiteering* – around the beginning of the last century. Some people have been idle from time to time ever since working for other people became a way of making a living; but the word *unemployment* was not in common use until around 1895 – the social problem gave rise to the name, and the name reified the problem. Reifying the problem called for reifying the solution: jobs. *Job* is a fairly new word for 'regular employment'. It is independent of operational terms like *TV serviceman, gas station attendant, coal miner, claims adjuster, cashier*, and *funeral director*. It is the democratization of a concept that formerly applied only to the genteel labor of government service, teaching, medicine, and law – in those occupations one had a *position* or a *situation*; the common run of humanity worked at *jobs* in the older sense of 'piecework'; but as the work became steady, so did the meaning of the word, and nowadays *job* is understood as 'steady' unless specified otherwise. One can speak of the job as a social value without examining what lies back of it. Reformers soon learn this when they advocate programs that may mean 'loss of jobs'. Productive work is esteemed regardless of the nature of the product – shoes or cigarets, tractors or tanks. Jobs are 'out there' for the seeking, and if they don't exist already, government should create them.

Some jobs cause *pollution*, which crystallizes its opposition in the name of *environmentalism* – a term not recorded in its modern sense in as recent a dictionary as the Merriam *Third New International* (1961) – only in the last few years have people conceived of contamination as a force affecting their lives. Or their *lifestyle*, as today's generation call it, reifying their preoccupation with 'doing their own thing'. All these concerns and discomforts existed before, but had not achieved the reality conferred by giving them their own names.

The staking out of new semantic ground can be seen most clearly in the making of compound words in English. For example, the language has a rule that permits the building of a certain type of compound by adding the *-ing* form of the verb to the noun that is its logical object: *fish-catching, bear-baiting, rum-running, nose-picking, book-burning.* But these terms are normally created only when the action achieves a certain status. One would not say *In our house we avoid floor-dirtying* – this action has not assumed the proportions of either a problem or a pastime. Compounds are the easiest of all 'new words' to create, and if we do not ordinarily create them till there is some more or less definite thing out there to name by them, then once again there arises a motive for pseudo-entities: if an existing name is a certificate of a thing, the making of a new name is a certificate for the making of a new thing. In the first case the language fools us, in the second case the fraudulent word-coiner does: it is unlikely that any of the bottled *hair-restorers* ever restored hair or that *consciousness-expanding* was quite what it pretended to be. Even the honest word-coiner may win by this kind of magic – the Johnny-come-lately who pins on the label all too often gets credit for the discovery.

Among the existing pseudo-entities, ghosts and unicorns are not especially dangerous. They can be frightened off with a denial: *I don't believe in ghosts.* The treacherous ones are those that are not all pseudo. They have a genuine side, and the false one hides behind it. Take the verb *to earn.* It occurs with its basic meaning in a sentence like *I have earned my wage and I expect you to pay it* – this is 'to merit as compensation'. It also occurs in *The president of Continental Motors earns $500,000 a year.* Does this represent a different meaning, simply 'to get' or 'to receive', or is it still the basic sense, implying that it is possible for someone's annual labor to be worth half a million? The two-faced verb sidetracks the question. Or take the verb *to own.* It relates to the adjective *own*, as in *She only claims what is her own, not what belongs to someone else,* where a genuine right is implied. But the verb is used in sentences like *They own half the state of Chihuahua,* which refers to asserting title yet trades on the other meaning. What is ownership? For that matter, what is possession? The language has a possessive case that imputes a property right to things: *my name, my dog.* In the spring of 1977, when gangster money was reported to be flowing freely in Arizona, some non-gangster beneficiaries were saying, '*His* money is as good as *anybody else's*' – this in the nine-points-of-the-law sense of possession, disguised as true entitlement.

Not all classes of words have the same capacity for deception. The names of qualities – adjectives and adverbs, mostly – are expressed separately from what they describe, and can be singled out and denied if they are false: *The man is old. – No, he is not old.* Even when applied attributively – *the old man* rather than *The man is old* – one can counter with *The man you are calling old is not old.* Adjectives are 'detachable'. Certain things about them can be EXPLOITED for deception – their vagueness, their tendency to imply values as well as to describe traits (is

Mary *good* or *goody-goody*? is John *easygoing* or *spineless*?), and their admission of exaggeration (is anything *perfect*, *unique*, or *irresistible*?) – but we are not apt to be taken in by the mere existence of a particular adjective in the language.

Not so with nouns. They are the hotbed of pseudonymy. This is to be expected, given their function, which is to lay hold of some portion of reality and hold it up to view. Hold it up, that is, AS IF it were a portion of reality. It may embody a slew of things. What is a *vitamin*? To define this word the Merriam *Third* requires a sentence containing a main clause and ten subordinate clauses, not counting a couple of dozen qualifying adjectives, adverbs, and prepositional phrases. Our confidence in the name emboldens us to talk about vitamins as if we knew what they were, and yet the disputes about them – is laetrile a vitamin or a drug? is ascorbic acid a vitamin or a metabolite? – prove that the chief claim to reality of this conglomeration of things is the name itself.

If what the noun collects under its wing is a jumble of mismated parts glued together with imagination, something can always be done to give it the appearance of consistency. Political entities are the leading examples of this, beginning with the State or Nation. Charles Osgood speaks of the *Nation* as 'the unit in international affairs':

> Since the flowing forests and oceans do not recognize these creations of the human mind, we put up boundary markers, erect walls and fortifications, establish border-crossing restrictions, try to impose language homogeneity within boundaries, define invisible territorial extensions into the seas and brightly color our maps in different hues so that children can learn just what is REALLY where – all to reaffirm that *The Nation* is indeed a unitary thing just like other things that have names. It then becomes easier to personify nations as Actors in a great global game, and harder to appreciate either the similarities across boundaries or the differences within.[8]

If some entities have no real unity, others have no substance. A process or an abstraction has to be caught on the wing. A term such as *air superiority* means 'having a superior number of planes', yet it is presented as if it could be produced, increased, controlled, or divided in half. *It took the subject two seconds to react* is worded – in a psychological experiment – as *The subject's reaction time was two seconds*. Science is forever having to pin down some form of elusive movement, or something that can be seen only by moving from point to point and summing up the glimpses. Its paths are strewn with the wrecks of old intellectual attacks and retreats – *calx*, *phlogiston*, *epicycle*, *phrenology*. They show to what extent nature is dependent on man's view of it. In the 'soft' sciences – sociology, political science, economics, psychology – and above all in philosophy, it almost seems as if the terms created the field. The phenomena are so complex that the manner of conceptualizing them becomes as powerful as the nature of the facts, and reformulations and renamings follow one another endlessly.

If the pseudo-entities of science are approximations to reality, those of commerce are parodies of it, with science as the model. The enterprise of concocting goods and promotional ideas is one vast exercise in pseudo-reification. Each fabricated pseudo-thing comes neatly wrapped in its noun – a nice grammatical analogy, because packaging is the typical result in the real world and the noun is a typical verbal package.

The packages contain SOMETHING, of course – the magician needs props for his illusions. But the entities are potentially random and limitless – a modern supermarket requires yards of shelf space just for its prepared cereal fantasies; the important thing is to make them APPEAR to have the same reality as an object of nature. A couple of generations ago, before the pseudo-entity explosion, all 'staples' were sold 'in bulk' – pickles came in barrels and flour in bins, and the merchant dipped or ladled out the buyer's portion; the product still took priority over the package.

The acceptance of packaging leads to the acceptance of the packaged object, promoted as having an existence of its own – capable of change in size, price, and quality. Milk chocolate sold in bulk could only vary in price and quality. A reified chocolate bar can also vary in quantity. So when the 'giant bar' shrank from eight to six ounces, and from six to five, the manufacturer reassured the public with impeccable logic: 'We reduced the size because we didn't want to increase the price.'

Fabricated reality has its visual and material illusions as well as its verbal ones. Pink toilet paper says, 'I am delicate', and when packed in a loose roll it says, 'I am soft' and 'I am larger than I really am'. The wasp-waisted bottle of salad oil says, 'I am not fattening'. Television newsman Daniel Schorr had this to say about the visual barrage: 'For many who have grown up in the media generation, the television reality is the only reality they have ever known. It may be the only reality that exists.'[9]

The chocolate bar is at least a real dollop of real chocolate. With many commercial pseudo-entities the contents are chiefly the evocations of scientific jargon or pure trademarked imagination – the mystery ingredients such as *irium*, the curatives such as *hexylresorcinol*, and the unadulterated hydromancy of *the water* in certain brands of beer. When the Shell Oil Company advertised that Shell gasoline with *Platformate* gave more mileage than any rival brand without that ingredient, it made an empty claim, because 'Platformate or its equivalent is present in virtually every gasoline refined'.[10]

The importance of the word in this scheme of things – even when the entity makes good on its implied claim of intrinsic value – can be seen in the litigation over trademarks and the vigilance that their owners keep to warn off poachers. Some names – *aspirin* and *linoleum* are the classic examples – have been captured for the public domain by individuals exercising squatters' rights, speakers who simply disregard the proprietary claim; in the long run the courts condone this, for they do not encourage private ownership of words of the English language. In 1978 the United States Supreme Court rejected the pretension of the

Miller Brewing Company to exclusive use of *Lite* or *Light* for its low-calorie beer. *Aspirin* and *linoleum* became common nouns by sheer weight of usage. But *Kodak* has been jealously guarded since 1888. *Xerox* holds its own. *Mimeograph* has probably lost the battle. More on this in Chapter 12.

Some names for concocted entities perform a kind of service. It is easier to remember and ask for *Clorox* than for *5.25 per cent solution of sodium hypochlorite*. The mixers and namers count on that. But the house brand comes cheaper.

What happens when views of reality change rapidly enough for us to be aware of it? The name that embodied the old idea comes to seem as if it no longer named anything. In English it is still possible to say that a person or an action is *wicked*, but no newspaper editorial or public address in a secular context is apt to deplore anyone's *wickedness. Sin* is obsolete and *evil* hangs by a thread. There is probably as much sin and evil as ever, but the behavior is seen in a different light. Some people still practice *discipline* and *character-training*, but might hesitate to call them that.

If a name can die and take its entity with it, it can also live on and color its entity; the result is different names for the same thing that produce quite different effects. Presumably the same deity is referred to in *God so loved the world* and *The Lord is my shepherd*. But *My God!* is a stronger expletive than *My Lord!*

From Plato on, philosophers have struggled with the relationship between things and names or ideas. Anthropologists speak of 'the constructed nature of all reality',[11] of humankind surrounded by its own products, whether confected outright, or remolded out of some primitive shape, or merely seen through eyes too human to conceive an object in its own terms – it must be used in some way, or exterminated as a danger, or at the very least entered into some classification, some conceptual scheme thought essential to it: the jawbone of a mammoth evokes endless vistas of evolutionary forms and lineal descendants. 'Except for the immediate satisfaction of biological needs,' says Ludwig von Bertalanffy, 'man lives in a world not of things but of symbols.'[12]

All this is carried in the picture gallery that is our memory for language. The non-human material world shapes it to some degree – there is little that we can do about a hurricane or a tidal wave – but it lays an indelible stamp on that world. Our reality is a product of ourselves, in large part a reflection of the categories, moods, and juxtapositions that our language provides us with or makes possible. And it is growing, as forests are stripmined, alluvial plains paved over, and life forms driven off the face of the earth. Nature recedes. A generation loses itself in an inner world of feeling and self-awareness, oblivious of outside forces. Technologies hypertrophy, and social scientists wonder if it is possible to 'determine the point at which changes in the environment are no longer adaptive and lead to breakdown'.[13]

The legacy of Babel can be drawn as a double arrow: meanings demand forms to represent them, but forms equally reach out to meanings. In large degree we find in the world outside us what our language leads us to expect to find.

What happens when the picture gallery begins to revolve? The mind is more than a collection of stills. It is a kaleidoscope, a free-wheeling spinner of ideas, rather like those computers that create novels or compose music by randomizing notes and chords. Our brains are terribly efficient mixers and combiners. One who would probably never murder a friend can nevertheless bring 'murder' and 'friend' together in his mind – the act becomes THINKABLE. Two and two in the head adds up to four in what we buy, sell, build, and carry. Or it may add up to three – the absurd is just as thinkable as the rational: it is language, according to Robert Ardrey, that 'made inordinately irrational beliefs possible'.[14] In children we call the product imagination. In adults it is sometimes called invention: the inner map is changed and the reality changes to match. Human creativity and human destructiveness alike depend on this.

Chapter 8

Guns don't kill people, people kill people

The folkloric title of this chapter is the standard argument of the gun lobby in the United States against efforts to restrict the possession of firearms. Other interests and occupations have their own versions. There used to be a saying about the automobile: 'It isn't the nut on the wheel but the nut behind the wheel' – speaking of responsibility for the annual slaughter in automobile accidents, now running close to fifty thousand lives a year in the United States alone. A spokesman for the Coors Brewing Company tells us that it is not beer cans but people that are responsible for littering parks.[1] Some careless groundskeeper must have said at some time or other, 'It wasn't the hole on the course that broke your leg, it was your stepping into it.' As it would be convenient for governments anxious about their food supplies to say, 'Food doesn't nourish people, eating does.'

Language begs off with its own folklore: 'Sticks and stones may break my bones but words will never hurt me.' The question is whether man is menaced by man's works – and words – as well as by man. It is hardly stretching what we know about causation to say that if the gun had not been on the mantelpiece, the victim would not have been shot. The adversaries might have come to blows, but fists and clubs are less apt to be fatal.

Are words, grammar, and the rest of language a threat just by being THERE? Do parts of language exist for the sake of mayhem? Is there an open invitation to abuse even in some of the innocent parts?

It would be surprising if the answer to all three questions were not YES. Words no longer have power in the magical sense – we cannot cast a spell by uttering a curse, or bring down the walls of Jericho by shouting, even to the accompaniment of trumpets. But latent power they do have, individually and in the way sentences are built from them. Language is not a neutral instrument. It is a thousand ways biased.

If so, how do we transact our business? The most essential part of any economy is the flow of information. If we cannot be sure when the FBI advertises openings for sixty marplots that the number is truly sixty and it is in fact marplots that are to be hired, the market for marplots may collapse. There must either be a core of neutral language somewhere, or people must somehow be able to discount the biases as they go about their practical affairs. Both ways are open, but need only be threaded to see how narrow they are.

One small corner is purely neutral: the language of mathematics. If I report rental income from six apartments, the number cannot be other than six, unless I am lying – provided we are agreed on what an appartment is. This depends on how pure the terms are with which we designate the objects of experience. Is it possible for a single room to constitute an apartment? As a landlord I might want to advertise it so. As a renter you might feel deceived if you answered the ad. But perhaps we can waive our definitions and come to an understanding on the basis of an adjustment in the rent. The meanings we attribute to *apartment* are not so far apart that we cannot bargain away our biases.

Mathematics gives us a neutral footing, and logic builds a neutral usage around it, with its techniques for winnowing out the biases: the definition of terms, the detection of fallacies, and the analysis of propositions to get at truth and falsity. If we are to live in a society we are forced to look more or less impartially at the things we deal with and to be more or less honest in the exchange of information about them. Truth in the marketplace, truth in the courtroom, contracts that are binding, standards that are set and maintained – these can be kept more or less uncontaminated so long as competing forces are in balance.

The logical, factual, and scientific language that results is so important that it imbues its users, even the most naive, with a keen awareness of language as such. The speaker who may live a lifetime without realizing that verbs agree in number with their subjects will give you a highly informed and highly charged argument if you try to pass off ten eggs as a dozen. The signification of *dozen* is something he can manipulate, on his fingers and toes if necessary. Or if you tell him one day that on the next he is to have the afternoon off, and then renege, you can count on his resentment; he knows what a promise is and will hold you to it.

The upshot is that the language of information, the language that we most readily talk about, has in the past been viewed as the whole of language. Abetting this is the fact that most of the contractual business of society is carried on in writing, which eliminates a good part of the bias to be found in speech. In particular, the tone of voice is squeezed out. The written sentence *The canned peaches were Grade C* conveys no sarcasm, disgust, or surprise – these must be infused according to the reader's whim or from clues in the context. The spacing of words gives an appearance of sharp segmentation, of beads on a string that can be measured and defined. We have a saying that apportions SUBSTANCE to this part of language and dismisses the rest as MANNER: 'I'm interested in WHAT she said, not in the WAY she said it.' As far as speech is concerned, there is no 'way' distinguishable from a 'what'; there are only different parts of the sound wave, each with its function. But the solidity of print, plus the need to talk more plainly about certain things than about others, creates the illusion that propositional language – the language that states facts – is all that needs to be accounted for. It was probably the practical importance of this part of language that caused it to be committed to writing in the first place, and caused the rest to be passed over. Only in novels and in the stage directions for plays do we generally find references to more than propositions – but even these must as a rule be expressed by additional propositions: 'The ring of fear was in her voice'; 'She spoke in a high, uncertain key'. The tone that is lost from propositional language is the purest form of bias; its purposes are emotional, attitudinal, and directive. It laments and exults, defies and coaxes. It has little to do with truth, and much to do with feeling.

What native speakers find hard to talk about – the parts of language they have no occasion to objectify – linguists find hard to describe, and that is another reason why we continue to be unaware of the subterranean world of the non-propositional. Take the experience of the linguist Michael Silverstein trying to get speakers of the Wasco–Wishram language to react directly to questions about something he needed to confirm: the use in Wasco–Wishram of shifting consonant sounds to convey augmentative ('big, awkward, clumsy') or diminutive ('small, graceful, cute') meanings in the words in which the consonants occur – a word containing a *p* sound, for example, could be made diminutive by glottalizing the *p*, or augmentative by changing it to a *b*. But though everyone used the device, none could isolate it from their speech and talk about it. The same speakers found it easy to comment on the meanings of complete words.[2]

The fact that other kinds of language are always judged by propositional language is a tribute to its importance, but there is no absolute reason why it should be taken as the standard. Sentences expressing will or interrogation could be used as a starting point rather than statements of fact. But linguists and others have always had the intuition that facts come first – unquestionably founded on the importance that facts and information have for getting on in an economic world. There are also negative tests of its impact. Propositional language is the language of RESPONSIBILITY; it invites probing for truth and accuracy. So if responsibility is to be evaded, other kinds of communication have to be cultivated. The most striking feature of advertising in the past twenty years has been the flight from propositional language toward no language at all. It used to be mostly offers of merchandise that had to be backed up with stocks of goods, and claims of quality that had to be fulfilled; it has become a conglomeration of testimonials and sound effects. The advertiser is probably today's best patron of the musician – directly in advertising, just as he is the best patron of the dramatist through the less direct medium of television programming. There are laws against false advertising, but a tune is neither true nor false, and the stricter the laws the louder the beat.

It is not easy to leave the familiar landmarks of fact and proposition, to talk about what is not ordinarily talked about, to see the catacombs under the propositional cathedral. If what we hide from ourselves were already well exposed, as speakers we might feel some shame at speaking in a way that others would clearly identify as self-interested, and as hearers we would object to being taken in. It will no longer do to imagine that well-defined words and propositions are the bulk of language and the rest can be ignored or easily held in check. They are the hard, bright core of our communications, but are dimmed by the fog around them and much of the time are scarcely visible.

Bias is so pervasive that hardly a sentence in normal speech lacks it, and many utterances contain little else. Take the sentence *Why did you have to go and let yourself be talked into that?* It swamps the hearer with a flood of accusations that are unanswerable because they are not stated but presupposed. The victim usually endures, but would be entitled to reply point by point:

As to *why*, I don't owe you any explanations.
As to my *having to*, there were no compulsions that I am aware of.
As to *go and*, you imply that I acted wilfully, whereas I was only trying to be reasonable.
As to *let myself*, you suggest that I was out of control, when I was just as responsible as the other person.
As to *being talked into*, I did my share of the talking, and I think I got a bargain.

The question is a mishmash of assumptions involving words-in-context, idioms, and constructions whose implications put the hearer on the defensive without saying frankly what he is accused of. The initial *why* sets the stage – by pretending that an explanation is called for, it implies that there is something to explain, that all the rest is factual and not merely a string of insinuations.

For a close look at particular kinds of bias, the place to start is with expressions that are clearly meant to be biased and are consciously chosen to PROJECT some inequality on the social situation. Typical examples are the honorific terms used in many languages, of which the Japanese are the best known and most frequently caricatured. The means of 'putting someone in his place' – high or low – extend all the way from selecting a particular pronoun of address (in Spain, *tú* for children, dogs, and other familiars, *usted* for superiors or strangers) to switching to a different language in cultures that happen to be bilingual or multilingual. The overtones are often so strong that speakers must strive hard not to seem obsequious or condescending. The effort is sometimes too much. In Java a generation ago the upper classes would shift to Dutch or Malay to avoid the elaborate formulas that would have been called for in Javanese. In the large cities of tropical Africa, where different ethnic groups with many different languages are thrown together in the workplace, the practice in speaking to fellow workers is to 'communicate in nobody's language' – to choose a language such as English, Swahili, or Pidgin, neutral in its values of status and familiarity.[3]

In English the distinctions of class and status are more subtle. The major English-speaking countries are nominally democratic. The standard language long since gave up the status pronouns *thou* and *ye*. Honorifics are mostly restricted to titles of address: *doctor, reverend, judge*, plus some remnants among the British nobility. But unwritten codes are numerous, and the fact that they are not formally codified conceals them from view; they are the more powerful for being insidious – they are rarely questioned. But when some upheaval brings them to the surface, we realize how pervasive they can be – the next chapter will show the extent of sexism in English, the ways in which language affects being female in our society. Being a child, being a farmer, being a politician or a minister of the Gospel – every role has its reinforcing linguistic forms.

But what of the common coin, the forms that belong to no particular segment of society and are freely bandied across every social class? These ought to be neutral, if any are.

Far from it. The words and the grammar are as full of bias as any overtly class-marked dialect. The rare person who on the rare occasion wants to be wholly neutral has to walk a tightrope.

First, words. A characteristic of free-floating meanings – those meanings cast loose from form at the Babylonian collapse – is the amount of semantic material that can entangle a word as it travels from one context or situation to another. It seems that few words ever remain as precise designations of something, but must always pick up an extra ingredient that is mostly irrelevant to their central meaning. Or words are preserved, perhaps through some occupational perversity, that mix totally inconsistent meanings. What does the fact that something can be measured in units of four inches have to do with horses? – a horse is so many *hands* high. Similarly a channel is so many *fathoms* deep – as if units of six feet had some special significance for water. So for *knots, nautical miles, forward* (for *front*), *below* (for *downstairs*), *astern*, and the rest of the seafarer's lingo that enables him to exclude the landlubber from his conversation.

But we were looking for a common coin, and have found ourselves in a specialized vocabulary again. Every profession has its in-group speech, which marks the professional and maintains solidarity. A lot of it blossoms in the language at large as jargon, which will have its turn in Chapter 11.

For the most widely diffused irrelevancy of all, we must look to the quirk of human nature that sees everything colored rosy or gray. Mixed in with most of the words in English – and very likely every other language – is some taint of liking or disliking. The psychologist Charles Osgood and his associates call this EVALUATION. Many concepts come in both shades, producing clusters of synonyms and antonyms, almost cell-like in the assemblies they seem to form in our brains. The popular expression is that words are LOADED.

Technically, loaded words are EUPHEMISTIC or DYSPHEMISTIC – they picture what they designate in a favorable or an unfavorable way. As Jeremy Bentham states it, 'In addition to the import which, in the character of a SIMPLE TERM, properly belongs to it, will be found involved in every such censorial appellation the import of at least one entire PROPOSITION: *viz* a proposition expressive of a judgement of approbation or disapprobation.'[4] So when the Health Director of the State of California accused his superior of *fibbing* about the appointment of two of his cronies to public office,[5] he meant 'telling an untruth' plus the proposition 'but I won't go so far as to call him a liar'. *To fib* is one of several euphemisms for telling an untruth; others include *to tell a white lie, to prevaricate*, and *to stretch the truth. To lie* is dysphemistic.

It is hard not to be aware of SOME euphemisms and dysphemisms, especially the more flattering, offensive, or otherwise colorful ones. Epithets are the obvious examples. To call a woman a *hag* or a man a *coward* or a person of either sex a *lush* is to lay on the bias so all can see. But as the shades grow paler they fade from notice and speakers tacitly accept and use judgments about others without being aware of it. The situation is worse than with the augmentatives and diminutives of Wasco–Wishram, where at least there was a recurring element of sound to which the meaning could attach. With the ordinary eulogistic or dyslogistic term there is no physical sign; the bias is below the level of awareness, and if we are to recognize it someone may have to point it out – as Canada's Prime Minister Pierre Trudeau did when he spoke on capital punishment before the House of Commons: 'To kill a man for punishment alone is an act of revenge. Nothing else. Some would prefer to call it retribution, because that has a nicer sound. But the meaning is the same.' The mere existence of such a term as *retribution* permits us to perceive a killing as something good.

A euphemism is most apt to be noticed if it is new. When an occupation once regarded as lowly wants to come up in the world, it may try to shed the name that signaled its humble status: *farmers* become *agriculturists, garbage collectors* become *sanitation engineers, janitors* become *custodians*. Our awareness of the euphemism is shown by our tendency to laugh at what we regard as false pretension. Yet other occupations that upgraded themselves in the past enjoy euphemistic names that are no longer questioned. One may laugh at an *undertaker* who calls himself a *mortician* or a *funeral director*, but not at a money-handler who calls himself a *financier* or a tradesman who calls himself a *businessman*. These euphemisms are accepted at face value – to the benefit of those labeled by them.

The cultivation of euphemism to paper over unpleasant reality leads – when the reality is truly unpleasant – to long histories of synonyms each of which started off as a euphemism and then, by intimate association with the unloved thing that it named, ended up as a dysphemism. Euphemism is a game played by adults. A child who hears someone behaving in a depraved manner called *sick* does not appreciate the attempt to avoid calling the person *evil* – the association is direct between word and meaning. The two are cemented; and later, for that child's generation of adults, the word *sick* has become as insulting as *verminous* or *rotten*. The downgrading is so regular that it invites a domino theory of euphemism: the fall of each term leads to the fall of the next, and in some areas of meaning we find an endless series of terms each of which had its day of innocence and then fell from grace. Sharon Henderson Taylor writes of the term *mentally retarded*: 'It is quite common now – although it was not ten years ago – to hear children say, "You're an MR," or "What's the matter, you retarded or something?" or even "What a retardo!" Such colorful use of terms meant to be bland and colorless is not what the educators intended, and it forces them to search out even vaguer substitutes – substitutes that only too soon will also depreciate. This process has led to a proliferation of educational terms [for low intelligence] – a sort of euphemism explosion.'[6] Bodily functions are a rich source – they are taboo in conversation, and have to be mentioned obliquely. An example in the domain of defecation (itself a euphemism) shows the death of euphemism at the hands of childish literalness: A parent was counting items and got as far as *Number Two*. His four-year-old daughter overheard and cried, 'Don't say *Number Two*!' Akin to bodily functions are habits, such as drinking, that affect behavior. One of Benjamin Franklin's earliest pieces (he later published a *Drinkers Dictionary*) contains the following:

> It argues some shame in the Drunkards themselves, in that they have invented numberless Words and Phrases to cover their Folly, whose proper Significations are harmless, or have no Signification at all. They are seldom known to be *drunk*, tho they are very often *boozey, cogey, tipsey, fox'd, merry, fuddl'd, groatable, Confoundedly cut, See two moons,* are *Among the Philistines, In a very good Humour, See the Sun,* or *The Sun has shone upon them*; they *Clip the King's English,* are *Almost froze, Feavourish, In their Altitudes, Pretty well enter'd,* &c. In short, every Day produces some new Word or Phrase which might be added to the Vocabulary of the Tiplers.[7]

The effect on the language is not only to multiply synonyms for the disagreeable, but to spoil a lot of otherwise good words. Like bad coin, bad meanings drive out good. Not bad intrinsically, since meanings are neither bad nor good, but bad in the sense that what is referred to is felt to be bad; linguists call this process PEJORATION. When a speaker in 1960 addressed an audience in Pocatello, Idaho, on the subject of special classes for children whose native language was Spanish, and said, 'They should be segregated,' the audience laughed. *Segregate* had already been ruined by its association with racial discrimination (just as *discrimination* has been ruined). The conspicuous example in the late 1970s was *gay*. Though it had long been used as a euphemism for *homosexual*, the current militancy of homosexuals gave it currency, and most people shied away from using it in its older sense of 'joyous'. To have a word and its precise area of meaning suddenly declared off limits, with associated terms such as *gaily* and *gaiety* left anchorless, is a loss that a sensitive user of the language feels keenly. Today's reader would be surprised to learn from Nathaniel Hawthorne that there are *saloons* in the Capitoline Palace in Rome.[8] We have been left with the ruins of this word after it was applied to grog shops to make them seem respectable. If Hawthorne were writing today he would have to say *hall* or *gallery*. The elegance of a grand old word is gone. (Sometimes the assault fails and a word strikes back. Look at *elegance* two sentences back – its adjective *elegant* almost went the way of *fabulous* and *out of this world* a couple of generations ago.)

If one were looking for examples to disprove the theme of this book, there could be none better than the euphemisms that flash over the horizon and end in the mire. They prove that there is something out there that is not made what it is by being given a pretty name. But they also prove that we never give up the BELIEF that we can do it the next time, that if a *second-hand* car is called *pre-owned*, or a *vacuum cleaner* is called a *sanitation system*, or a *neutron bomb* an *enhanced radiation warhead*,[9] the humble will be raised and the horrible will be transfigured. And when we begin to trace the tentacles of 'goodness' and 'badness' as they creep through the meanings of the majority of our words we realize how much of our awareness of their presence is due to a few outrageous cases of obvious fraud, areas already notoriously euphemized where we are on the watch for euphemism and can drag it to the surface with comparative ease: addiction to drugs and alcohol, idiocy, bodily functions, bathrooms, prostitution, strong emotions, political propaganda. It would not occur to us to wonder why instead of 'We are going to have some *people* over for dinner' we prefer 'We are going to have some *friends* over for dinner', or why there is an impudence in a *grin* that is lacking in a *smile*. Readiness to accept the other person's concealed proposition – 'This is pleasant, that is unpleasant – makes us easy prey to contrivances like taking an old *Department of War* and renovating it as a *Department of Defense*, or airing testimonials for a brand of soup that have been '*selected* from calls made at *random*', where *selected* conveys delicacy and precision and also suggests, but does not literally claim, that the selection was random when in fact it was only the calls. It also blunts our curiosity when we hear the same action referred to one day as *hoarding* (when people stored up goods for their personal use in the Second World War) and the next as *stockpiling* (when they were urged to supply their bomb shelters), or when the objective marks of *chauvinism* and *patriotism* are the same. These are of course a deliberate manipulation of biases, but the existence of the terms invites it.

The widest spread (though not the deepest penetration) of hidden bias is in the English adjective. The typical adjective is SCALED – it comes in a 'more' and a 'less', and this pale coloration readily takes on the deeper tinge of 'better' and 'worse' (not necessarily respectively). We do find a few adjectives that are like most nouns in not being scalar –

physical education, *comparative* anatomy, *civilian* clothes (the proof is that one does not say **The education is very physical*), but the majority express degrees and are highly susceptible to losing their virginal neutrality (*The man is old, The man is very old, The man is old and decrepit*). It is hard to think of an adjective in common use that does not bring to mind some biased meaning. Here is the result of five minutes of random searching:

old (and worn out)	blue (and downhearted)
long (and tiresome)	strong (and heady)
green (and inexperienced)	heavy (and dull)
tall (and handsome)	sweet (and lovely)
plain (and tasteless)	rough (and uncultured)
deep (and learnèd)	smooth (and velvety)
straight (and true)	level (and judicious)
slippery (and unreliable)	

The associated adjectives here are overtly biased, but their 'neutral' partners are obviously tilted in the same direction. Not that we are unable to clean them up if the occasion demands strict neutrality – this can be done in various ways: by intonation (just the way we SAY words like *strong, rough,* and *deep* can infuse them with bias or partially free them of it), by gesture and facial expression (avoiding, for example, the almost automatic tendency to grimace when uttering the word *sour*), by explicit disclaimers (*muscular but not muscle-bound*), and by stereo-typing in syntax. The best example of this last device is found with the set that is required to be most objective and precise: adjectives of measurement, including pairs like *old–young, tall–short, wide–narrow, deep–shallow, thick–thin.* Despite what would seem to be a need for adjectives to refer just to the dimension without committing the speaker to either the plus or the minus direction on it, the language has none. Instead, it adapts the positive end to a neutral purpose in such relatively neutral expressions as *How old is she? She is five years old.* A child of five is obviously not *old*, but we make do with the biased adjective in the set expressions that refer to measurement. Sometimes this forces us into odd poses when we feel a need to eliminate all trace of bias. The second sentence in

> Jackie Smith had his fourth birthday yesterday. I wouldn't have guessed he was that old.

is normal, but it signifies 'farther along the scale of age than I would have expected'. (Replace *that old* with *so old* and you get the absurd 'really advanced in age'.) To be completely neutral, one cannot use a straightforward STATEMENT, but must hark back to the stereotyped question *how old*, putting it in indirect form: *I wouldn't have guessed that was how old he was.* (It sounds a bit technical to resort to the noun *age* and say *I wouldn't have guessed that was his age.*)

The remarkable thing is that our adjectives are so contaminated that these hedges are necessary. Nouns as a class are substantially less biased – ideally they are designations of segments of reality, and should present their entities more or less in the pure state. A thumb is a thumb – how can one put irrelevant plusses and minuses on it? Rather easily, as it turns out – the lack of bias is only relative: some people *thumb their noses* at others, extracting a biased verb from the noun; others are *all thumbs*. Nouns, like all other words, get mired in context and come away with biases clinging to them.

Just as with adjectives, there are overtly biased nouns, and it comes as no surprise that they are the ones that most resemble adjectives in the way they are used. They form the class already introduced, that of EPITHETS; and like most adjectives they can be compared for degree:

(Adjective) I didn't think she was so dumb!
(Noun) I didn't think she was such a dumbbell!

Here is a pair that illustrates the difference between a noun that is an epithet and one that is not:

John is an awful fool.
John is an awful teacher.

The word *awful* expresses a DEGREE of the first noun (we could also say *John is a big fool* without referring to his size), but in the second it has its literal meaning and describes the quality of John's teaching – *teacher* is not an epithet.

Epithets are overtly biased and it is not hard to detect the hidden proposition that they embody. If I say *Did you see that idiot try to cross the street ahead of me?* I am calling your attention to a PERSON (and might have used the word *person*), but I am insinuating a judgment: 'That person is an idiot!'

On the other hand, how are you to respond? An exchange like the following is impossible:

Did you see that idiot try to cross the street ahead of me? – *No he isn't!

Even if the 'idiot' is a friend of yours, by using an epithet instead of an explicit proposition (*Did you see that man . . .? He's an idiot!*) I have deprived you of the chance to defend him. You could of course say, a bit lamely, *I don't think he's an idiot*, but you might hesitate to for fear of seeming rude. We EXPECT our listeners to agree with our assumptions, our hidden propositions – it comes so close to being a rule of discourse that we take offense if they expose us. The consequence (or perhaps the cause!) of our not being brought to book is that we can use such expressions without realizing ourselves how we have loaded the conversational dice.

Bias in nouns does not stop with epithets. The effect of substituting *female* for *idiot* in the passage above hardly lessens the accusatory effect:

Did you see that female try to cross the street ahead of me?

In ordinary conversation, *female* for 'woman' is derogatory in any case,[10] but there is more: instead of a single underlying proposition we now have a whole syllogism:

Did you see that person . . .? Said person is a female. Females are (stupid, unreliable, troublesome, etc). Therefore said person is stupid (unreliable, troublesome, etc).

More gems of this kind will be offered in the next chapter. The adjective that forms part of the syllogism is one that has come to form a sort of collocation with the noun. It names a quality that is frequently associated with the noun, and often appears along with the noun in cases of what the linguist J. P. Maher calls 'salient feature copying':

stubborn ox	proud father
scared rabbit	dirty tramp
flighty girl	dumb broad
irresponsible child	lazy foreigner

Since the syllogism is more indirect and harder to unwind than the single proposition that underlies the epithet, using such expressions leaves the victim even more powerless to fight back. And the speaker may be totally unaware of laying a trap. Something like the following actually has the feel of an 'explanation':

Why is she so giddy? – Because she's a girl.

Girls are SUPPOSED to be giddy. With some individuals the reputations revealed in salient feature copying may be well earned. With others we have prejudicial associations at the level of racial stereotypes. J. D. McClure mentions 'the Pavlovian conditioning . . . by which we are led to feel such collocations as *sturdy Saxons, hardy Norsemen*, and *wild Highlanders* to be natural and inevitable'.[11] The *wild Highlander* of Scotland is matched by the *wild Indian* of North America. These expressions have a special intonation that shows that the adjective is not in contrast, that is, it does not add anything to the meaning of the noun but just expresses the way the thing named by the noun 'really is':

You're be ^{hav}ing like a ^{wild} High land$_e$ $_r$.

– the adjective is higher in pitch than the noun. The noun already carries our 'approval' or 'disapproval' in its semantic makeup. (Contrast:

wi^{l}$_d$ High land$_e$ $_r$.)

Partly because it is found there less frequently, a bias hidden in a noun is more potent. But there is another reason for its power: the noun OBJECTIFIES in a way the adjective cannot. A quality may come and go. If we are disappointed at Jane's lack of appreciation we can call her *ungrateful*, or solidify it a step further and call her *an ungrateful person*. But if we call her an *ingrate* we put the brand on her: the noun implies that the world puts people like this in a class by themselves. The heavier loading of the biased noun is most visible with names of nationalities. In the following, the nouns are more apt to suggest the racial stereotype than the adjectives:

Noun	Adjective
He's a Jew.	He's Jewish.
a Swede.	Swedish.
a Turk.	Turkish.
a Mexican.	Mexican.
a Dutchman.	Dutch.

The noun *Jew* has been degraded to the extent that speakers often rephrase a sentence to use *Jewish* instead. It is as if, being the sign of a 'quality', the adjective made it possible for one to be, say, 'just a little bit Turkish', whereas *a Turk* has to go all the way. When speakers really want to be insulting, they produce disparaging nouns, not disparaging adjectives: *Kike*, *Wop*, *Spik*, *Bohunk*, *Jap*, *Chink*, *Dago*, *Greaser*. A mispronunciation can do the same: *A-rab*, *Eye-talian*.

The branding power of the noun stands out in the epithets that pair with adjectives and verbs having approximately the same meaning, and sometimes with other nouns that are not quite so hardhitting. *Jane worries* is a feeble way of saying that *Jane is a worrier*; but more potent still than the latter is *Jane is a worrywart*. The epithet tends to have a marked form – *worrier* is a regular derivative of *worry*, but *worry-wart* has a unique morphological makeup. Many pairs and triplets show the relative strength of the noun:

Jill fusses.	Bill takes his time.
Jill is fussy.	Bill is slow.
Jill is a fussbudget.	Bill is a slowpoke.
The boat leaks.	Willie cries.
The boat is leaky.	Willie is a crybaby.
The boat is a sieve.	Henry blathers.
Jerry is extravagant.	Henry is a blatherskite.
Jerry is a spendthrift.	Melinda is easy.
	Melinda is a pushover.

The effect of this is to give the advantage to the person who is skilled at calling names. If you and I embark on some dangerous undertaking and I get cold feet and want to back out, you CAN of course say *Don't quit!*; but you are more apt to say *Don't be a quitter!* The noun becomes a way of anathematizing things that we disapprove of by making qualities seem to be permanent. As we saw in Chapter 7, the mere existence of a word carries the implied proposition 'There is such a thing'; and when the word belongs to the category of names of things par excellence – nouns – the proposition is firmly anchored.

Of the three major classes of words, verbs seem least hospitable to bias. This is probably due to the relatively transitory nature of what they name. A THING, designated by a noun, and a QUALITY, designated by an adjective, are stable enough to build up associations of approval or disapproval; a process is not. We are more apt to link an extraneous value to the result than to the process:

to grow – growth (tumor)
to cut – (a bad cut; the
    unkindest cut)
to find – a find (treasure)

to choose – choice (a choice
    bit of beef)
to lose – a loss
to fill – full (a full life)

But this is relative, and more evidence is needed to prove the case. It hardly matters, because examples of bias are there in abundance, and some take fairly systematic forms.

First, there are the cases of action in some direction viewed as positive or negative. While the positive direction is not necessarily 'good' (something can even be called *positively bad*), the tendency is to view it as such and to associate the negative direction with 'bad':

improve – deteriorate
build – destroy
help – hinder
succeed – fail

praise – blame
alleviate – exacerbate
win – lose

The goodness-badness is the embodiment of the speaker's biased view of the action: *to improve* means 'to change in direction *that is good*'; to *succeed* is 'to have an outcome *that is good*'.

Next are verbs where goodness-badness does not adhere to the action but to some other aspect of the situation. It may be the speaker's view of the actor:

They found the treasure (neutral).
They stumbled onto the treasure (they found it accidentally, which is
    not to their credit).
She is resting (positive).
She is loafing (taking it easy when she should be working).
He is protesting (positive).
He is complaining (protesting in a disgruntled way).

Or it may be the speaker's view of reality. This is the aspect of bias that has most interested logicians and the logico-linguists whose main preoccupation in meaning is truth value. The verbs entail the speaker's view of the truth or falsity of what he says. Like positive-negative, true-false are not fully synonymous with good-bad, but they lean in that direction. There are verbs that entail the truth of the proposition – the speaker does not use them unless he believes the claim to be true:

> He thought it was too late (no entailment).
> He realized that it was too late (and I, as speaker, accept that it was too late).
> It struck me that I was being made a fool of (no entailment).
> It dawned on me that I was being made a fool of (I consider it a fact that I was).

(The entailment can be tested by negating the proposition: *It struck me that I was being made a fool of, but I actually wasn't* makes sense; **It dawned on me that I was being made a fool of, but I actually wasn't* is contradictory.) There are verbs that entail the speaker's denial:

> She said that I had lied to her (no entailment).
> She pretended (let on) that I had lied to her (but I hadn't).

And there are verbs that entail the speaker's skepticism:

> They represented that the signature was genuine (no entailment).
> They claimed that the signature was genuine (but I doubt it).

There are verbs that simply take the speaker's acceptance of the fact for granted. These tend to be emotional – they are EXPLICITLY biased in the attitude of the SUBJECT (not necessarily the speaker) toward the fact:

> He is sorry that she is not well (bad from 'his' viewpoint; an accepted fact from mine as speaker).
> They were outraged that the gossip had been published (bad for 'them', a fact for me).
> How nice that you could come! (this is said from my viewpoint – it is nice for me, and the being able to come is a fact).

Even in the negative these verbs entail the acceptance of the fact: both *He is glad that she is well* and *He is not glad that she is well* entail her being well. The same is true of *dawn on* and *realize*. (So the class has been called 'factive'.) There is another class that entails the fact (or non-fact) when affirmative but not when negative:

> I managed to get control of myself (I made the effort, and I did get control).
> I didn't manage to get control of myself (I didn't get control).
> She failed to get the part (non-fact entailed).
> She didn't fail to get the part (non-fact not entailed – she got the part).
> They got to see Niagara (a privilege was desired, and they got the benefit – they saw Niagara).
> They didn't get to see Niagara (they missed out on a privilege; they didn't see Niagara).

These verbs have been called 'implicative'.[12]

Whatever the entanglements – whether simple approval-disapproval or more abstract truth-falsity – the fact is that the speaker is communicating on more than one level at once, and that the hearer may be lulled into accepting both communications while listening to just one. Some expressions are not too difficult to drag to the surface. English has a number of adverbs that nudge the hearer into adopting this or that attitude toward what the speaker is reporting, and a little reflection makes us aware of the trick. Take a simple statement of fact such as *It costs ten dollars* and add to it:

It costs only ten dollars.
It costs all of (no less than) ten dollars.
It actually costs ten dollars.
Sure enough, it costs ten dollars.
It even costs ten dollars.
It clearly costs ten dollars.

The hidden propositions go roughly like this:

It costs ten dollars and
. . . that amount is not very much.
. . . that amount is a great deal.
. . . that fact is true despite contrary assumptions.
. . . that confirms what had been predicted.
. . . that makes the fact more extreme than had been supposed.
. . . there is no doubting of the fact.

Other expressions – notably verbs – are more difficult to strip of their disguise. Imagine a courtroom in which the following unlikely scene takes place:

Counsel: So you admit that you were at the scene from two minutes before the explosion until one minute after.
Witness: No.
Counsel: No? Didn't you just say that you were there?
Witness: Yes.
Counsel: Then why do you deny it?
Witness: I don't deny it.
Counsel: Then you admit it?
Witness: I do not admit it. I assert it. The person who admits something concedes that it is embarrassing to him to do so, that it is damaging to his position. The fact that I was there when I said I was is not embarrassing to me and is not damaging to my position.

A duel of this sort would probably not get very far without the court's intervening. To admit something is to grant its truth, isn't it? So what is the witness complaining about? Yet the questioner, perhaps unconsciously, has reached for the verb that puts the witness on the defensive. A similar verb is *to bother*:

Did the clerk find your purse? – He didn't bother to look for it.

The bare fact is that the clerk did not look for the purse. The *bother* part is the speaker's effusion of reproach. If the hearer does not question it – and being implicit it is not easily open to question – the clerk's reputation suffers.

Consider the verb *to point out*. Superficially it appears to be the same as *to indicate*, but there is a subtle difference:

> The manager pointed out (indicated) that it would be necessary to raise the rent.

With *indicate*, though the speaker is not unsympathetic to the manager's viewpoint, he does not guarantee it. *To point out* is a factive verb; the speaker adopts the manager's point of view – and the hearer, unaware of the flimflam, tends to go along.

Or take the phrase *perfectly well* attached to *know*, a highly frequent collocation:

> She knows perfectly well that I meant it.

This does not add to the factuality (*know* by itself is virtually factive), but it tells something about HER: she has been resisting her supposed knowledge. If the nearer accepts it she is branded as a liar at worst and as stubborn at best.

Or take the scene in a New York police station as portrayed in a television comedy. The white inspector comes in with an announcement to make, and the Black policeman starts to leave on an assignment. The inspector asks him not to 'go shuffling off' before he makes the announcement. The policeman is incensed and a couple of minutes of altercation follow in which he insists, to the bewilderment of the other man, that he 'does not shuffle'.[13] The inspector's attempt at humor was offensive because *shuffling gait* had become one of the denigrating stereotypes about Blacks in the United States.

Whether formally as part of their semantic structure, or through associations picked up along the way, the meanings of words lie at varying depths. To traverse them is to cross a minefield where every step triggers a silent explosion in the brain.

Given their specialized uses, it is not surprising that words develop such complexities. We saw earlier how easy it is for a fragment of sound symbolism to attach itself to a word – the verb *to sunder* is a synonym of *to sever* but it echoes *thunder* and *blunder* and suggests a more radical or violent cutting or tearing apart. So it is natural for some very peculiar specializations to develop, such as our tendency to use the verb *to hop* with a conveyance only when the journey is viewed as accomplished (*I hopped the plane and got to Cincinnati at six*, **I hopped the plane but it never got off the ground*), or the distinction between *unless* and *if not* which requires that *unless* look affirmatively on the possibility referred to (*If it isn't going to rain, we'll have a picnic*; ?*Unless it's going to rain, we'll have a picnic* – doubtful because we have too little knowledge of the chance of rain to look affirmatively on it) – as well as the infusion of goodness-badness which is so general and which, to drive it home with one more example, spells the difference between the adverbs *roundly* and *soundly*:

> He roundly berated them (he did it thoroughly, and I as speaker relish it).
> He soundly berated them (he did it thoroughly, and I as speaker relish it, and he was right).

But what of CONSTRUCTIONS? Can syntax be loaded – given the variety of conditions and purposes that it has to mind? The answer is yes, provided the definition of 'syntactic pattern' is not conceived too abstractly, and one is permitted to class as *loaded* a pattern that is rarely used without some special intent beyond informing, inquiring, and commanding.

English has a pattern of TAGGING that is used to 'get around' the defenses of a hearer in several ways. The most familiar is the TAG QUESTION, which pleads for agreement by pretending to offer the hearer a choice between a positive and a negative answer. The tag has the opposite polarity from the rest of the sentence (if one is negative the other is affirmative, and vice versa), it is in question form, and it consists of a pronoun and an auxiliary (or a form of the verb *to be*):

> It will be all right, won't it?
> He hasn't a chance in the world, has he?
> You like him, don't you?
> It wasn't Jill, was it?

The intonation of the tag can be either rising or rising-falling – the latter for when one is pretty sure of the hearer's agreement.

This same device of reverse polarity is used in questions without tags, to appeal for agreement or just to state something that is so obvious that agreement is assured. The question is negative, and the expected answer is affirmative:

> Isn't it a nice day?
> Wouldn't you like to try some of these almonds?

– but by overreaching itself, 'appealing' sometimes becomes the opposite; the question is insincere and is taken at its real value:

> Can't you be a little more careful?

Tags – with or without reverse polarity – are used with commands to soften them or to plead for compliance:

> Give our product a try, won't you?
> Hand me the basket, will you?
> Let's go, shall we?

Similar tags, but in statement form, are used with statements to emphasize the speaker's conviction. This pattern is no longer familiar in its basic sense in American English, so that when the British television program 'That Was the Week, That Was!' became popular in America, most Americans were simply mystified by the title, if they thought about it at all. For Americans, the emphasis has been reinterpreted as 'irony':

That's just perfect, that is!
She's a great one, she is!
You know everything, you do.
Oh, yes! I have talent, I have!

Another pattern that can almost be marked 'ironic' is one that has no tag but puts the complement before the verb. Irony here depends partially on the stereotyping of particular expressions. The first example below is ironic regardless of the tone of voice:

A lot you care.
A fine friend she turned out to be.
A lovely fix you left me in.

Partly the effect depends on the specialization of certain words for ironic use: *fine, precious, lovely,* and *a lot* are frequently used this way. Further, the complement is indefinite. When any of these conditions is broken, the result may be ironic but need not be, and sometimes is simply perplexing:

A lot of good will come of that. (This is ironic or non-ironic: *a lot of good* is subject, not complement; compare the unambiguously ironic *A lot of good that will do!*)
A wonderful meal she served. (Not ironic unless with heavy intonational or gestural overlay – *wonderful* is not specialized for irony.)
This fine product we offer for sale. (Not ironic. *This* is definite. Compare *A fine product THEY put out!*)

A likely story is another ironic stereotype, possibly a shortening of *A likely story that is!* Compare *A plausible story*, where *That is a plausible story* makes a good match but ?*A plausible story that is!* seems odd. These ironic expressions are on the borderline between syntax and idioms.

So where do we make contact with pure syntax? One purely syntactic construction that has been widely examined for its potential for bias is the passive voice. When complete with all its trappings, the passive is no more open to bias than the active:

The reports were handed in by the students (passive).
The students handed in the reports (active).

But the active voice requires the speaker to be explicit about who performs the action; the passive does not:

The reports were handed in. (The agent, 'students', is omitted.)
The students handed in the reports. (The agent is expressed.)

It is of course possible to be noncommittal and say *Someone handed in the reports*, with indefinite *someone*; but that is a plain invitation to the hearer to ask *Who?* The active cannot simply omit the agent as the passive does and say **Handed in the reports*.

In itself there is nothing deceitful about omitting the agent. It is handy when the audience already knows who the agent is, or when it doesn't matter, as in the second sentence of the last paragraph, with the expression *has been examined*, where what counts is the result, not the examiner. Bias enters when the passive is used to conceal the agent. It may be some nonentity whose views are exploited to make a headline: 'Senator Accused of Bilking Constituent' – where the agent turns out to be the constituent's grandmother, who bears a grudge. Or it may be a case not of conscious concealment but of accepting uncritically some popular judgment whose dubious status would be evident if the agent were focused on: *Woman is intended for reproduction* – by whom? God? men? *People should not try to live where they are not wanted* – by the people who don't want them, of course; the passive is a handy way of serving up prejudices as if they were universal truths. *This information was not meant to be divulged* – by whom, a bureaucrat who might be embarrassed by it? *I was told that you didn't do very well on the exam* – by some gossip, of course. Deliberate use of the passive comes easy to officials who want their acts to have the ring of higher authority and not to appear arbitrary. A dean wrote to a complaining professor, 'Your approach was to write an intemperate letter . . .; such letters are *appropriately disregarded*.' [14] This example not only makes the implied claim of an authoritative disregarder, but uses an adverb to insinuate an extra claim, 'It is appropriate to disregard such letters', which by not being frankly stated easily slips by the reader's guard.

The agentless passive is one of the worst plagues of irresponsible journalism. Here is an instance where a journalist was the victim:

> In August 1976, the chief European correspondent for Herald and Weekly Times Proprietary Ltd newspapers (the largest chain in Australia and the South Pacific) filed a story saying that Wilfred Burchett, who claims to be a professional journalist, 'lived in Hanoi' during a time which concerned a law court 'and IS UNDERSTOOD [emphasis added] to have drawn at least some of his income from North Vietnam Government sources'. For Burchett's professional standing and for his Australian citizenship, the implications of such a charge – and it is a charge – were momentous. The correspondent, Garry Barker, did not actually say Burchett was a North Vietnamese hireling, yet his choice of words tacitly endowed the claim with credibility. [15]

Not all passives exhibit the formal passive construction in full grammatical form. There are implicit passives lacking a normal spot where the agent MIGHT be expressed. If we hear the sentence *He is one of the chosen* it might occur to us to ask *Chosen by whom?* But if we hear *He is one of the élite* we have visions of a superiority that floats free of any granting agent: *élite* means 'elect, chosen', and the hearer is invited to suppose that it is by heredity or divine grace. Who elects the 'power élite'? When we read *In the Fifth Century the known world was limited to Europe and small parts of Asia and Africa* we are told to exclude the whole civilization of China from the knowers.

The suffix *able, -ible* in many of its uses is a curious implicit passive that takes an agent more or less for granted. Things and persons have certain qualities that lead to actions and are named accordingly. The performer or performers of the action are left unspecified, and invite the inference that they may be anybody or everybody. *Intangible* is the quality of not permitting the act of touching by anyone. *Contemptible* is the quality of incurring everyone's contempt. The existence of countless perfectly rational cause-effect connections of this kind (what we can drink is *drinkable*, what we can discover is *discoverable*, what the post office allows to be mailed is *mailable*), where the cause is a quality more or less evident to the mind or senses, is a wedge that permits entry to fraudulent connections or connections based on prejudice or highly personal viewpoints. '(Not)-*able* for me (or us)' is transferred to '(not)-*able* for anyone', on the theory that all right-thinking people will think as I (we) do. The fact that the agent is unexpressed enables the transfer to be made by sleight-of-hand, and a quality is imputed that only reflects the prejudice. One egregious instance is the adjective *undesirable*, also used as a noun: *We want no undesirables around here* is a sentence that chases its tail – 'We don't want the people who lack the capability of being desired by anyone', for which read 'by us'. The quality is a projection of the eye of the beholder. The moral effect of such a label can be seen in the American military, which created an *undesirable discharge*, which, unlike a *dishonorable discharge*, required no court-martial proceeding and thus deprived the veteran of a legal defense.

The language is full of cases like this. No disease is known to be *incurable*, yet many are labeled so, and this makes it easier not to worry about a cure. A prisoner classed as *incorrigible* can be disposed of without further attempts at reform. Many overt good-bad adjectives are formed with *-able, -ible*: *likable, detestable, abominable, admirable, intolerable*. Other adjectives lack even this formal clue to their bias. When we hear *an unwelcome guest* we visualize the person as having some quality of unwelcomeness about him; yet no more has been said than that some person or persons unknown have failed to welcome him.

What a language permits us to CONCEAL is only the other side of what it forces us to REVEAL, and the revealing side is what has always concerned linguists, first because it is visible and requires no probing, and second because there is too much anyway to talk about for a language not to have to take some of it for granted. And languages differ in what they force speakers to be frank about. If there were no passive in English, the agent would have to be named for every action. If English re-quired – as some languages do – that all nouns be marked for gender, it would be impossible to reply truthfully to *Who were you out with last night?* with *A friend* without revealing whether the friend was male or female. If English required that an indirect object be expressed whenever the situation implied one, we would not be able to get away with saying *Mary seems unfriendly*; it would have to be *Mary seems unfriendly to me* (or *us* or *them*) – the responsibility for the seeming would have to be fixed. This has been called 'experiencer deletion' and applies to verbs like *seem, appear, look, be surprising, be obvious, be amusing, stand to reason, be convincing,* etc.[16]

Mostly the reason a language does not force us to do this or that is to avoid the bother. Constructions are created by abbreviation, as shortcuts. We have neither time nor energy to say everything. But this leaves unfilled gaps where the creeping motives of deception and concealment can make their way. The simplest form of abbreviation is the attributive adjective: *She told a harmless lie* replaces *She told a lie and it was harmless.* We are less apt to question the concealed proposition than the explicit one.[17] This of course is a syntactic example of the suppressed proposition, which we found so abundantly in single words.

Abbreviations of one kind or another – whether represented in the over-compactness of word meanings or the omission of elements in syntax – are only the most obvious breeding grounds for bias. There is probably no syntactic pattern that does not offer some foothold. The mere arrangement of a sentence can do it: *The Cubans have enough to eat but don't have political freedom, The Puerto Ricans have political freedom but don't have enough to eat* – what comes last is what is most persuasive: the first sentence gives the greater importance to political freedom, the second to food. Even an explicit proposition may betray us, by overgeneralization – by presenting reality as if it were not limited by time. If John steals once and we say *John is a thief,* we go beyond the fact that John was a thief WHEN he stole and carry his guilt forward in time. The simple 'X is Y' contains a world of overstatement.

Loaded language, like loaded firearms, can be hidden where least suspected, and the laws against concealed weapons do not apply.

Chapter 9

A case in point: sexism

Those who were children before the 1920s – and many later than that, no doubt, in some localities – remember the innocent merriment of racial slurs:

> Eenie-meenie-miney-mo,
> Catch a nigger by the toe.
> If he hollers, let him go.
> Eenie-meenie-miney-mo.

> Smarty, Smarty had a party;
> Nobody came but a big fat darkie.

'For a black writer in this country to be born into the English language,' says James Baldwin, 'is to realize that the assumptions on which the language operates are his enemy. . . . I was forced to reconsider similes: as black as sin, as black as night, blackhearted.'[1]

What breeds contempt is misfortune and weakness; familiarity perpetuates it. The language that white children heard taught them to despise their former slaves as surely as parades and band music taught them to respect the flag. The attitudes were implicit in the symbols. It was enough for the words and phrases to be THERE.

When Moses said to the children of Israel, among other injunctions to righteousness, 'Thou shalt not curse the deaf, nor put a stumblingblock before the blind' (Leviticus 19, 14), he was countering what seems to be a universal flaw in human nature: to build self-esteem by looking down on those less fortunate. The misfortune may take any form; there is always an abundance of derogatory terms attached to it. People who are ill 'HAVE diseases' – the expression conjures visions of possession by evil spirits – that are generally viewed as loathsome, and unpleasant adjectives are attached to the afflicted themselves: *scurvy, pock-marked, consumptive, parasitic, leprous, rickety, anemic, gangrenous, syphilitic, rheumatic, scrofulous, mangy, scabby* – some of which have become free-floating synonyms of *disgusting*. The reaction of disgust no doubt arose naturally as a help to avoiding contagion; but it was just as surely a hindrance to early understanding and prevention, and its extension to the persons of the sufferers was of a kind with taunting cripples and ridiculing the feeble-minded. While the fears of some diseases have been allayed, others are as virulent as ever. In our time cancer has the leading place, and terms consecrated to it aggravate the dread: *terminal, growth, metastasize*; even the word *cancer* itself carries a kind of taboo.[2]

The humble and the poor come in for their share of contempt. Just the names for farmers are a spectrum of disparagement: *hick, hayseed, yokel, clod, bumpkin, countryjake, rube* – and older terms that have been generalized such as *clown, churl, boor*. Some were applied in contempt to begin with; others were relatively neutral terms which by association with the despised class have become derogatory. The same is true of servants, whether bound or free: *villain, knave, varlet, caitiff, scullion, lackey, henchman, flunky, potwalloper, underling, errand boy*.

Extreme youth comes in for equal parts of disparagement and endearment. With their dependency, children share some of the traits of PROPERTY; like domestic animals, they are apt to be cherished when they keep their place and disciplined when they do not. Terms for 'young' are easily degraded. The apparently neutral *child* yields *childish*, biased when applied to an adult (to call a grown man *childish* is insulting; to call a boy *mannish* is merely inappropriate, and *manly* is a compliment). To find unfavorable terms for children we go a step lower on the social scale, into the animal kingdom: *cub, whelp, puppy, fledgling, kid. Callow* covers more than hair and feathers, and the cries and tears of infants give adjectives for 'weak, spiritless': *whimpering, puling, mewling, blubbering, sniveling, weepy. Brat* may originally have referred to a ragged garment.

Disease and infancy can be outlived. Race cannot. Neither can sex – which will be our showpiece, because thanks to the feminism of the past decade, more is known about sexual bias than about any other kind. The views in this chapter bring together ideas from a number of linguists who are also feminists. They are views from inside, and convey a sense of the oppressiveness that women themselves – those most sensitive to language problems – believe exists in our linguistic heritage. Male readers may find some degree of zealous overstatement, but this should be weighed against equal degrees of male complacency in society at large – along with a lingering of the sentiment expressed by the courtly white Southerner confronting charges of racism: 'Why, we LOVE our Nigras!'

Before looking at the details of anti-feminism in language, we should remind ourselves that where one part of the problem is concerned – that of the language OF women, the language that women USE rather than the language used about them – the very posing of the question is apt to conceal a bias. When linguists talk about sex differences, they almost always look for a distinctive FEMALE speech. This is true of English – it does not surprise us that the grammarian Otto Jespersen in his book *Language*[3] has a chapter titled 'The Woman', but no corresponding 'The Man'. It is equally true of books and articles about other languages, and of course it implies a standard of comparison: male language. So at the outset we are equating male language to the norm. Since male and female divide the species evenly, the comparison might as well be in the other direction, but even linguistics has been till now so dominated by men that female speech has always been regarded as the 'marked' or supposedly exceptional form. (That it also works out to be marked in the actual grammar and vocabulary of the language testifies to the dominance of men in other fields than linguistics. *Aviatrix* is certainly marked by comparison with *aviator*. More examples later.)

First, how do WORDS for women differ from words for men? As with other relatively powerless classes, there is a heavy representation of epithets and similar unfavorable terms, more than for men. One would think that untidiness was not preeminently a female quality, yet most of the words for 'untidy person' listed in Roget's *Thesaurus* are words for women – *slut, slattern, frump, drab, dowdy, draggletail, trollop, bitch.* Not one of those currently in use is marked as masculine. Similarly learning and scholarship would seem to be asexual, yet while Roget lists a number of terms in ordinary use that are mainly or exclusively masculine, only two are feminine, and they have to do with PRETENSIONS to knowledge: *Pedantess* and *bluestocking*. Many loaded terms, particularly those referring to women as sex objects, reflect women's status as property, kept or rented for sexual services: Roget's *Thesaurus* lists roughly twice as many female terms as male under *libertine*. Furthermore, all the female terms are fully disparaging, whereas a number of the male terms imply a boys-will-be-boys tolerance: *rake, skirt-chaser, old goat, gay dog, gay deceiver, Don Juan.* When we think of *gay dog* we mentally punctuate it with a snicker or a jab in the ribs. As for the adjectives, the very heading of the section in Roget has sexual overtones: *purity*. This is a term that is rarely used for sexual inexperience in males; and as for the entries that are directly associated with one sex or the other, hardly any are like *satyrish, goatish* in applying primarily to males. Female terms abound: *of easy virtue, fallen, whorish, on the streets, unchaste, wanton*. Though *loose* looks to be an impartial modifier, *loose woman* is readily understood as 'immoral woman', but *loose man* would probably be taken as a fugitive. The simple word *woman* itself is listed as a synonym of *prostitute*. Most indicative of the attitude toward women as sex objects is the history of terms that started out as relatively unbiased or even favorable and were gradually degraded. Barrie Thorne and Nancy Henley quote Duncan McDougald on the word *tart*, originally meaning a small piece of pastry. It 'was first applied to a young woman as a term of endearment, next to women who were sexually desirable, then to women who were careless in their morals, and finally – more recently – to women of the street'.[4] '*Queen, madam, mistress*, and *dame* have all acquired degraded meanings, whereas *prince, king, lord*, and *father* are exalted and applied to God.'[5] In separate studies, Julia Stanley and Muriel Schulz found 320 terms in English for 'sexually promiscuous woman'.[6]

Being old puts one in another class of the powerless. Being old AND female puts one on the verge of being an outcast. There are no male terms to match the contempt embodied in the words *hag, crone, witch, warhorse, biddy*, and *beldam*. There are sexual connotations here too: 'old and unattractive', 'old and sexually useless'.

Not all semantic areas put women on the down side, but the ones that favor them still have the tinge of male appreciation – what is good is what men admire in women as women, not as persons. (A stock joke in movie comedy is to have a Marilyn Monroe type say 'He loves me for my mind'.) Among the 'terms of endearment' listed by Roget are many that are applied exclusively to women or children (*sweetheart, jewel, sweetkins, babe*, etc), none that are applied exclusively to men. The skin-deep phenomenon of physical beauty is overwhelmingly feminine, but the same proportions – though the numbers are fewer – are found in the words for 'ugly person': Roget lists one for males (*satyr*) and four for females (*hag, harridan, strumpet*, and *witch*). Women carry the burden of opposite stereotypes. They are angels, because they are beautiful – and also long-suffering and uncomplaining in their subordinate role. And they are devils, when they scheme to win by guile what they cannot take openly. Deception is seen as a feminine trait, but it is a recourse of the weak. Angel or devil, on pedestal or in pit, women in Western society have had the greatest trouble simply being accepted as human, and the language records all their manifestations as the 'sex with a difference'.

Epithets are the tip of the women-as-property iceberg. The language is mined with expressions that reflect women's status as a commodity, despite the disappearance long since of prearranged marriages and the obsolescence of promises to love, honor, and *obey*. A radio ad for 'home owner' loans carries the sentence *We married off our last daughter.*[7] The phrase *marry off* would never be used of male offspring except as a joke; it smacks of *auction off* and *sell off*. The word *wife* itself, though it has escaped signifying 'property' in a direct sense, is often encountered in statements like the following: *The brave pioneers crossed the plains with their wives, their children, and their cattle.*[8] Similarly *women*, as in this from the television series 'Star Trek': *Our people are the best gamblers in the galaxy. We compete for power, fame, women.*[9]

Status as property is seen as devaluation by the possessed, not necessarily by the possessor. From the male viewpoint a woman may well be a cherished object (and note the term *object*). The man's role as protector harks back to hunting and gathering, tribal wars, and life on the frontier. In today's society, needing protection is not an enhance-ment of a woman's self-respect, and this is the measure of value as feminists see it. A good exercise for the male reader who may doubt the lingering ties with property and protection is to put interpretations on the following sentences:

We have to take care of our women.
We have to take care of our men.

How free are the two *we*'s to refer to either men or women or both, and what are the appropriate contexts?

Commodity status is not the only form of depreciation. Terms for females – even apparently objective and neutral ones – are subtly devalued. If a woman driver makes a bad maneuver, a man may be heard to say *What does that woman think she's doing!* with *woman* lengthened and pronounced with a rise-fall-rise intonation – which makes it an expression of disregard. A similar use of *man* would be taken as an emphatic way of expressing the emotion of the whole sentence, not as a reflection on the man's sex. On page 86 of this book there occurs the following passage:

> Bias enters when the speaker or writer uses the passive to conceal the agent. It may be some nonentity whose views are exploited to make a headline: 'Senator Accused of Bilking Constituent' – where the agent turns out to be the constituent's grandmother. . . .

The effect would have been lost if *grandfather* had replaced *grand-mother*. The little old lady is a standard topic for jokes. When a woman is at fault, it is often because she is a woman; when a man is at fault, it is more often because he is cruel, or dishonest, or cowardly, or ambitious.

In most forms of literature, devaluation through words related to sex takes a more subtle form which can be exposed only by collecting and counting. From the time they begin to read, children are submerged in stories and textbooks that emphasize sex roles, that use male terms preponderantly, and that present males as dominant: 'when adults write for one another, they refer to young people as *children*, almost as often as they call them *boys* and *girls*. When writing books and stories for children, however, adults use the gender words *boy* and *girl* twice as often as the neutral words *child* and *children*. . . . Overall, the ratio in schoolbooks of *he* to *she*, *him* to *her*, and *his* to *hers* was almost four to one.'[10] The same heavy weighting of male terms is found in the 200 million achievement test forms used annually in the United States.[11] Even the terms that are not explicitly male are interpreted that way if their referents in the past have been predominantly male. An item in *Our Sunday Visitor* reads as follows:

> The Catholic Theological Union in Chicago showed an increase in students from 168 to 189. But don't cheer. Among the students are twenty-two women, subtract them and the total showed a loss.[12]

From words that reflect the status of the sexes we cross the thin boundary to grammar that does the same. Gender-marking in English syntax is limited to the pronoun system, and it is there – with the use of *he, she, him, her,* and *his* – that sex usages have raised the greatest controversy. Modern English has no pronouns in the singular that can refer indifferently to male or female – *X prides Xself on X's good sense.* The practice has been to insert the masculine. Its use has even been made official. An Act of Parliament in 1850 decreed that *he* should be used for both sexes in all parliamentary language.[13] The Associated Press Stylebook published in 1977 does the same: 'Use the pronoun *his* when an indefinite antecedent may be male or female: A reporter attempts to protect his sources.' The masculine goes for indefinite nouns as well, so that *man* occurs widely with the presumed sense of 'person, human being' – *Every man (every person) has his self-esteem; he prides himself on his good sense.* The hearer or reader is supposed to interpret this 'common gender' use of the masculine as 'he or she', 'his or her', etc.

But it is doubtful that very many do, at least consistently. Expressions like the one from 'Star Trek', or like the ad for a hotel offering *Anything any businessman or his wife would want*,[14] show all too clearly that women are on the sidelines and that the mental picture we get when *he, him*, or *his* is used is male. Given the approved interpretation it should be just as easy to assume 'she' as 'he', but the fact is that we tend to assume 'he' unless it is LIKELY that the individual referred to is female. This explains the oddity of a sentence like *The nurse put on his hat.*[15]

It was natural for feminists to pick the 'common gender' as one of their main targets. Distrust of it dates back many years. Helena Maria Swanwick wrote in 1913,

> the common pronoun is non-existent and I have not used the neuter [*it*], lest it should alarm nervous persons. Perhaps when we have got over the panic fear of unsexing ourselves, we may find it safe to speak of a human, just as we do of a baby, as 'it'.[16]

Some publishers and public bodies have tried to remove the bias. The United States Department of Labor in 1977 revised about 3,000 of its approximately 30,000 titles for occupations. Terms such as *bus boy, foreman, salesman, boom man*, and *bobbin man* were replaced with *dining room attendant, supervisor, salesperson, log-sorter*, and *bobbin winder tender*. (But nothing was done to the title of the bureau in charge of these changes: the *Manpower* Administration.)[17] Publishers urge authors to paraphrase, and, if necessary, to repeat the combinations *he or she, his or her*, etc.

The problem was not discovered by the feminists. It is an old one in the language, and has one popular solution: the use of a plural when the antecedent is indefinite. Instead of *Everybody will choose his partner* we have *Everybody will choose their partner*. Sinclair Lewis described Doremus and Emma as having *each their own bedroom*, and Sir Walter Scott complained of being *shut up in a nasty Scotch jail, where one cannot even get the dirt brushed off their clothes*. Most speakers are unconscious of any inconsistency in a sentence like *Nobody is blaming you, are they?* where a singular *is* is repeated by a plural *are*. But the more definite the person referred to, the less acceptable the plural form becomes. The following go from normal to impossible:

> If anybody wants their phone number changed. . . .
> If a person wants their phone number changed. . . .
> ?If a man or woman wants their phone number changed. . . .
> *If a subscriber wants their phone number changed. . . .

The clash is worse when a singular verb collides with a doubly plural *themselves: When a person can't think what to do with themselves*, with its *can't*, which may be either singular or plural, is not as bad as **When a person doesn't know what to do with themselves.* For some obscure reason, the more logical *themself* is less used.[18]

The last example can of course be made passable with *When a person doesn't know what to do with himself or herself*, and this solution too is an old one. Jespersen quotes a line from Henry Fielding: *The reader's heart (if he or she have any).*[19] But Jespersen called the double pronoun a makeshift, and H. L. Mencken condemned it as 'intolerably clumsy'.[20] Another possible recourse would be to use the grammatically neuter form *it*, as Swanwick recommended. But besides wrenching our lifelong habit of restricting *it* to things, animals, and occasionally infants, this collides with two other ingrained habits. One is that of extending *it* to grown persons only as a sign of contempt. (On being jeered at by a passing motorist, you catch up with him and say, with a lofty stare, *From a distance I could have sworn it was human.*) The other is that of NOT using *it* even with animals when the wish is to personify. You observe the antics of a squirrel working on its nest and remark, *I saw him climb the tree with his mouth full of building materials.* You have not determined the sex of the squirrel so you personify with the masculine. To use the double pronoun would be absurd by today's standards: **I saw him or her climb the tree with his or her mouth full of building materials.* And to substitute *it* and *its* for *him* and *his* would destroy the personification.

The real difficulty with the double pronoun must be looked at in the light of what is meant by 'clumsy'. Anything that speakers are not used to is 'clumsy', and it might be argued that all we need to do is keep saying it and eventually it will sound all right. But this overlooks one of the two main functions of the pronouns in English. The first, of no interest here, is the distinction of a particular individual, male or female. The other is anaphoric: the function of standing for and pointing to an antecedent. English syntax requires that all finite verbs have explicit subjects and that most verbs have complements. We can manage this by repeating the noun: *When I saw Mary, Mary was getting Mary's self ready to go visit Mary's cousin, and I asked to go along with Mary.* (Even this would require the effacement of another habit, that of taking repeated *Mary's* to refer to different persons with the same name: *Mary [Jones] met Mary [Smith].*) To avoid the repetition we use the corresponding pronouns: *When I saw Mary, she was getting herself ready to go visit her cousin, and I asked to go along with h .* The pronoun adds no information; we could as well substitute a mathematical symbol. Such virtually empty words behave as empty words normally do: they are de-accented, to attract as little attention as possible. The grammars of some languages allow one or more of them to be omitted altogether – in Spanish no word for 'she' would need to be expressed at all. English downplays the *h* pronouns by dropping the *h* when it is not directly after a pause: *she was getting 'erself ready to go visit 'er cousin, and I asked to go along with 'er.* It would be unnatural to pronounce the *h* here.

But the double pronoun compels full accent and full-blown *h*'s; we cannot say **If you see the manager, call imorer,* for *call him or her.* The 'clumsiness' of the double pronoun is not only that we are un-accustomed to it but that it refuses to take the back seat that all languages reserve for pure anaphora.

There has been no lack of quixotic inventions as substitutes for the double pronoun. A few writers (including males), though nowhere in the popular press, have adopted *she* as common gender, presumably to even the score. The dialectal pronoun *thon* was once proposed, as was the French *on*. The latest at this writing is *e*, for research on whose feasibility a professor at the University of California has received a grant.[21] This appears to merit the Proxmire Golden Fleece Award, because *he* is already pronounced *e*, and hearers would simply infer that the speaker intends *he*.

So no solution is in sight. The writer or speaker has to choose between perpetuating sexist language and making a mess of the grammar. The kind of expedient that might work is the one proposed by a feminist of another era, Ella Flagg Young. She suggested dropping the *or* and combining: *himer, hiser* (and, supposedly, *heshe*). These could be played down as pronouns normally are, including dropping the *h*. It is enough to make a barely distinguishable noise in the proper slot. The problem is the same as with any other direct intervention in language: first agreeing on the expedient, then getting used to it.

What people are not used to is generally good for a laugh, and the feminists have been showered with barbs from female as well as male humorists looking for an easy joke. Even those sympathetic to the cause are sometimes intolerant of any reforms that might cause temporary discomfort. The former managing editor of the Washington *Post*, Alfred Friendly, offers the feminists a lesson in historical grammar: 'The suffix *-person* is a needless bastard born of ignorant parents. For several millennia, back to the Sanskrit word *manu, -man, man-* and the word *man* standing alone meant "person, one, human being of either sex". They still do. That *man* has the additional meaning, when used in a different context, of an adult human male is beside the point.'[22] Unfortunately, etymologies are irrelevant, and *man* suggests its own contexts.

The sexist use of the pronouns goes beyond straightforward male–female reference. It also extends to the personification of inanimate things. Ships are often called *she*. The imagery is fairly obvious: sea captains, sailors, and shipping clerks are traditionally men, and the ship is pictured as something alive that works for them and toward which they feel a certain affection. The feminine can be used for any fairly elaborate workhorse contrivance: *Look at my new power mower; ain't she a beaut?* As the linguist Uriel Weinreich points out, this usage is particularly common among male speakers to refer to objects 'lovingly handled'.[23] But if the workhorse is pictured as having a rudimentary intelligence, then the pronoun switches to masculine. Here is a conversation about a game-playing computer:

> 'I usually win,' the teacher continued. 'But he can play quite well some times.'
> 'He?'
> 'Yes, that's odd, but most people call computers "he" and ships "she".'[24]

The bestowing of feminine names on objects such as airplanes and car trailers follows the same tendency, which also doubtless explains why meteorologists have given us such things as *Hurricane Edith* but not *Hurricane Elmer* – it takes a meteorologist to view something as destructive as a hurricane with affection – HIS property, of course. But the winds are changing: in 1978 the weathermen (*weatherpersons) agreed that male and female names would henceforth be balanced.

A similar personification is found with abstractions, especially the names of political entities. But rather than the 'faithful slave' metaphor, this is probably connected with the notion of 'mother country': *China and her millions*. Sometimes the neuter *it* works well enough instead, but in the following, where the writer was obviously trying to avoid *her*, it does not:

> As one American Embassy counselor says, '90 per cent of our problems would disappear if we could convince Japan that our policy was not aimed especially at it.'[25]

This ignores two rules of English: *convince* requires an object with something resembling a mind, and *it* is usually avoided where it would occur in the position of the main sentence accent.

Superficially, the use of *man* in the names for occupations seems as biased as the 'common gender' *he*, and some feminists have attacked it just as vigorously. But there is an important grammatical difference: *he* belongs to syntax, *man* to morphology or wordforms. *He* has to be coordinated with some other reference in the sentence or nearby – an antecedent – and this brings it to more or less conscious attention. *Man*, used as a kind of suffix, is affected as such elements usually are: it tends to be swallowed up in the larger word. *He*, too, in its normal anaphoric use, tends to fade, but it always CAN be pronounced with its consonant and vowel unabated. But a word such as *workman* would sound strange with *man* not reduced to *m'n*. Newer forms do have the full *man* – *garbage man, meter man, ice cream man*; but the commoner ones lose the vowel: *doorman, lineman, postman, workman, chairman, trainman, chapman, fisherman*. With this less obvious suggestion of 'man', it would appear that the masculinity of the term is more a function of the word as a whole than of the suffix. If *She is the chairman* sounds odd, it is for the same reason that *She is the commissioner* sounds odd – both words refer to posts once held almost exclusively by men. So it might have been better to leave most of the *man* words alone, trusting to the future feminine occupants of the positions to feminize or neutralize them. Some feminists agree that *person* was a dubious choice to replace *man*. As one feminist who is also a linguist says, 'Terms like *chairperson* seem to be specializing to women, while *chairman* is reserved for men. All that has been accomplished is the self-conscious avoidance of *chairwoman*. Meanwhile, we are subjected to a rich assortment of jokes about *Freshpersons, personhole covers, postpersons,* and *person-eating sharks.'*[26] A local woman official in California declared that she and another female official 'both hate the term *chairperson*'.[27]

All in all, the troubles with pronouns, sex-marked nouns, and other such biases in language prove how important it is, when trying to intervene in the way people speak and write, to know something about linguistics.

The language ABOUT women reflects the attitudes of men toward women, and, to the extent that women accept them, the attitudes of women toward themselves. The language OF women is evidence of women's perceptions of themselves however derived – whether by acceptance of the social type-casting to which women are subjected, or through inherent differences between the sexes.

This is the inveterate nature-nurture dispute, as difficult to settle in sex as anywhere else. 'It is woman's nature to be thus' has always been the justification for discriminatory treatment, yet very little is known about the real biological differences between male and female. Mary Key cites some views that persisted well into the present century:

> Some scholars had come to the conclusion that genius could only be a masculine trait. This was 'documented' by Weininger,[28] along with his other ideas that women did not have souls and that they were incapable of true love. . . . To be fair one should say that Jespersen tried to have a more balanced perspective about genius – and he pointed out that 'idiocy is more common among men',[29] another myth that he would have been unable to prove. Nevertheless, these ideas about intellectual potential influenced the statements about language and promulgated weird conclusions: the vocabulary of a woman is smaller; male language is more constructive, useful, and abstract; male language has more complex, embedded constructions, while female language is simple-minded with much emotional emphasis.[30]

The reproductive differences between male and female are obvious, but the evidence is inconclusive on differences that might affect intelligence or the ability to acquire or use language in a distinctive way. It may be that male and female brains are organized somewhat differently, especially where 'lateralization' is concerned. All human beings use the left side of the brain to process language more than they use the right side (except that with some left-handed people this is reversed). The right side of the brain appears to control non-analytic functions such as space perception and musical appreciation. The process of lateralization – of firming up the two sides for their separate functions – is gradual and is complete about the age of five. If there are differences in lateralization, there might well be differences in language ability or language use.

There seems to be some evidence for this. In a series of experiments it was shown that four-year-old girls had a lower right-ear advantage than four-year-old boys. (This can be interpreted to mean that the specialization for speech perception has not progressed as far at that age as for boys. The right ear 'feeds' into the left hemisphere of the brain.) But by the age of five this difference between boys and girls had disappeared.[31]

Other experiments point to a difference in rate of development of the two sides of the brain, with the right side maturing faster in boys and the left in girls – regardless of left- or right-handedness. This seems to be correlated with differences in the abilities controlled by each side. Dr Jerre Levy claims that 'there is no way child-rearing could produce the differences we see in left-handers' and therefore 'these differences must be genetic (inborn)'. She concludes that 'even in the total absence of social discrimination, men, on the average, probably make better architects and engineers, and women better social workers and teachers'.[32]

There is no comfort to male supremacists if the side of the brain controlling language reaches full development earlier in girls than in boys. But the current state of brain research gives no good reason for complimenting either sex on its special abilities. Whatever initial advantage one or the other may have in its equipment for language is unlikely to override the massive influence of socialization as children grow up.

Female speech is stigmatized, in somewhat the same way as Black speech. A woman may feel miffed, but is not apt to be outraged if another woman imitates her using a mannish tone of voice; but for a man to use the 'swoopy' tone associated with women's speech when he mocks the speech of a man is 'one of the most infuriating acts of aggression one person can commit on another'.[33] It is like clothing: a woman can wear a mannish suit and be admired for it; a man in a woman's dress is an object of ridicule. Yet the traits that make a style of speech sound masculine or feminine are resources for all to use. They derive their quality from the PREPONDERANCE of their use by one sex or the other – in amount or intensity. In this respect the stigma differs from that of Black speech: a woman is not apt to be more esteemed by a man if she sounds less feminine, whereas a Black is apt to be more esteemed by a white if he sounds less Black. Black speech is outside the standard; female speech is not. But for a man to use feminine tones and forms in any consistent pattern is taken by most other men to be grossly inappropriate, and this tells us something of men's regard for women and their place in society, as well as men's regard for men.

One hereditary difference between male and female speech is unmistakable: the pitch range for adult males averages about an octave lower than that of females, owing to the lengthening of the vocal folds during puberty. This difference defines sex so sharply that it tends to be cultivated and the initial difference may be increased by females speaking in a somewhat higher register and males in lower – already boys tend to have lower-pitched vowels,[34] and adult males in some societies (speakers of Arabic and Spanish, for example) frequently glottalize their speech, exaggerating the low range for the *macho* effect. Even in this one conspicuously physiological difference, the cultural influence is evident.

Their higher pitch prompts the view that women are more childlike than men. Girls' voices do not change at puberty, so they sound more like children. '"Baby talk" in both English and Arabic is perceived as more appropriately used by women than by men. Additional documentation that the use of language suggests that a female never grows up is provided . . . in a sample of job advertisements in the Los Angeles *Times*: 97 ads used *girl* or *gal* while only two used *boy*.'[35] The reasons for the popularity of *girl* are more complex than this, but it is nevertheless a stereotype, and women who are aware of it frequently protest against being referred to as girls. An angry letter-to-the-editor about a meeting at a local parish church ends with this: 'I do credit the San Andreas clergy with enlightenment to the point of referring to black adult males as men rather than boys. When will they with equal consistency pronounce the word *women*?'[36]

In a word, female speech lacks the ASSERTIVE tone of male speech. The following characteristics have been noted:

1 Women use more tag questions than men.[37] Where a man says *This is better*, a woman will tend to say *This is better, isn't it?* or *This is better, don't you think?* Tag questions leave the issue open; they contain assertions but are not assertive.

2 Women use more reverse accents than men. Where a man says

        TRY

I ^{wish} you'd

           it

with the most prominent word at the highest pitch, a woman will tend to say

  wish

      you'd

I

          i t

TRY

with the most prominent word at the lowest pitch. This is one reason for the 'swoopy' effect of women's speech. A reverse accent says, in effect, 'This is important, but I don't want to be pushy about it.'

3 Women use the falsetto range of voice more than men do. It has been claimed that women have a greater tendency to end a sentence with a rising pitch, but this may not be true.[38] A rising pitch indicates incompleteness, and men and women both need to convey meanings that are incomplete and uncertain. But the rise into the falsetto range has another function: it adds a kind of pleading sweetness, so long as it is not over-loud. The distinction is not so much in the presence of the rise as in how far it goes. This is another reason for the 'swoopy' impression. Actually our description here may be confusing cause and effect. It is possible that falsetto is 'sweet' because women use it. It is more accessible to their voices, and women are judged to be sweet when they plead. But it forms part of the general repertory of sounds; men can draw on it – sparingly: in this case, to sound sweetly reasonable or placating (a good source of examples is the man's end of a telephone conversation with his wife). It is more common in the speech of Black than of white males, among speakers of American English.

4 Women make a heavier use of the inconclusive intensifiers *so* and *such*. These were originally demonstratives that required a correlative *that* clause: *Mary is so bright that everybody is astonished.* But the clause was omitted, leaving the degree of whatever it was up to the imagination: *Mary is so bright!* The speaker does not have to commit herself. It would be hard to say whether women's speech carries a greater load of intensification in general. Probably it contains more VERBAL exaggeration – intensifiers such as *very, awfully, terribly*; repetitions such as *very very, so so, much much*; and highly eulogistic words like *georgeous, superb, divine.* But this is conspicuously POLITE intensification, and the reason for it may lie in women's exclusion from the kind of non-verbal intensification that men freely use: loudness and roughness of voice, alongside the assertive tone referred to earlier and forms of verbal 'coarseness' such as cursing – which takes no imagination; a woman has to work harder at being emphatic than a man. Mary Key notes the hyperbole in women's speech, 'accompanied by strong emphasis patterns': *I'd just DIE!, He'll NEVER forgive me!*[39] Hyperbole is another harmless form of intensification; but as for the emphasis, identical patterns are found in men's speech: *It's the SHITS!, That SON of a bitch!*

5 Women are more careful to follow prescriptive rules. A man's *Are you comin'?* is matched by a woman's *Are you coming? He walks too slow* is matched by *He walks too slowly.* Women are more apt to make mistakes in the direction of AVOIDING mistakes, that is, to use hypercorrect forms such as *You gave it to June and she* (this comes from trying too hard to avoid things like *June and her received it from you*). A form such as *I done it* is heard less from women of whatever class than from men.[40]

6 Women's speech shows a more refined perception in certain areas. Specifically, colors have been mentioned: women are said to have 'a color vocabulary that contains items such as *azure* and *turquoise*; men are thought, by and large, not to have these words in their lexicon'.[41] But

it is hard to disentangle the appreciation of color from the use of certain exotic NAMES for colors. A man would not hesitate to use a highly specific color term such as *cobalt* or *ultramarine*, but would avoid the foreign-sounding *mauve* or *magenta*.

Till recently, the interest in women's speech has been more theoretical and political than immediately practical. But with the growing freedom to change sex physically as well as mentally, men who make the change are demanding to be taught female ways of speaking. It was having to learn foreign languages that led to linguistic analysis in the first place, centuries ago, and the situation here is similar. In a program of classes for transsexual males at Stanford University, the instructor, Maureen O'Connor, uses 'contrastive analysis' – the analytical comparison of languages or dialects – much as in foreign-language teaching.[42]

To end this lengthy example of a particular kind of loaded language, we must ask again the question posed at the beginning of Chapter 8: Does the mere EXISTENCE of a linguistic form produce a social effect, when speakers are free to use it or not? Most feminists are convinced that the language about women and of women is a form of enslavement. 'Our speech not only reflects our place in society,' says Sally McConnell-Ginet, 'but also helps to create that place.'[43] Julia Stanley adds, 'At its most "trivial" level, the vocabulary provided by our culture limits severely the kinds of experience we can express for ourselves.'[44] And this from Thorne and Henley: 'Language helps enact and transmit every type of inequality, including that between the sexes; it is part of the "micropolitical structure" . . . that helps maintain the larger political-economic structure.'[45] Though a consensus does not make a fact, the evidence is pretty conclusive. Women are required, by the conventions of the language, to identify themselves as

polite
unobtrusive
correct

and above all AS WOMEN, to the point of advertising whether they are marriageable or not: a woman is addressed by titles of nubility, *Miss* or *Mrs*. A man's noncommittal *Mr* implies that he is a free agent in his sex life.

Women are the 'marked', the 'different', sex – woman's language is described against man's as a standard, not the reverse. And this is not just a whim of linguists when they analyse – it inheres in the language. Being a Miss or a Mrs is more exceptional than being a simple Mr. The usual pronoun is *he*, not *she*, when sex is unknown. Women are 'objects' rather than 'subjects' in almost all metaphorical discourse – the property rather than the possessor, the moved rather than the mover (the Prime Mover is endowed with the pronoun *He* and pictured with a beard – a child's letter reads, 'Dear God, is it really true that boys are better than girls? I know you are one, but try to be fair. Love, Sylvia.'[46] The human race is *man* and *mankind*. In the Creation, woman came from man. The word *pioneer* is used of a group if any males at all are present, but if only women are involved, they are *pioneer women*.[47] The same was true till recently of many professions: *woman doctor, woman lawyer* – including marked feminines like *aviatrix, authoress, poetess, seamstress* (where sex is relevant, these persist: *actress, majorette, madam*). Linguistic asymmetry is everywhere.

Whether it can be done away with is an economic question as much as a linguistic one. Many families now require more than one wage earner, which has forced more and more women into the marketplace, in competition with men – inflation is the current equivalent of the wars that put minorities in uniform and gave them a power they had never had before. Sexism in language will grow less as women are accepted more, in the roles that men have traditionally occupied. This is a safe historical prediction – but it will come about by applying pressures, of which awareness of the stereotypes and protest against them is one. In the long run, reducing asymmetry will probably take the form of women laying equal claim to masculine characteristics in language, rather than the deliberate neutering of sex markers. Male forms are esteemed by BOTH sexes as better for the self-respect that goes with independence; the 'feminine whine' is not for today's professional women. The language is intricate, cumbersome, and strongly resistant to interference; it changes its values more easily than it changes its forms.

As for the sore points, attempts to remove the more obvious indicators of sex have been mostly cosmetic. We have seen the problems of trying to change the 'common gender' *he*. Even as simple an expedient as using *Ms* to avoid the distinction of *Miss* and *Mrs* has run into trouble. Ann Holmquist points out that *Ms* seems to have backfired – it has come to be associated with 'divorcees, widows, businesswomen, feminists and others who may be supposed to have sexual experience and to be either available or militantly liberationist'[48] – in other words, the attempt to get an unmarked term has simply resulted in a new and different form of markedness. Robin Lakoff feels that some of the sexist aspects of language 'are too common, too thoroughly mixed throughout the language, for the speaker to be aware each time he uses them'[49] – and correspondingly difficult to root out. But Julia Stanley says that people had better be MADE aware of them. As Holmquist says of *his or her*, it is admittedly cumbersome and 'grates on editors' nerves'; but it is still a 'necessary, if temporary, expedient – for raising consciousness'.[50]

The inertial mass of language is like the inertial mass of society. Women inherit their place as speakers inherit their words. We drag a vast obsolescence behind us even as we have rejected much of it intellectually, and it slows us down. Language is a stage built over a graveyard from which fossils rise and dance at night. A part of our reality is the unreality of archaic language about sex. Roles are made over but stereotypes remain – epithets we no longer use but that linger in consciousness, attitudes that prevent the full realization of our beliefs, weapons still – in the hands of the ignorant, or of those who feel threatened by change. The rehabilitation of names of things and of creatures comes in part automatically as the things and creatures are rehabilitated, but it is a factor too in their rehabilitation – no amount of enlightened animal husbandry can erase overnight the associations of *swine*, *pig*, *hog*, *sow*. The gun of sex-biased language may be rusty, but it is there, and the greatest danger is unawareness that it is a gun, and is loaded.

Chapter 10

Power and deception

On 10 May 1978 a nuclear bomb, code-named Transom, was scheduled to go off at the bottom of a two-thousand-foot shaft in the desert at Yucca Flat, Nevada. Preparations apparently went well, and the Department of Energy announced that the explosion had taken place according to plan, at 8 am. But seismographs throughout the West told a different story; no tremors were detected. The bomb was a dud. The Department of Energy was caught in a barefaced lie.

Why a modifier like *barefaced* on the plain unvarnished *lie*? It is because lies are modified by their aims, and come in varying shades of intensity, detectability, literalness, and social acceptance. One may admit to lying and justify it as a social necessity, as when the painful facts are withheld from someone who is dying. Or one may call a lie by another name – a *fib* for one told in jest, a *white lie* for a serious falsehood where no harm is meant, a *terminological inexactitude* to spare one's parliamentary colleagues, or *dancing on the edge of the truth*, as one advertising man describes what he does 'for dramatic effect'.[1] One may falsify for self-preservation, or for someone else's good, or for the good of the state. The prince, wrote Machiavelli, should always have 'legitimate grounds . . . for the non-fulfilment of his promise; . . . those that have been best able to imitate the fox have succeeded best. But it is necessary to disguise this character well, and to be a great feigner and dissembler; and men are so simple and so ready to obey present necessities, that one who deceives will always find those who allow themselves to be deceived.'[2] Deception for reasons of state has been called 'plausible denial' in the United States.

It will not do to condemn all lying. But it is necessary to understand the lie, for protection against it – if one prefers not to be among 'those who allow themselves to be deceived'.

Suppose we take the broadest definition possible of truth and falsity, to embrace the gradations and locate them in Verity Space.

A has information that may be useful to B. B may inquire of A, or A may volunteer. A is truthful to the extent that he conveys the information that he supposes B wants in the form and manner he believes B wants it. Complete truthfulness is synonymous with complete sincerity.

But ahead is a fork in the road. In one direction lies information about what has happened or is happening in the real world. In the other lie the intentions of the speaker toward FUTURE events. The first is the domain of reports, the second that of promises. It is possible to go with untruth in either direction, but promises are never objectively true or untrue, because intentions are private. If I promise to be loyal to King Mboto II and have no intention of fulfilling my promise, I am of course telling a falsehood, but it is not open to inspection. My being loyal later would not make me truthful. Nor would my being disloyal make me a liar if when I said I would be loyal I meant it – for a promise is essentially a PREDICTION of future behavior, which is subject to future events. A meteorologist is not a liar when the fair weather of his promise turns into rain.

The confusion between truth in reporting and performance in promising may be in part deliberate or at least not discouraged, as a way of making promises more binding. Some of the purposes of a society are served best when the behavior of its members can be predicted, especially in critical matters such as payment of debts, adherence to the law, and the carrying out of contracts. Much of the same terminology is used in both kinds of veracity – one *gives one's word* that a fact is so or that something will be done. One *signs* an affidavit or an agreement. One *swears* to tell the truth or to be loyal. In fact, the history of oath-taking is a study not only in ways societies have devised to extract the truth from unwilling witnesses but of efforts to make future behavior contingent on telling the truth about intentions now.

Ultimately, intentions are the arbiter of truth in the broad sense, in reporting as well as promising. Only the person who makes the statement knows whether he is speaking truly or not. There may be external evidence of the ACCURACY of the statement, and this is called 'objective truth'; but the fact that the statement does not conform to the evidence does not make it a lie – the speaker may be honestly mistaken.

What is the nature of intentions? At the extreme of utmost sincerity one can imagine a witness who does not take advantage of a flaw in his interrogator's question but points it out and answers accordingly: 'You have asked if I was there on the fifth of June; you must mean the sixth, and it is true, I was there that day.' At the other extreme is the intention not merely to withhold information but to represent the facts as exactly opposite to what they are: the barefaced Yucca Flat lie.

Between the extremes are all the shades of evasion, which come in two styles, propositional and non-propositional. The non-propositional evasion supplies suggestive images and lets the viewer or hearer make up his own false proposition. An outdoorsy type is pictured smoking a cigaret against a background of lake, cliff, and campfire; inference: cigarets are good for you. Or a toothy six-year-old rushes to its mother's arms with the cry, 'Look, Mom, no cavities!' This is the testimonial, and whether it is verbal or visual the inference is 'What applies to that or them applies to me', the viewer or listener. Some non-propositional responses approach total irrelevance, and in effect are the same as saying 'I refuse to answer', though the disguise may be skilful enough to make the words seem to say something. A quotation that mystifies: this is sham profundity – you can't figure it out, so it must harbor some unfathomable truth. Or an anecdote, especially one containing a personal gibe. Cyrus Stuart Ching annihilated a heckler with this: 'My friend, I'm not going to answer any more of your questions. I hope you won't take this personally, but I am reminded of something my old uncle told me, long ago, back on the farm. He said, "What's the sense of wrestling with a pig? You both get muddy all over, and the pig likes it."'[3] Contending with the non-propositional is difficult because it has to be done propositionally, and the defenders can always say they 'did not mean that' – if they HAD given their message propositionally, it would have been perfectly innocent. The Deputy Director of the US Federal Trade Commission created a furore when he proposed to look for ways to deal with 'unspoken promises' in advertising. As one advertiser complained, 'You would have to do away with all perfume advertisements and all cosmetic advertisements. You're selling a woman a bottle of promise.'[4]

The propositional evasion leans on the crutch of LITERALISM. Here we have STATEMENTS that purport to represent reality, but are skewed by some linguistic mismatch – a word with a double meaning or a construction that makes a false connection. The liar adopts the pose of telling the literal truth or acting according to the literal instructions. Suppose a government agency has been illegally collecting and storing intelligence on private citizens. A suit is brought, and the courts order the agency to destroy *the documents*. The agency proceeds to destroy them – after making a copy for posterity. This evasion hinges on the sense of an abstract noun that can also be taken concretely. The court intended the abstraction: there was to be no record left; the agency obeyed by destroying the concrete documents. Or take the concept of *self-incrimination*. The Fifth Amendment of the US Constitution provides that no person may be 'compelled in any criminal case to be a witness against himself'. This broad right is abridged by literalism. First, *witness against* refers only to 'testimonial utterance' – that is, to the STATEMENTS made by the witness; he may still be compelled to speak as a test for recognizing his voice or to try on a shoe that will put him at the scene of the crime. Second, *incrimination* is reduced to literal PROSECUTA-BILITY – a witness can be compelled to give testimony that may ruin his reputation, so long as it cannot be used in criminal charges against him.

Literalism in rules for conduct is a necessary evil. Much of the involved and redundant language of the law is to make conditions as explicit as possible, to leave no ambiguities for either side in a controversy to exploit. The ideal is a literalism that can be trusted for its impartiality. The reality is too often an ambush that defeats the framers' intent by diverting it into a verbal bypath that was not foreseen.

Retreating behind an unguarded literalism is a form of defense that children learn as soon as they become aware of the meanings of words. In fact it most likely is part of the process of learning how far a meaning can be stretched. A child has been warned not to *dig holes in the yard*. He proceeeds to dig where a playmate has already dug a hole and filled it in. Enter adult, who scolds child for digging hole. Child replies, 'But Mrs C, I didn't dig a hole, I just cleaned the dirt out of it.' How does one define the word *hole*? If a glass can be full of water, why can't a hole be full of dirt?

Literalism is a common safeguard in commercial advertising and labeling. An ad or a label is ambiguous – possibly false on the interpretation most favorable to the product, but true on some other interpretation. When an unmodified plural noun in English is used as the subject of a sentence, it can refer to 'all' or to 'part' of what it names. In the sentence *Athletes are subject to muscular strain*, the reference is to all athletes – it implies 'If you are an athlete you are subject to muscular strain'; but *Athletes were running around the field* refers only to the ones who were there. So how is an ad like *Athletes Use Sayers Liniment* to be understood? The advertiser would like us to infer 'all athletes' – the statement would not be worth the boast otherwise; but it is literally true even if only two athletes in the world use the product. This kind of literalist evasion leans on an ambiguity in English. Other kinds use evasive word meanings. In the United States, sugar is marketed in several forms, one of which is called *brown sugar*. All packages bearing this label contain a product that is brown in color. So it is brown sugar – just as a polar bear painted brown is a brown bear. But all the major English dictionaries except one follow the *Oxford* in defining *brown sugar* as 'unrefined or partially refined sugar' – the meaning that probably comes closest to the popular conception of what brown sugar is, on the strength of which many people buy it as a health food. The one exception among the dictionaries gives a clue to what has happened: 'Soft sugar whose crystals are covered by a film of refined dark syrup that imparts color, flavor, and moisture' (Merriam Webster *Third New International*). Instead of an unrefined or partially refined product, this describes a doubly refined one: refined sugar to which a refined syrup has been added. The Webster definition is known to lexicographers as a 'constructed definition': instead of incorporating, as it is generally thought dictionaries should, the meaning that most people have in mind when they use the word, it adopts the industry's description of its product. The sugar industry has double insurance – brown is brown, and if you don't like that, Webster says brown sugar is what we make.

Advertising aimed at children is a rich source of evasion by literalism. Television ads for breakfast cereals in the United States are supposed to include 'at least one audio reference to . . . the role of the product within the framework of a balanced regimen'. The reference usually takes the form *X part of Y breakfast*, and a lot can be done with *X* and *Y*. One such ad is worded *The good part of any good breakfast*. As Professor Michael Geis points out in testimony to the Federal Trade Commission, *good* in this context is ambiguous between 'good-tasting' and 'good for you', and the words *the* and *any* make their own special claims. The result is a four-way ambiguity that pretends to meet the broadcast requirement and wheedles the viewer at the same time.

Literalism is also a smokescreen for certain government activities. When the Central Intelligence Agency was suspected of paying journalists to perform services, the director of the Agency, William Colby, 'would say things like "Nobody on the staff of Newspaper X is on the CIA payroll", when in fact four "stringers" for the newspaper were being paid by the CIA'. A stringer is not technically a member of the staff. Or the Agency would deny that *reporters* had worked for the CIA, when 'photographers from the same publications had performed clandestine tasks'.[5] In one interview, when Mr Colby was asked, regarding CIA operations, 'Do we have to kill people or break bones?', he replied, 'The rules are very clear today that there will be no assassinations.'[6] The definition of *assassinate* provides a loophole: according to the *American Heritage Dictionary* it means 'to murder (a prominent person)'. Intentionally or unintentionally, Colby's answer was beside the point. In 1943, when General Dwight Eisenhower rebuked General George S. Patton for striking an enlisted man, an Army official in Algiers denied that General Patton had 'at any time been reprimanded by General Eisenhower'. In Army parlance, a *reprimand* involves a formal proceeding.

A form of defensive literalism in common use is REDUCTIONISM. It is a projection of literalness out of language onto the real world. If the literal meaning of *hit* is expressed in terms of its elements – something like 'to make a thrust that comes intentionally in contact with an object' – then the act itself can be decomposed, and when the culprit is asked, 'Why did you hit your sister?' he can deny any intention by picturing himself as part of an impersonal chain of events: 'I didn't! I just poked out my hand and there was her face.' The refrain of reductionism is 'All I did was'. Imagine that you are bent on mischief and pronounce the name of a friend's town, *Pismo Beach*, with a voiceless *s*. Your friend is duly annoyed, but you say, 'All I did was devoice the *s*.' Your behavior deserves to be judged at the level of WORD MEANING, but your game reduces it to the level of phonetics. A bit of probably unconscious reductionism occurred in a US court case that was reversed on appeal. The police had raided a house occupied by a family suspected of trafficking in heroin and in spite of a thorough search had found nothing. Then it occurred to one of the policemen to offer a bribe of five dollars to the five-year-old son of the occupants, who promptly led the way to the cache of drugs. The lower court ruled for the defense, scoring 'police conduct that amounted to denial of due process'; but the court of appeals returned a conviction, explaining that the policeman had 'simply removed the boy's reluctance to cooperate'.

Propositional language, as we saw two chapters back (pages 69–70), is what speech shares most fully with writing. *Literal* refers to *letters*; the literal truth is the letter of the truth. So another aspect of literalism is that it pays little heed to the normally unwritten parts of language – tone of voice, emphasis, and interlocking gesture. A spoken advertisement for a patent medicine runs like this:

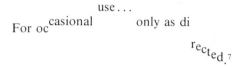

The ostensible meaning of this is 'Don't worry about using this now and then, just follow the directions'. But the legal safeguard depends on the proper intonation, which should be something like

$$\begin{array}{cccc} & ca & & \\ & & use & on \\ For\ oc & sion_{al} & & as\ di\ ^{rec} \\ & & ly, & ted. \end{array}$$

The ad misleadingly intones *occasional* as if it were of no more importance than *casual*, instead of giving it the contrast needed for a proper warning. This on top of the mildness of the words themselves, when compared with the forthright *not for frequent use*.

Evasion is the same, whether practiced by high or by low and whether meant to persuade or to defend. In either case there is a violation of some responsibility of disclosure. The persuader conceals the drawbacks of his product or policy. The defender protects himself against the extractors of information – prosecutors, employers, labor bosses, military interrogators, high school principals, angry parents. What is defended is privacy, the most private world of all: if a man's house is his castle, a man's mind is his castle keep, the last fortification when he is under attack by the seekers of unwilling information. He is expected to 'tell the truth', 'come clean', 'confess', to produce statements that fit the facts.

A damaging truth most people will naturally evade. Short of telling a literal lie, Western society generally permits this with a clear conscience. The agile player on literal truth who reveals nothing of substance is usually admired for it, particularly when the interrogator is not felt to have a right to the information. Conscience is implanted when children are punished for deception, and authorities that replace the parents in later life continue to encourage the idea that it is wicked to lie. As a rule, social interests benefit. No society could endure that made deception the rule; and the dissemination of news – everywhere one of the most powerful institutions – survives only to the extent that it is believed to be truth-telling. But the individual may be hurt. And as usually happens, the one hurt most is the one with the fewest defenses. It is the petty liar who is most often caught and branded. He does not know his right to remain silent and is not skilled at evasion when cornered. He is not one of those 'whose eccentricities are excused because they are the holders of power, and are able to label others rather than be labeled themselves'.[8]

As with other defenses, those of the mind are breached through bribery or by force. Most societies limit or – at least nominally – prohibit the use of physical torture, and the information it produces, as far as testimony is concerned, is apt to be unreliable. Milder persuasions are employed everywhere, and mostly take the form of instilling fear. The threat may be direct or indirect. Later punishment for perjury if one is caught is a direct inducement. Even more direct were the tests to which witnesses were once subjected – the ordeal by fire, the ordeal by drowning (the person telling the truth could walk through fire and not be burned, or would float if thrown in the water). Though not classed as torture, the prospect of such a test was usually enough to loosen a tongue.

The indirect compulsions are more interesting in the manner of their evolution as social beliefs have changed. Moral suasion depends on beliefs. There is no use in threatening an atheist with hellfire. But a religious person who puts his hand on the Bible and swears to tell the whole truth so help him God, is more apt to be true to his oath. This has been the purpose of swearing on sacred things – such oaths 'induce witnesses, especially the ignorant and superstitious, to give evidence more truthfully'.[9]

The oath is still a formality in courts of law, though its power has come to depend on fear of prosecution for perjury more than fear of eternal damnation. For the 'ignorant and superstitious' we now have the God of Science. The fear that haunts the defenseless today is having a probe inserted into their heads. This has been the age-long dream of enforcement agencies, and if the promotional literature is to be believed, the dream has finally come true. Since a branch of science very close to linguistics is involved in the machines and techniques, the claims for them deserve our attention.

The readings of a lie detector are not direct. There is no chemical that precipitates a cloudy deposit when catalyzed with a falsehood. What the machine does is measure physical stress under interrogation. The best-known instrument is the Keeler polygraph, first successfully tested in 1923, which registers changes in blood pressure, pulse rate, and respiration. The theory is that telling a lie makes one nervous, and the symptoms cannot be hidden.

A more controversial machine – or group of machines – is that of the so-called stress-analyzers, which register changes in the voice rather than the body as a whole and do not require the physical presence of the person being tested. They are an offshoot of devices for analyzing the sound wave; one version produces a spectrogram of the sound called a VOICEPRINT (a bit of promotional association with FINGERPRINT). This type of analysis has been widely used in the identification of suspects in criminal cases, using recordings of voices which are later matched with the live voice. For example, knowing that rapists frequently call their victims on the telephone, the police are able to tap a victim's line and get a recording that can be used for testing later if the suspect is caught. Taking all the voice characteristics into consideration – and sometimes quantifying them on a computer – frequently yields enough evidence to make an identification that will impress a suspect and lead to a confession. Some of the best work of this kind at present is being done by two linguists at the University of California in Los Angeles, Peter Ladefoged and George Papçun, both specialists in phonetics.[10]

Voiceprint identification is not refined enough to establish guilt – it cannot approach the accuracy of fingerprint identification – but it can help to point the finger and it may be strong enough to establish innocence. Unfortunately, it is widely misused. One well-known forensic phonetician charges that voiceprinting is 'a fraud being perpetrated upon the American public and the courts of the United States'.[11] In about half the cases in which his testimony has been sought, the indictments have been withdrawn as soon as it appeared that the voiceprint identification of the defendant would be challenged in court.

The stress-analyzer is a stepchild of the voiceprint that undertakes a much simpler kind of detection than the identity of a speaker with all the fluctuations that make identification difficult (such as the fact that the accuracy of a comparison drops about 50 per cent when the compared samples are taken at widely different times); its sole function is to indicate whether the speaker is lying. It looks for symptoms in the voice comparable to the emotional reactions of the body as a whole registered by the polygraph.

A number of such machines are on the market and both their reliability and the nature of their use have caused widespread controversy. George Papçun, the UCLA phonetician, says the makers of the devices 'are just putting out hooey to fog the truth that the device can be put together for $65 or $75'.[12] But there are plenty of takers, even at fancy prices (as high as $4,000) – police departments and detective agencies as well as private employers who would like to enforce honesty (the National Retail Merchants Association estimates thefts by employees at 500 million dollars a year).

Papçun considers the stress-analyzers worthless as lie-detectors, and one investigative reporter did his own experiment using a brand of analyzer called the Hagoth. He made some autobiographical statements, and the first couple of answers activated the green-for-true and red-for-false lights as advertised. But, he says,

the device later began to flash red on some truthful statements as well. For example, it went red when I mentioned the name of a high school I attended. At the time I could think of no good reason for the stress the machine picked up in my voice at that point. Later, it occurred to me that I had recently driven past the school and had been deeply angered to see the once beautiful lawns of its campus blacktopped into parking lots.[13]

Some lawmakers have taken alarm. California now has a law banning the use of stress-analyzers without the consent of the speaker. (Law enforcement agencies are exempted.)

In short, the stress-analyzers and polygraph machines can register physiological changes, but truth and falsehood are not wired directly into the nervous system. If the subject believes the machine will register a blip when he tells a lie, it probably will – and this is the same 'ignorant and superstitious' subject who was frightened into telling the truth by fear of the wrath to come. At the 1977 murder trial of Ronnie Zamora in Dade County, Florida, which made news because the proceedings were telecast locally and later nationally, one of the defense witnesses, Dr Jack Jacobs, Director of Psychological Services for the Catholic Service Bureau, objected to having the results of the tests made public. He argued that exposing a subject to an open discussion of his responses and their psychological meaning would tend to invalidate any future evaluation of the same subject – and would have a similar effect on anyone else watching and listening to the discussion. The more one knows about how the responses can be interpreted psychologically, the easier it is to control them so as to influence the results. In the long run, the more naive the subject, the more potentially effective the test.[14]

Every force seems to develop its counterforce, and the stress machines come at exactly the time when more and more is being learned about how to deal with stress. The practitioners of yoga have shown that it is possible to bring the 'involuntary' muscles under voluntary control, including those responsible for the three main reactions measured by the polygraph: blood pressure, pulse, and respiration. Reciting a mantra, meditating, Transcendentally or otherwise, and similar methods of relaxation can bring tension under the dominance of the will. The power of the machine, like the power of the oath, extends only a little way beyond the belief in it. The defenses are there, for those with the strength and knowledge to use them. The castle keep of the mind's privacy is still well-nigh impregnable for the person who knows how to guard it.

What of those with the power to prevent even the outer wall of the castle from being attacked? They know that not having to defend oneself at all is half the battle.

The best recourse is to declare the premises off limits to controversy. The doctrine – inherited even by democracies – is that the king can do no wrong, and his chief of security is Ritual, who oversees what is done because it is done, and, even more potent because unseen, what is not done because it is not done. The powerful make the rules, from what is the polite or correct thing to do (including correct language) to the legal safeguards protecting person and property and warding against perjury and treason. When the power resides in a system, the individuals at the controls come and go, and the rules gain the appearance and some of the reality of justice and impartiality. But the system is its own justification, and is generally proof against the questions that may be raised against it and against the class of its principal beneficiaries.

The anthropologist Maurice Bloch compares systems of authority to systems of religion,[15] and indeed among the institutions sheltered by what is not done, religion has the most advantageous position of all: it is not merely objectionable, but wicked, to question. The doctrine of *heresy* imposes virtual thought-control. Bloch argues that ritual is the enemy of propositional language, through which human beings grasp reality. The more formalization there is of what can be said and done, the less there can be of questioning and change. Traditional authority needs SOME propositional language, but secures itself by ritualizing what it approves and tabooing what it does not. The rituals are less obvious than those of religion, but more numerous and sometimes just as powerful – those associated with *patriotism*, for example. A society can be known by its unthinkables, by what its members will react to by repeating a formula or by saying *That simply isn't done*.

When a challenge to power is met and defeated, its programs and its language are written off as well, and can hardly get a hearing even when the prevailing system later adapts to them. Some aspects of American society seem to outsiders (Latin American conservatives, for example) to be socialistic if not downright communistic – the right to strike, to speak one's mind openly, to initiate a law. But if a new reform – say in health care or in taxation – can be linked firmly enough to socialism or communism, it will be rejected. There is a psychological 'throughness' once an issue has been decided; the problems may remain, but the ideology is closed to discussion and can be reopened only with great difficulty. An example of how this works to the advantage of a commercial power is the resurgence of the liquor industry in the United States after the defeat of prohibition in 1933. Every subsequent effort to cope with the problems of alcohol and alcoholism had to overcome the bluenose image of the Women's Christian Temperance Union and the Anti-Saloon League; even the medical evidence associating alcohol with other drugs was of little use – the arguments against alcohol were 'tired' arguments, and young people frightened off marijuana by draconian penalties felt no guilt in taking to drink. The typical tired argument is one tied to a moral stance that has been passed by. *Honor, virtue, uprightness, transgression* – however real such concepts may be, they are seldom invoked in today's truce between religion and secularism, from having been too long invoked from the pulpit.

'What ever became of sin?' Karl Menninger has asked in his recent book. Of course, there IS no such thing as 'sin'; it is a *faux pas*, a peccadillo, a lapse, a slip, a breach, a misdeed, an impropriety. One does not 'sin'; one is simply 'being human'. The 'Seven Deadly Sins'? Don't be quaint! It's not Gluttony but 'overindulgence', not Covetousness but 'getting ahead', not Lust but 'girl-watching' and not Adultery but 'an indiscretion', not Pride but 'an accentuated self-image', not Envy but 'keeping up with the Joneses', not Sloth but 'indiscreet employment of leisure time'.[16]

So much for the justification of what is by the fact that it is. The important thing is that truth and accountability are not exacted evenly. And that some individuals and institutions in a society are in a position to use falsehood and concealment not only for self-defense but for aggressive self-promotion. And to use the biases of language toward that end.

The impact of AGGRESSIVE falsehood is a matter of size, spread, and timing. The Hitlerian *big lie* traded on credibility-through-outrageousness. No one would dare to say such a thing if it were not true! But the small lies that find their way into the streams of public information can be more harmful than the literal mendacity of one person defending himself against a just charge. It is not that the only lies affecting large numbers are those spread by the media, but other means – posters, circulars, word of mouth – are ineffectual by comparison. As for timing, a truth that comes too late is equivalent to a lie; like justice, truth delayed is truth denied.

We speak now, obviously, of *propaganda*, another of those tired expressions one seldom hears nowadays because *public relations* has taken its place (or *education*, or *consciousness-raising*: the propagandist does not coax, wheedle, indoctrinate, or inveigle the public into accepting his point of view, but *educates* it or *raises* its *consciousness*). The ultimate in power is achieved when a publicity apparatus is set up to generate its own financial feedback. Various government agencies in the United States are engaged not only in promoting their activities but in promoting their promotion – some of the tax money coaxed from the public is used to subsidize further coaxing, making counterefforts heartbreakingly laborious and expensive. The ultimate insult is that public talk is one-way talk: a television set can be silenced, but is not equipped to listen. Institutions and individuals of power command the microphones, teletype machines, and computer networks (giving rise to some of the pathetic and often atrocious publicity stunts by the Unheard, such as hijackings and kidnappings), and their responsible or irresponsible use of the media in news, advertising, and official messages raises vital questions of survival.

All the biases outlined in previous chapters invite exploitation in public language for what Tony Schwartz, publicity agent for President Jimmy Carter, called 'the real question in advertising', namely 'how to surround the individual with the proper auditory and visual stimuli to evoke the reaction you want from him'[17] (Schwartz spoke of *political* advertising and *voter* rather than *individual*; but the qualifications are unnecessary).

Among the auditory and visual stimuli are the music and visuals designed to attract or repel, to hint rather than to say (see page 70), as well as the linguistic stimuli, which include all shades of bias, starting with the biases of words. First among these is euphemism, thanks to its cultivation in advertising, whose business is to praise qualities and gloss over faults. Some examples of euphemistic terms and what they substitute for:

Crafted for *manufactured*. 'The use of *crafted* is an attempt to delude the public into believing that something has been made by hand, in a carefully old-fashioned way.'[18]

Fun size for *small* (candy bar). The selling of objects or packages that come in more than one size boasts a long history of how not to say *small*. For items like olives, cakes of soap, and eggs the word *small* is either avoided altogether or restricted to the lowest point on the scale, with *large* starting midway and expanding to *extra large, jumbo, mammoth*, etc. The word *pint*, which has become a synonym of small (*pint-sized*), has virtually disappeared from beverage labels – pints are now *half-quarts*. (Compare the psychological suggestion of the *half-full* versus the *half-empty* glass.)

Standard for *average* (beef). There is also a history of how not to say that anything is less than very good. The grades of beef are *prime, choice, good, standard,* and *canner's*.

Rinse for *dye*. The practice of dyeing the hair is a deception that one hesitates to admit, even to oneself. So the deceiver is willingly deceived by products advertised as *rinses*. *Painting* the face likewise, and the French word *rouge* was substituted; the earliest citation in the *Oxford Dictionary* is from the Earl of Chesterfield, 1751: 'to lay on a great deal of rouge, in English called paint.' If attitudes had not changed, *rouge* would have yielded long since to some other term; but tinting the face is accepted, and the word has settled into a neutral groove.

Advertising requires no microscope. Its euphemisms add up to a world of promise grander than life. Here are the ten most frequent adjectives in a study of two hundred US television advertisements, with their frequency:[19]

new 42	beautiful 19
better 28	free 19
extra 25	good 19
fresh 23	great 18
clean 23	light 17[20]

The ten most frequent in a British study were the following:

new	full
good-better-best	sure
free	clean
fresh	wonderful
delicious	special[21]

One could also list the terms that are avoided, as was done in the title of an article on commercial euphemism: 'Cheap Clothes for Fat Old Women'.[22]

The term earns a second plus if it can be trendy as well as euphemistic. In times of scarcity, imitation goods and products are substituted for those in short supply. As these are often inferior, *imitation* and *substitute* have acquired a bad name; *imitation* leans toward such real dysphemisms as *sham*, *bogus*, *counterfeit*, and is euphemized, for certain objects of commerce, with *simulated*: *simulated* pearls – compare also *costume* jewelry, *man-made* material (imitation leather in handbags). The disrepute extends to the process: imitations are made by *artifice*, and *artificial* is dragged down too. The substitutions may be for only some aspect of a product – say, freshness, where a chemical is added to 'retard spoilage': the item is no longer fresh, but it appears to be. The counter-culture of the 1960s rejected artificiality and all its works, in family, social relations, and daily living, including food, which had to be grown *organically* and prepared *naturally*.

The food industry was a little slow to react, but when it realized the potential of the market it embraced the *natural* with the same devotion as a Gentile bakery producing matzos for Passover. *Organic* too became part of the ritual, but was dangerously close to having a meaning that imposed certain standards. Since everything, including fire-retardant chemicals as well as wheat germ, is a part of nature, no one could say precisely what was not natural, and the euphemism was perfectly safe. For the Food Marketing Institute's displays at its convention in Dallas, Texas, naturalness was everywhere, including an ice cream with an *all-natural flavor* (inviting one to infer 'all-natural product') and a brand of bread made of *100 per cent natural ingredients*, including *100 per cent natural fiber* – which turned out to be powdered wood pulp.[23] In the study of US television reported above, naturalness was second only to sex appeal among the themes that were stressed.[24]

The din of euphemism in advertising leads to a merciful deafness toward some of its tones – even legal deafness. The most euphemistic word in the language, in its literal sense, is *best*. One would expect it to be used sparingly, but for certain products it is commonplace, those indistinguishable in quality because ingredients and processing are virtually identical. They are called PARITY products, and they infuse *best* with a new meaning:

> In parity claims, *better* means best but *best* only means 'equal to'. If all the brands are identical, they must all be equally good, the legal minds have decided. So *best* means that the product is as good as the other superior products in its category. When Bing Crosby declares Minute Maid orange juice 'the best there is', he means it is as good as the other orange juices you can buy.[25]

Advertising turns a timepiece into a jewel, a motor car into a symbol of prestige, and a mosquito swamp into a tropical paradise. Its euphemisms are all in high colors. Other fields tend to euphemize not for visibility but for concealment. Reality, drab or unpleasant, is not to be gilded but made to pass unnoticed or at most to seem harmless. Taxpayers – or non-payers – who can afford expert advice are guided into financial havens known as tax *shelters*, which has a homey sound, unlikely to alarm those who must foot the bill. The military is noted for the studied innocence of its vocabulary. A bombing *raid* is renamed a *mission* (no one yet dares to call the raiders *missionaries*). *Dead bodies* are *casualties* or *fatalities*. An explosion does not have *power* or *force*, but *yield*. The military of course only have to work harder because they have so much to tone down. Other agencies play the same game. The police no longer have *informers*, but *informants*. The insurance business sells *life insurance*, not *death insurance* (*accident* does not sound as bad as *death*, so we are spared *survival insurance*). The US Law Enforcement Assistance Administration, called to account for supporting the use of aversive drugs and other mind-bending techniques in prisons, saw fit to demand reforms in the programs it was subsidizing. Some of the programs merely changed their names and continued to receive aid. In place of *behavior modification*, 'One behavioral spokesman, Leonard Krasner, proposed *environmental design* or behavior influence.'[26] A local school board, not wishing to upset parents who might otherwise object to letting their thirteen-and-fourteen-year-olds attend a class on sex, sent out requests for consent in which the class was labeled *Family Life Education*.[27] Most newspapers have avoided calling the shooting of students at Kent State University in 1970 a *crime*; the accepted euphemism is *tragedy*, which implies no blame.

It is hard to draw the line between euphemism and mystification. Technically, euphemisms are terms with a pleasant meaning. But pleasantness is relative. It often comes to the same thing to resort to a misleading term or to pure nonsense – a code name, for example, such as *Codeword Dora*, *Operation Sunflower*, *Operation Camelot*, *Operation Keel-haul* (the US Army's cryptogram for the repatriation – sometimes forced – of Russian nationals after the Second World War). An advertising man describes the virtues of nonsense in promoting a parity product:

> Our research had shown us that it would be impossible to convince people that Salada tea really tasted much better than any other tea. So our strategy was to develop a high-impact campaign that was so wacky that people would still be remembering the commercials when they walked by the Salada display at the supermarket.[28]

The same author reports an instance of nice-sounding illogic, the parity product in this case being a candidate for the US presidency. Steve Ford, he says, was very articulate. He was filmed urging farmers to vote for his father:

> 'You'll get to keep a heck of a President,' he said, 'and I'll get to keep a heck of a father.'

'What do you suppose he means by that?' I asked Doug. 'If the
President loses, is he going to get another father?'
'Well,' Doug said thoughtfully, 'it looks so darn good and it SOUNDS
so darn good that nobody will stop to think about that.'[29]

Stopping to think is just stopping to ask what the words mean.
Obfuscation in general is treated in the next chapter.

Euphemism is everyman's sin. Dysphemism is more selective. There
is little bad-naming in advertising, for example, but a great deal of it in
the angrier verbiage of politics and the courts. Jeremy Bentham
identifies its users as 'politicians, lawyers, writers on controversial
divinity, satirists and literary censors'.[30] It also tends to be more
personal – among epithets the unfavorable far outnumber the favorable.
Typically, these dehumanize – *nigger, tart, kike, hick, retardo,* and other
examples in Chapter 9. One deliberate case is that of Hitler labeling the
Jews as *creatures.* At first this aroused no concern because the word was
not a recognized dysphemism, but it had the deadly effect of
depersonalizing its victims and was all the more sinister because there
existed no institutionalized rejection of it – an epithet of long standing
tends to develop its own antibodies. 'Hitler specified that creatures are
those who must be treated like parasites, vermin, and bacilli. They
cannot be seen. They are everywhere. Hence, they warrant separation.
They must be suppressed. . . . And, because they are invisible they can
only be detected by those who are especially trained in their detection.'[31]
Enter the SS troops.
  Political propaganda is a battleground of good- and bad-naming.
'Republicans have *associates,* Democrats have *henchmen,*' writes the
columnist Herb Caen.[32] The struggle between the haves and the have-
nots brings a new confrontation of word-images in every generation. At
the present time its most glaring form is *terrorism,* as seen from one side,
the *struggle for liberation* as seen from the other. An instructive example
is Cuba before the downfall of Fulgencio Batista. A small fighting force
was able to win over larger and larger segments of the population by
attacking the abuses of power and sparing the lesser individuals
supporting it. When a police patrol was captured, the individual
policemen were often lectured and let go. Instead of the image of a
terrorist, Fidel Castro acquired that of a *Robin Hood.* The fear of this
euphemistic symbol is evident in a highly publicized sequence of events
in California. In February of 1974, Patricia Hearst, daughter of the
wealthy publisher Randolph A. Hearst, was carried off by kidnappers
who identified themselves as members of the Symbionese Liberation
Army. The condition for her release was food for the poor, and
Patricia's father distributed two million dollars' worth in low-income
sections of San Francisco. The California Senate hastily approved a bill
making it a crime merely to ACCEPT a gift under such conditions. (It was
later defeated in the Assembly.) The pursuit of SLA members nation-

wide and their tracking down and killing in Los Angeles was a more relentless action than that taken against ordinary crime for profit. And Miss Hearst herself, for apparently throwing in with her kidnappers, was severely punished despite the initial coercion. The Robin Hood image was tarnished by later events, but it was a brief propaganda triumph, as was the general acceptance of the euphemistic name the guerrilla group bestowed on itself: a mystic *Symbionese*, a sloganeering *liberation*, and an exaggerated *army*. The counterpart urban guerrillas in Germany never got beyond being recognized as the Baader-Meinhoff *gang*.

For rival political systems, the entire rhetoric of the adversary becomes tinged with dysphemism, but special epithets are reserved for the routine taunts. In a capitalist society, trouble is caused by *radicals* and *outside agitators*; in a communistic society, by the *lackeys* and *running dogs* of imperialism. Small-scale rivals behave the same. Opponents of nuclear power deplore the *nukes* – a nice bit of sound symbolism trading on *fluke, gook, spook, kook* (see Chapter 3, page 20 for the symbolism of *oo*). Advocates decry *nuclear safeguards* as a threat of *nuclear shutdown* – industry will grind to a halt, jobs will be lost. Dysphemism of course runs deeper than epithets. One of the means used to defeat the creation of a Consumer Protection Agency in the United States was a national opinion poll conducted by the US Chamber of Commerce. The results purported to show that 81 per cent of the public were opposed to such an agency. But the key question in the poll asked how many were in favor of 'setting up an additional consumer agency on top of all the other agencies'.[33] Everything in this question represents the new agency as 'excessive', and *on top of* contains a biased ambiguity: it means 'subsuming' and is also the slyly unfavorable synonym of *in addition to*.

Editorializing in newspapers is theoretically limited to the editorial page, but the sympathies of editors and publishers are subtly conveyed in the biased language used for reporting the news. This is not necessarily intentional; one reaches instinctively for words favorable to one's point of view. Most of the American press is just anti-labor enough to give an unfavorable twist to much of its labor reporting: '[George] Meany . . . is often characterized as "cigar-smoking", which would be a trivial detail were it not a sort of shorthand for "boss". [I.W.] Abel's name is often preceded by phrases like "$75,000-a-year steelworkers chief", which is presumably intended to mean "overpaid".' On the other hand, 'Rarely . . . is the reader introduced to US Steel Corporation chairman Edgar B. Speer as "$425,000-a-year steel company chief".'[34] To refer to a corporation executive in such terms would be 'lacking in *respect*', a manifestation of the off-limits taboo mentioned earlier. One who espouses consumerism, however, is fair game. Ralph Nader is frequently referred to as the *so-called* or *self-styled* consumer advocate. Though literally signifying only that *consumer advocate* is not a recognized title, these modifiers manage to cast doubt on Nader's legitimacy in the field itself. It is usually what the privileged class or some locally powerful segment of it is afraid of that inspires these editorial leanings in the news columns. The fear of Robin Hood that leads to the murder of charismatic figures such as Malcolm X and Martin Luther King makes objective reporting of related events hard to come by. When various Third World countries are sent 28,000 Cubans for military defense (less than a tenth of the American NATO presence in Europe), a headline reads 'Castro Hordes Swarm Globe'.[35] The word *horde* is defined as 'a vast number', and is used only when the intended image is that of an irresistible mass of rabble. (Note the euphemisms on both sides in the sentence before last – *defense* rather than *aid* or *reinforcement*, *presence* rather than *forces* or *garrison*.)

One curious variety of dysphemism trades on what might be called auditory malapropisms. Technically a malapropism is the misuse of one word for another that resembles it in sound and is vaguely similar in meaning (see pages 23, 42): *economically depraved* for *economically deprived, spreading like wildflower* for *spreading like wildfire*. But one may also MISUNDERSTAND one word for another, and be deliberately steered toward a damaging inference. One of the schemes used by George Smathers to defeat Claude Pepper in the race for US Senate was to accuse him of rightdoings, so to speak:

> A scenario of the spring of 1950: George Smathers, eyes glinting like Clint Eastwood in an Italian-made Western, entertains – and confuses – a gathering of North Floridians with the most famous phraseology of the campaign. 'Are you aware that Claude Pepper is known all over Washington as a shameless extrovert? Not only that, but this man is reliably reported to practice nepotism with his sister-in-law, and he has a sister who was once a thespian in wicked New York. Worst of all, it is an established fact that Mr Pepper, before his marriage, practiced celibacy.'[36]

Loaded words can influence memory as well as perception. In an experiment to test this, 150 viewers were shown a film of a multiple-car accident. After seeing it, fifty of the subjects were asked 'About how fast were the cars going when they hit?' and fifty were asked 'About how fast were the cars going when they smashed?' (The remaining fifty were controls.) The *hit* subjects averaged 8.00 miles per hour for their estimate; the *smash* subjects, 10.46. Both groups were also asked 'Did you see any broken glass?' (there was none in the film). Of the *hit* subjects, seven said yes; of the *smash* subjects, sixteen. Another experiment revealed a steady increase in the estimated speed for the following words, in the order given: *contacted, hit, bumped, collided, smashed*.[37]

The *good-bad* of euphemism-dysphemism is the outer coating of suasive language. Most other biases work on us under cover of darkness. Take the factive verbs (page 81). A radio advertisement for a publishing firm went as follows: 'Professor William Wood of the Columbia

University School of Journalism would remind us that government regulation of gas at the wellhead would lead to disaster.' This has the appearance of an ordinary testimonial in the form of an OPINION from a person of authority. But the verb *remind* makes a difference. It is not like *assert* or *claim*; it pretends that the facts are TRUE. *Remind her that it's six o'clock* cannot be said if the speaker believes it is five or seven.

Of the syntactic devices, all those described earlier (Chapter 8) – and more – can be found nudging our minds in advertising and propaganda. Questions with reverse polarity are commonplace: *Aren't you glad you use Dial?* The passive is found wherever it is convenient to conceal the agent of an action, or where mentioning the agent might contradict the aseptic image of a product that emerges untouched and uncontaminated by human hands:

> You'll taste the sunshine in K-Y peaches, pears and apricots. Only K-Y fruit is ripened ON THE TREE to capture the full, natural sunshine flavour of tree-fresh Australian fruit. K-Y fruits are picked and canned fresh from the orchard the very same day.[38]

In the following passage from a newspaper account of the conflict in Zaire in the spring of 1978 we find a nice blend of lexical and syntactic euphemisms and dysphemisms:

> The likes of Nyerere, who sees himself as Africa's conscience, will want to condemn the West while ignoring Soviet and Cuban intervention in Africa.
>
> The respected President Leopold Senghor of Senegal, on the other hand, will demand condemnation of Russia and Cuba . . . .[39]

The dysphemistic *likes of* contrasts with the euphemistic passive *respected* (by whom?). The reflexive *sees himself* has the opposite effect to that of an agentless passive – it suggests that the sole agent is Nyerere himself.

A device similar to the missing agent in the passive is the missing conclusion in a comparative construction. Advertisers use it constantly: *Queasies Are Munchier, Crunchier, Fun-chier!* (munchier, crunchier, fun-chier than what?). Since any point of comparison is grammatical and a safe one can always be found, the advertiser is protected. When the Ford Motor Company advertised that the Ford LTD was *700 per cent quieter*, one might have presumed that the model was 700 per cent quieter than some competing car or, at least, 700 per cent quieter than some other model of Ford. But when the Federal Trade Commission demanded substantiation of the claim, the Ford Company 'revealed that they meant the inside of the Ford was seven hundred per cent quieter than the outside'.[40]

The comparative suffix *-er* has the further advantage of combining in jingles with other instances of *-er*: *Bounty, the quicker picker-upper.*[41] The constant play of sound symbolism is the most effective diversion from logical language and critical attention. Violations of grammar are sometimes used for the same purpose or just to catch the ear. Chunky Candy advertises that it is *thickerer*.[42] The dispute over the 'ungrammatical' *like* in *tastes good like a cigaret should* was an advertising coup for Winston cigarets. A brand of pillow advertised as *huggable*, *snuggable* is a triple threat: it is a jingle, the *snuggable* part is ungrammatical though clearly related to *snuggle*, and the *-able* suffix is an implicit passive that projects an action into an object as a quality of it. Advertisers venture into obvious ungrammaticality only now and then, for fear of offending the purists; but they fight many a skirmish on the brink. An example is the copious invention of compounds and derivatives, which is found in ordinary language only to designate some new reality, but is freely indulged in advertising, where the naming so often IS the reality:

> Cool, thirst-quenching cucumber. Taste-tempting tomatoes.
>   They go for its fresh, wake-up tang.[43]
> Lovely, oveny biscuits.[44]

The agentless passive and the incomplete comparative do not exhaust the list of constructions where something is left unsaid, to tempt the imaginations of the unwary or the uncharitable. The military has its *undesirable discharge* (page 87), where not-desired-by-whom is unmentioned. Also its category of *unfit*, without disclosure of unfit-for-what. It would be hard to expose all the kinds of suspended sentences, of not-sayings and pregnant silences, from the child's unfinished answer *Because!* to the inclusiveness of undefined terms, that fill the arsenals of verbal warfare.

And it would be just as difficult to discover all the ways in which the syntactic functions of elements of the sentence can be used to partisan advantage. In newspaper reports of collisions one can usually tell where sympathies lie by observing which vehicle is the subject and which is the object: *Bike collides with car, Car collides with bike.* If both are moving, the collision is mutual; it should make no practical difference which comes first. But the responsibility is shouldered by the subject: *Bike collides with car* suggest that it is the bicyclist's fault. We find *The boy rode his bicycle into the path of an oncoming car* normal, but *The motorist drove his car into the path of an oncoming bicycle* strikes us as odd – it is up to the little fellow to look out.

Subject and object are grammatical functions. The sentence also has DISCOURSE functions – different parts carry out different communicative intentions. The two main ones are the topic (what is spoken about) and the comment (what is said about the topic – see pages 20, 30). In both *I forgot his name* and *His name I forgot*, *I* is subject and *his name* is object; but the first answers 'What did you forget?', the second 'What about his name?' Inside the comment is an element that is the semantic peak, where the main accent of the sentence falls: *name* in *I forgot his name*, *forgot* in *His name I forgot*. For an advertiser there are multiple advantages to using short sentences or sentence fragments (which are usually sentences without a topic). One is that they are more easily understood by the average listener. Another is that since each has a separate comment and therefore a main accent of its own, the more there are the more accents there will be, and the message is made louder and clearer. Instead of *Crisp, tasty Cubs might have been made for your children* the ad reads *Crisp, tasty Cubs. They might have been made for your children.* The brand name gets the extra accent.[45]

A grammatical device much exploited by advertisers is the attributive adjective with its concealed proposition (page 88). The ad that reads *Delicious, light-as-a-feather Nimble bread* could have been worded *Nimble bread is delicious and light as a feather*, but that would have exposed it to the question 'IS Nimble bread delicious and light as a feather?' The adjective in front of the noun wakens no doubts.[46] In fact, verbs, with their assertive and open-to-question meaning, are infrequent in advertising by comparison with nouns and adjectives.[47]

Keeping close watch on the exploitation of bias tends to make one a bit paranoid. After an NBC television program about the plight of migrant workers, the Coca-Cola Company moved a million dollars' worth of its advertising to competing networks. 'Some of the filthiest and most dilapidated migrant camps shown on the documentary were owned by Coca-Cola's Minute Maid division. Coke, of course, denied that the sudden switch in ad money had anything to do with the unfavorable publicity in the documentary. But the message of their action was a clear "let the broadcaster beware". But broadcasters and news outlet owners seldom have to be reminded of their own dependence on advertising revenue.'[48] A high-level conspiracy among corporate executives? One is strongly tempted to think so. But all it takes is a consensus, a strong self-interest plus large amounts of inertia. The corresponding actions follow in all sincerity, with no cooking of plots. Backs are turned, minds are turned off, taboos become inviolate, logical language gives way to noise, and the kingdom of What Is Because It Is extends its domain.

For self-protection, if not for the general good, we need spies in that territory.

Chapter 11

Another case in point: the jargonauts and the not-so-golden fleece

When the US Department of State appointed a Consumer Affairs Coordinator to look after the Department's interests in what has come to be called consumerism, it fell to the Deputy Secretary for Management, Lawrence Eagleburger, to draw up a description for the job. Here, in part, is what he wrote:

> The purpose of the Department's plan is two-fold, to confirm and reinforce the Department's sensitivity to consumer rights and interests as they impact upon the Department and to take those steps necessary and feasible to promote and channel these rights and interests with respect to the maintenance and expansion of an international dialogue and awareness.

The Coordinator's duties were to 'review existing mechanisms of consumer input, thruput and output, and seek ways of improving these linkages via the consumer communication channel'.[1] For this achievement in prose, Mr Eagleburger was presented with the annual Doublespeak Award from the National Council of Teachers of English, through its Committee on Public Doublespeak.

That there should be such a committee – formed in 1971 – is one of many signs of growing irritation and alarm at the spread of obscure language. Next to 'Why can't Johnny read (or write)?', the most-debated question of language today is 'Why can't officials use plain language?' Not that officials are the only offenders, but their pronouncements affect the general public and the general public feels it has a RIGHT to understand what is going on.

Jargon – gobbledegook – doubletalk – doublespeak. Johnny's encounters with English are part of the problem. Writing is such an alien activity that he overreaches himself. Stepping into a written paragraph for him is like stepping into a Paris salon – to play safe he dons the most formal style he can lay hands on, and since he has little acquaintance with formal styles, he combines purple tails with a frilled shirt and forgets that he is still wearing his work trousers. As more and more Johnnies spread by capillary action through the professions, the level of prose sinks with a dead weight.

By sheer numbers, Johnny's ineptitudes are transformed. The more

Johnnies there are in contact with one another and performing the same activities, the more their altered language becomes a badge of their class. Jargon takes on the functions of a SOCIOLECT. The same can be said of jargon as of another sociolect, the slang of marijuana-users: that it becomes 'one of the most important active media for transmitting certain kinds of social awareness through the culture'[2] – a Solidarity of Bureaucrats, whose bureaucratese is their password. Like other forms of secret language – the slang of the 'now' generation, the argot of pickpockets, the Latinisms of medicine – it identifies its users to one another and shields them from intrusion. Combating it calls for something more than instruction in English. The anti-jargoneer encounters the same obstacles as the campaigner against environmental pollution: success is not a question of eliminating a few supposed errors but of changing a way of life.

Except that all play their part in group reinforcement, there would seem to be little in common between jargon and other secret languages. Yet there are so many of them that it is easy to find unofficial styles that share the sources of jargon as well as some of its purposes. Take the language-for-sociability that the anthropologist Bronislaw Malinowski called 'phatic communion'. Its main purpose is not to exchange information but to warm the conversants to each other and keep the talk going. Ostensibly conversation has to be about something, so phatic talk – when it gets beyond the standard greetings and leavetakings – makes a stab at being informative; but content is outweighed by sound and stroking. In California, phatic communion luxuriates in a rank growth of 'psychobabble', as R. D. Rosen calls it (see his book listed on page 203). The topics follow the latest psychic fad, disdaining precision, affecting modish variation of the same trite ideas, a music to accompany the clink of cocktail glasses:

> At a dinner party, a new acquaintance tells me about her intimate life. Although she is still 'processing' her ex-husband . . . , she just spent a weekend with another man from whom she gets 'a lot of ego reinforcement. My therapist keeps telling me to go where the energies are,' she says, 'so that's what I'm doing, because that's what went wrong last time. I didn't just kick back and go with the energies.'[3]

The mark of pseudoscience is on this passage, and reading another, from McFadden's book *The Serial*, one understands why. It lists the character Rita's curriculum of psycho-courses; Rita had 'been through'

> Gurdjieff, Silva Mind Control, actualism, analytical tracking, parapsychology, Human Life Styling, postural integration, the Fischer-Hoffman Process, hatha and raja yoga, integral massage, orgonomy, palmistry,

and she was commuting twice a week for 'polarity balancing manipulation'.[4]

For jargon, science is both source and motive. The social sciences imitate the hard sciences, the pseudo-sciences imitate the social sciences, and the mod speaker takes his cues from all three. Why does an ordinarily plain-spoken person advise keeping detergent away from indoor plants because *it causes an adverse reaction* instead of *it is bad for them*? The metaphors of scientism tempt us with a sham authority; they keep the ordinary from sounding commonplace. English is particularly susceptible because of its openness to borrowings from everywhere, and scientists are notorious for their snatches of Latin and Greek, and for applying rules of affixation that result in verbal monstrosities. Their nomenclatures are intended to be internally consistent – *deoxyribonuclease* is made to have each of its elements, *de + oxy + rib + nucle + ase*, relate the compound to some trait in the whole family of organic compounds. But this goes counter to the essential contrastiveness of words; in natural language it is more practical to keep things apart than to show their interrelationships, and when such terms are taken into everyday speech they trade the reality of scientific precision for its pretense. The charlatan passes for a scientist by sounding like one, and writing and conversation swell with the concepts, metaphors, and polysyllables of our white-coated oracles. In some professions – notably those dealing with public safety, such as fire and police – the affectation becomes comical: *At least seventy-five people evacuated safely from the premises*, goes a radio report,[5] to let us know they all got away.

The full riches of jargon are best savored in the softest of the soft sciences, sociology and its branches. An anonymous wag a few years ago circulated a 'Folklore Article Reconstitution Kit' consisting of four sections which, when compiled phrase by phrase in 1–2–3–4 order, would yield sentences suitable for a folklore article. Readers can try their hand:

Section 1

1 Obviously,
2 On the other hand,
3 From the intercultural standpoint,
4 Similarly,
5 As Lévi-Strauss contends,
6 In this regard,
7 Based on my own field-work in Guatemala,
8 For example,
9 Thus, within given parameters,
10 In respect to essential departmental goals,

Section 2

1 a large proportion of intercultural communicative coordination
2 a constant flow of field-collected input ordinates
3 the characterization of critically co-optive criteria
4 initiation of basic charismatic subculture development
5 our fully integrated field program
6 any exponential Folklife coefficient

7   further and associated contradictory elements
8   the incorporation of agonistic cultural constraints
9   my proposed independent structuralistic concept
10 a primary interrelationship between systems and/or subsystems
      logistics

Section 3

1   must utilize and be functionally interwoven with
2   maximizes the probability of project success while minimizing
      cross-cultural shock elements in
3   adds explicit performance contours to
4   necessitates that coagulative measures be applied to
5   requires considerable further performance analysis and computer
      studies to arrive at
6   is holistically compounded, in the context of
7   presents a valuable challenge showing the necessity for
8   recognizes the importance of other disciplines, while taking into
      account
9   effects a significant implementation of
10 adds overwhelming Folkloristic significance to

Section 4

1   Propp's basic formulation
2   the anticipated epistemological repercussions
3   improved subcultural compatibility-testing
4   all deeper structuralistic conceptualization
5   any communicatively-programmed computer techniques
6   the profound meaning of *The Raw and the Cooked*
7   our hedonic Folklife perspectives over a given time-period
8   any normative concept of the linguistic/holistic continuum
9   the total configurational rationale
10 Krappe's Last Tape.

Not to be outdone, the Open University's magazine *Sesame*
published the following reduced-complexity homeomorphic covarying
exercise in sociological conceptualization:

The Instant Sociological Jargon Matrix

0 relative	0 charismatic	0 model
1 peripheral	1 hierarchical	1 regression
2 traditional	2 bureaucratic	2 alienation
3 internalized	3 conceptual	3 paradigm
4 functional	4 homeostatic	4 reification
5 normative	5 pre-industrial	5 hypothesis
6 symbolic	6 deviant	6 commitment
7 multi-variate	7 anomic	7 expectations
8 reciprocal	8 empirical	8 syndrome
9 affective	9 psychometric	9 deprivation[6]

Jargon spares no institution, not even the sacred ones, where, we are told, the minister of the Gospel

> lives in a *pastorium*, *interacts* with and gets *input and feedback* from his *prayer-cell circle of the Committed* in a *Christian Life Center*, *raps* with *teens* in special *after-glow* services, *opts for alternatives* to *implement*, *restructure*, *finalize*, and *firm up* a *meaningful Operation Involvement Outreach Explosion* to *bridge the Generation Credibility Gap* of the *unchurched* through a *Koinonia, Agape Multimedia Thrust*.[7]

The organ supplies strains of rock music in the background.

Most jargon is not quite so condensed – it takes rhapsodic compilations like these to make good reading. The anti-jargoneer is not above exaggerating a bit to make his point. Here is a 'translation' of the beginning of the Twenty-third Psalm from the Gospel according to Alan Simpson, former President of Vassar College:

> The Lord is my external-internal integrative mechanism.
> I shall not be deprived of gratifications for my viscerogenic hungers or my need-dispositions.
> He motivates me to orient myself towards a non-social object with affective significance.
> He positions me in a non-decisional situation.
> He maximizes my adjustment.[8]

But the real thing is almost a match for the caricature. Here is a true-to-life sentence from an article on linguistics:

> In traditional linguistics it has been assumed that the analysis of sentences can be performed upon examples isolated from the process of interaction within which they naturally emerge.

Deflated, this means 'Traditional linguists thought that sentences could be analyzed out of context'. Appropriately, the next sentence from the same passage reads *Indeed this has been stated as an explicit tenant by Chomsky*.[9] Malapropisms – like *tenant* for *tenet*, where the writer could just as well have said *principle* – are a regular adornment of jargon. The writer or speaker strains for the more erudite and exotic synonym, but has no sure idea of what he is looking for. An official of a chemical company boasts that *During our 33-year history, only one employee died of chemical exposure and his death was largely due to panic on his behalf* – jargon in the phrase *chemical exposure* as well as in the malapropism *behalf* for *part*.[10] A caller on a radio talk show says *It becomes inherent on us* – stumbling on the way from the simple *It is our duty* to the elegant *It is incumbent on us*.[11] Another true-to-life passage:

> Over the past ten years the school has evolved a child-centred individual-learning situation with a degree of integrated day organisation and close co-operation between each year's mixed-ability classes. Basic-work morning programmes are carefully structured but allow for integration ... .[12]

The spelling tells us that jargon is firmly established on both sides of the Atlantic, with roots deep in the educational establishment – as yet another true-to-life passage extravagantly proves:

> Our school's Cross-Graded, Multi-Ethnic, Individualized Learning Program is designed to enhance the concept of an Open-Ended Learning Program with emphasis on a continuum of multi-ethnic academically enriched learning, using the identified intellectually gifted child as the agent or director of his own learning. Major emphasis is on a cross-graded, multi-ethnic learning with the main objective being to learn respect for the uniqueness of a person.

This was in a letter received by a Houston, Texas father inviting him to a meeting about a new high school program.[13]

Like any other style, jargon is complex and hard to define. Pure jargon would have to be a condensation of only those ingredients shared by no other style, and obviously such an extreme would be annihilated by its own density, a sort of verbal black hole. But take certain qualities and pack them close together, and you get a pretty solid approximation of the undenatured thing:

First, basic words – pseudo-scientific, much of it layered with Greek and Latin prefixes and suffixes, most of it a substitution of the unusual for the usual. Not that unusualness is bad if the ideas are unusual: the rarity of the words hardly counts against a sentence like *The piebald mare trampled the yarrow underfoot.*[14] But *The identical theory offers a basis for development of X* is authentic jargon: for *identical*, read *same*; for *offers a basis*, read *from*; for *development*, read *develop* – which translates to *From the same theory we develop X*. Jargon even invades the prepositions: *before* becomes *prior to*, *after* becomes *following* or *subsequent to, from* in a causative sense becomes *due to* (*She broke down due to overwork*), *in* becomes *as far as* (*It is striking as far as appearance*). The unusual soon becomes usual – statistically – as the jargon word catches on and becomes a vogue word. *Government programs impact on people's needs. Things are prioritized and reprioritized. Bureaucrats coordinate, facilitate and disseminate, especially on the interface.*[15] The lexicon of jargon quickly degenerates into a catalog of clichés.

After basic words come the compounds. Here thrive the hyphenations that make it appear as if every passing encounter between two ideas deserved a permanent record in the dictionary. On a Greyhound bus appears the sign *This coach is restroom equipped for your convenience – to have a restroom* becomes a new verb, *to restroom-equip*. The city jail in Madison, Wisconsin is called a *total-incarceration facility. Correctional facility* has become a kind of standard euphemism for *jail* or *prison*.

Third, the syntax of phrases. Richard Nixon's lieutenant Gordon Liddy, outlining *Operation Diamond*, aimed at preventing demonstrations at political conventions, explained a bit of strategy:

We will have a second operational arm that could be of even greater preventive use. These teams are experienced in surgical relocation activities. In a word, General, they can kidnap a hostile leader with maximum secrecy and minimal use of force.[16]

The simple noun *kidnapping* grows to a noun modified by a noun modified by an adjective. A radio station announces a new venture in religion: *Program emphasis will be on Christian living:*[17] we have a new technical entity, *program emphasis*, to replace the humdrum activity of emphasizing something in a program. An ad for a magazine inquires, *How can you tell if you are heart-attack prone?*[18] Piling up plethoric adjectives gives a similar effect: *ambient noncombatant personnel* for *refugees*[19] and *waterborne logistic craft* for *sampans*,[20] both from the rich harvest of jargon from Vietnam. A common practice in these phrases is to attach heavyweight modifiers to lightweight nouns. The noun *facility* covers virtually anything intended for general use and having an established location, from an insane asylum to a lavatory: *sanitary facility, health facility* (hospital), *parking facility* (public garage), *recycling facility* (junkyard), besides Madison's *incarceration facility*. A traffic-spotter helicopter, reporting light rain, observes *a lot of wind-shield wiper activity*. We hear *firefighting operation* for *firefighting*, *supervisory personnel* for *supervisors*, *age level* for *age*. Among the most frequent empty nouns are *phase, process, condition, nature, phenomenon*. In advertising the favorite is *system*: a motel calls its beds *sleep systems*, and a water bed is a *flotation system*; a vacuum cleaner is a *sanitation system*. But the general favorite for a number of years has been *situation* – empty enough to cover any situation. When the telephone lines were jammed during a heavy storm in the winter of 1977–78, a patron called the company to complain, and the operator explained, *Yes, we know, everyone's having the same trouble – we're in a slow-talk situation.*[21] A radio report says that *the weather does not permit a helicopter to maintain a landing situation.*[22] Two people in a fight are in a *conflict situation*. The result of no rain for six months is a *drought situation*. The nice thing about *situation* is that you can add it to any self-sufficient action noun: *crime situation, inflation situation, strike situation, attack situation, retreat situation*.

Verb phrases are like noun phrases except that the lightweight is an empty verb instead of an empty noun. A passage quoted earlier had *perform an analysis* in place of *analyze*. *To be in receipt of* substitutes for simple *receive, to have need of* for simple *need*. In some cases there is a true contrast; for instance, *They had an argument* pictures the argument as finished, *They argued* suggests that there is more to the story. But this does not explain why the San Francisco police chief who wanted to get rid of prostitutes referred to *having an absence* of them.[23]

Many phrases are hard to classify, but all are the same in substituting the roundabout for the direct: *other considerations to the contrary notwithstanding* for *in spite of other considerations, over and above* for *more than* or *beyond, from this it follows that* for *so* or *therefore, it is a function of* for *it depends on.* In the larger unit of the sentence the combined resources are infinite: in the Nixon era, *The input process is going on* stood for *The president is listening.*

As for the syntax of jargon, it predictably circumnavigates. There are passives in abundance (*it is thought that* for *I think that*), double negatives (*a not unintentional remark* for *an insult*), inversions and extractions (*It is security that people want* or *What people want is security* for *People want security*), repetitions of words that could be dropped or replaced with pronouns (*They accepted the document and said document was affirmed*), continual admonitions to the hearer or reader that the speaker or writer means what he is saying (*it should be understood that, it is noteworthy that, it is necessary to be aware of the fact that, bear in mind that, it cannot be stressed too strongly that*), transitions pointing to what is obvious on inspection (*to begin, we next turn to, in conclusion*), phrases with which the author pats himself on the back (*interestingly enough, the important fact is, we have made it clear that*). And so on. For every way of driving straight to a goal, jargon discovers a dozen ways of beating around the bush – for whatever reason: self-importance, obfuscation, ineptitude. Expanded constructions have their place, but not whole colonies of them.

The most consistent feature of jargon is SEMANTIC. It is elevated, ameliorative, euphemistic in the most general sense. It tries to improve appearances, both in what the message is about and in the message itself. The listener is reassured that reality is at worst not threatening and at best attractive, and that the message and its giver have authority. The first purpose is served by avoiding the unpleasant, and the second by sounding weighty. The ideal piece of jargon does both at once. There are not supposed to be secrets from the American people – so *secret* is removed from the secret file and replaced with *classified*, which makes things seem less conspiratorial and at the same time creates visions of busy, efficient people classifying documents in a scientific way. The Department of Physical Education of the California State University at San Jose covers its sweat and dons academic respectability as the *Department of Human Performance* (*physical education* was already the jargon of another era, when *physical exercise* was seeking status in institutions of higher *education*). The *Bay Area* (San Francisco) *Air Pollution Control District* went itself one better in 1978 as the *Bay Area Air Quality Management District.*[24] For many years now we have dialed *Directory Assistance* when all we want is *Information.* Vietnam was a verbal as well as a military minefield, a place where

> troops were advisors, where men were not murdered but wasted, and where the CIA shunned assassination in favor of termination with prejudice .... 'You always write it's bombing, bombing, bombing,' Col David H. E. Opfer, air attaché at the US Embassy in Pnompenh, complained to reporters.'It's not bombing. It's air support.'[25]

Business uses glossy jargon for advertising, but evasive jargon for self-protection. When the Ford Motor Company recalled their Torinos and Rancheros,

> They sent out a letter: '. . . Continued driving with a failed bearing could result in disengagement of the axle shaft and adversely affect vehicle control.'[26]

Adversely affect vehicle control is a pseudo-scientist lecturing a moronic public, and *continued driving* puts the responsibility on YOU. George Herman, on the Washington staff of CBS News, tells of a business executive who erected a verbal screen at a Senate hearing by promising the optimum maximization of the potentialities or the maximum optimization of the potentialities, he wasn't sure which.

> I tried to figure out what it meant either way. Optimum maximization, I figure, is the best possible way of making something big, whereas maximum optimization is the biggest possible way of making something the best. Neither way does it make much sense. I listened some more and eventually I realized that it wasn't supposed to make much sense – it was part of a new language of anti-semantics, a strange hybrid tongue designed to keep your meaning so unclear that if anyone tries to quarrel with you, you can hastily beat a retreat by saying that that wasn't what you meant at all.[27]

Herman errs only in thinking the language to be new. It is more rampant now, but it is as old as speech, renewing only its manifestations.

There is always some obstacle to penetrating the essential meaning of a piece of jargon. As with the last example, likely as not when we have got to the center of it we find the room empty. This happens most often in advertising, as in the pure illogic of *Not everybody likes Kava but Kava likes everybody*, or *People eat more MacDonalds than anybody*. Or the nonsense may be added on. Intonation can be used for this: an advertisement for Chevette cars went *A choice of TWO engines instead of no choice at ALL!*[28] The least possible choice is a choice from two, but least is made to sound like most. As these examples show, the conjuring of something out of nothing can be done with plain words as well as with woolly abstractions; the gobbledegook is in the logic rather than in the terms. Whether this should be called jargon is a matter of definition. It lacks the ingredient of impressiveness. The brand of soup that carries on its label the wording *Full strength; no water needs to be added* is merely aiming to deceive, with its substitution of *full strength* for *already diluted*.

Who the first jargoneer was, nobody knows. He – or as likely she – probably antedated articulate speech, and substituted fancy gestures for plain ones. No one has compiled a history of jargon, but recorded objections to it go back a long way. Over two hundred years ago the Secretary to the Commissioners of Excise admonished an official of the town of Pontefract to stop his 'schoolboy way of writing', with 'affected phrases and incongruous words, such as *illegal procedure, harmony*, etc.'[29] A century ago, the Director of the US Geological Survey, Dr George Otis Smith,

> chided a colleague for writing 'The argillaceous character of the formation is very prominent in some localities, although it is usually subsidiary to the arenaceous phase.' What he meant was: 'At some places the formation included considerable clay, but generally it is made up chiefly of sand.'[30]

Jargon at its worst is partly a product of unfinished education, and if we have more of it today, one reason is that we have more half-educated people in a position to afflict the public with their words – and, as often as not, a wish to hide something.

Reaction was inevitable, and it has taken two forms: an effort to reeducate, and an attack on deliberate unclarity. Industry and government are concerned about the bad impression their employees make on the public and the trouble they have understanding one another. President Carter made it official by demanding that Federal regulations be written in plain English, and a number of agencies looked for ways to reform themselves or called in outside help. The Federal Trade Commision hired Rudolph Flesch, author of *Why Johnny Can't Read*, as consultant, the Department of Housing and Urban Development began taking advice from the former head of the English Department at Goucher College, Ruth Limmer, and the Department of Health, Education, and Welfare launched an 'Operation Common Sense' directed by a lawyer and writer, Inez Smith Reid, in a five-year plan to reedit six thousand pages of regulations. Its office of Civil Rights employed a former reporter and editor, Norma Mohr, to help 'push back the tide of turgid prose'. Here is an sample of an old regulation on hearing aids, and its new rendition by Flesch:

> No seller shall represent that it or any of its employees, agents, sales persons and/or representatives is a physician or an audiologist, unless such is the fact.
>
>   Don't say or hint that you or anyone in your firm is a doctor of medicine or an audiologist if is isn't so.[31]

Some local governments too began taking stock of their language. The Planning Division of San Mateo County, California, hired a specialist in plain writing whose blue pencil 'regularly changes *utilize* to *use*, *inaugurate* to *start*, and *at this point in time* to *now*'.[32] In Milwaukee a consulting firm was set up by a journalism graduate, Caroline Poh, to serve business clients in rewriting such products as advertisements, articles for trade magazines, and executives' speeches.[33]

Conspicuous by their absence among these experts are the professional linguists. It cannot be just because linguists are among the worst offenders themselves – as claimed by David Ferris of Exeter University, who devised a scale to measure jargon and put theoretical linguists at the top.[34] It is partly because linguists have not come forward with advice, and partly because shamanism is still the rule in treating the ills of language – glottotherapy, if you please.

When jargon is deliberate, education in direct, unambiguous speech and writing is of little use. If the deliberate jargoneer is a diplomat, he needs his indirections for the sparring matches he has to play with others of his kind. Here, perhaps, jargon has its place, in encounters where suspicion is high and talk has to be kept going without presuming on a frankness that might cause offense. But deliberate jargoneering 'to advance the career of the speaker (or the issue, cause or product he is agent for) by a kind of verbal sleight of hand', as L. E. Sissman describes it,[35] calls for countermeasures. There is one response that offers at least psychological relief: a public that feels put upon but helpless to do anything about it strikes back with gallows humor. Professor Don Nilsen of Arizona State University collects anti-jargon graffiti:

> When in doubt, do as the President does – take a guess.
> Studies at the University of Michigan have proved that the average blond has an IQ equalling that of a medium-sized radish.
> There is a relationship between stable government and horse sense.
> Bureaucrats never change the course of the ship of state; they simply adjust the compass.[36]

But sarcasm is too often an admission of defeat, and besides, not every public servant deserves to be publicly ridiculed. The logical target of the anti-jargoneer is specific jargon and its motives. Frankness and honesty are more apt to come in our one-way language-consuming world when we demand them frankly and honestly. And if the deliberate jargoneer cannot be educated, his victims can, to recognize what is being done to them. When Edwin Newman says of jargon that 'it serves as a fence that keeps others outside and respectful, or leads them to ignore what is going on because it is too much trouble to find out',[37] he exposes the attitude that makes this kind of deception possible. We are surrounded by the products of scientific magicians whose methods and formulas we do not understand and are afraid to question lest we expose our ignorance. Confident that if the scientific is accepted as unintelligible the unintelligible will be accepted as scientific, the pseudo-scientists parade their pseudo-formulas, persuading us to buy their products on the basis of misleading claims, or to accept a course of action that we would never endorse if it were clearly labeled. Jargoneering deception depends on ignorance; seen through, it collapses. We are the students in a class where the professor talks over our heads. We have paid our fees, and have a right to stop his lecture every time he gets ahead of us.

But to catch jargon aimed at us we must understand our own all too easy retreat into it. Words pass for solutions because we permit language to become automatic. This too we inherit from science – applied science, that is, which is forever on the lookout for tricks that will save people from having to do for themselves – in transportation, food preparation, computing, pest control, child rearing – even to brushing teeth and opening a tin can. We have convenience foods and we want a convenience language, one with a formula for every emergency. For all things there have to be specialists, and specialists are those who have mastered the incantations of their science. If formulas have that power, how is the ordinary word to stand up against them?

The answer is to renew our own faith in ordinary language as the most powerful instrument we have. It produced all those special languages in the first place and can recall them when they prove defective. Formulas are good for putting ideas into a small space and testing them for consistency, but the formula that defies translation into intelligible prose is probably a fraud. The test of survival is to face the world of problems unarmed except with a functioning brain and the birthright of a common language. It is the unrestricted code, the organizer of our universe, not to be shamed by false notions of refinement nor cowed by the condescensions of those for whom promises are commitments and driving the Blacks out of the slums is urban renewal in the inner city.

Having battered jargon for all these pages, is there any good we can say of it? Perhaps that along with slang it is part of the exuberance of language always striving to keep one jump ahead of reality. If the expressions are there, even though vague and often deceptive at first, some of them may serve as half-finished material for ideas that are steadily refined. As we saw in an earlier chapter, things are not only assigned their words, but words reach out to things. The process of adjustment is never-ending – and what other word can we use here than *process*? In its day, *complex* was a jargoneering loan from psychology. *To contact* was jargon fifty years ago, but now we find it a useful abstraction a level higher than *to call*, *write*, or *see*, all unnecessarily specific; and it is certainly less clumsy than *get in touch with*. Today's *lifestyle* instead of *way of living* dramatizes what a whole generation insists on as its right, a new conceptual entity. Though terribly overused, *viable* in its proper sphere has no substitute. Jargon is an ABUSE of terms whose main fault is that some of them tempt us to abuse them. Otherwise they have a certain right to protest their innocence, for their other faults are no worse than those of hundreds of terms that pass our lips daily, unnoticed because we are used to them. A new word, or an old one that rockets to popularity, like *meaningful*, flags us down because we expected something else. With our attention riveted on it, there is no way for it to hide the semantic vagueness that afflicts all abstractions. Yet *meaningful* comes as a potentially useful antonym of a term that no one would think of as jargon. When Britt Ekland declares, *My love affairs have always been meaningful*,[38] she is saying that they were not *frivolous*. *Serious* will not quite serve. Old vices are accepted, new ones viewed with horror – the familiar jargon is the alcohol of our verbal drug culture, the unfamiliar jargon is its marijuana.

For all that one would like to throttle them, it would neither be good nor possible to ABOLISH the special ways of talking and writing that serve little purpose except to set groups apart from one another. But it is essential to learn when not to be fooled by them. It makes no sense for a society to spend millions on bilingual programs to break down the barriers between languages, and do nothing about the rank growth of sociolects that raise new ones. Or do nothing about the oppressive side of the standard itself, which in some of its forms – and to some degree in the scheme as a whole – is designed as a barrier of social class. The standard, too, is a sociolect.

Chapter 12

Rival metaphors and the confection of reality

In October of 1973, a seventeen-year-old woman presented herself at the City Hospital in Boston, Massachusetts and requested an abortion. This was legal under Massachusetts law, and the operation – one of many at that hospital – was perfomed by Dr Kenneth C. Edelin, an experienced surgeon. Afterwards the fetus, which was more than twenty weeks old, was taken to the hospital laboratory to be kept for research. Investigators from the district attorney's office were touring the hospital, saw the fetus, concluded that some attempt should have been made to keep it alive, and promptly charged Dr Edelin with manslaughter. He was tried and found guilty. At the trial, one point of contention was the prosecutor's insistence on *baby*, *child*, and *subject* to name what the defense called a *fetus* or a *product of conception*.[1]

Though Edelin's conviction was later reversed, the moot question remained: WAS what Edelin removed a *fetus* or was it a *baby*? And why such passion over the choice of a word? A fetus is what an embryo becomes after the eighth week of pregnancy, and is what the unborn remains till it is born. But since the doctor 'delivered' it, it must have been born, hence was no longer a fetus. Along with the tangle of *baby*, *fetus*, *product of conception*, *life*, and *birth* went the complication of *manslaughter*: what kind of act makes one guilty of it?

Something more that euphemism and dysphemism was involved in this dispute. Both sides were determined to be in the right: one, opposed to abortions under any circumstances except perhaps to save the life of the mother, chose language that would put the doctor in the wrong: he had ended the *life* of a *baby*. The other, in favor of terminating pregnancies undesired by the mother-to-be, claimed that the doctor was *disposing of* a *fetus* that could not have survived in any case. While a number of rather explicitly euphemistic and dysphemistic expressions have emerged from this nation-wide controversy – *abortion on demand*, *right-to-life*, *right-to-one's-own-body* – the terms in dispute were potentially neutral ones being used in a favorable or unfavorable way. Somewhere in a continuum of good-to-bad, of life-to-death, and of embryo-to-child, a legal dividing line has to be drawn.

Dilemmas of this sort are commonplace. They are the heart of most legal disputes. A has killed B. Was it *murder* or *self-defense*? The State of

California imposes a sales tax on most items sold, but not on *food*. For many years sales of candy were taxed – candy was not a food. Naturally the sweets industry resisted – what really distinguishes a box of chocolates from a box of some other confection such as chocolate-coated marshmallow with a cookie base? The state finally capitulated and accepted candy as *food*.

The dilemmas make news when feelings run high. Asked whether they believe in the *right to life*, most people would answer yes – and would give the same answer if asked whether they believe a woman should *have control over her own body*. The conflict between the two beliefs does not become apparent until some other value intervenes – the rights of the unborn, the need to avoid overpopulation, the interest of the state in maintaining its armies, religious doctrine, sentimental attachment to young and small things. Then the epithets begin to fly: *slum-breeding, racial suicide, clerical meddling, socialized medicine*. At this point, labels are ATTACHED. It is no longer a question of deciding whether a given act should be viewed one way or another; the contending sides have already made up their minds, and look for terms to stigmatize the opposition. The following letter-to-the editor reveals the tactic, adding another invented term, *pre-born* – to preclude the term *unborn* with its negative prefix *un-* which might suggest that the fetus is not fully entitled to be called a *baby*:

Editor of the Times:

I must disassociate myself from the 'pro-abortion' element of the AAUW. I recently attended the California State Division Conference in San Jose and, at the workshop entitled, 'Women and Free Choice – The Abortion Issue,' was informed by the moderator that it was a meeting to decide how to further the abortionists' cause in regard to legislation and there would be no discussion of the moral issues of abortion.

That had been my reason for attending this particular workshop – to put forth the consideration for the right to life of each individual including that of pre-born babies. Nevertheless I stayed to observe the tactics of this group of women. They described themselves as a silent majority but they are not silent and I fervently hope not a majority.

The slogan 'Women For Free Choice Over Their Bodies' is one which any woman will agree with but the body in the case of free choice for abortion is not hers – it is the child's within her. From conception to death you are you – whether you are called a fertilized egg, a zygote, a fetus or any other rose. The deliberate termination of this pre-born individual by vacuuming, saline solution or any other method is murder and certainly a deprivation of human rights which so many of these women are championing in the ERA movement.

Even the pro-abortionists balk at the killing of the unborn after a certain period – the trimester is the magic word; however, who are they to say that before that time the pre-born baby is not an individual and so can be done away with, and, after this time lapse, the same unborn has at last gained the human right to life? By eight weeks all the baby's body systems are present including the brain.

Free choice for women over their own bodies, 'Si,' but not at the expense of destroying another's life. Pre-born infants are individuals; in birth they simply change their living quarters from their mothers' wombs to the outside world – if allowed to do so. The pro-abortionists say 'No.' I regard their stand as Medean.[2]

Euphemism-dysphemism turns out to be a kind of polarized NAMING. But naming is more than that. When a psychiatrist recommends a *surrogate wife* for a male patient he considers to have a legitimate need for sexual experience, is he using a polite term for *prostitute*? Probably – but not merely. Prostitutes tend to be promiscuous in their favors, a surrogate wife presumably is not. Prostitutes may incidentally teach, but that is not their function. Surrogate wives have a certain respectability; prostitutes have none. There are legitimate reasons – shaky, to be sure – for putting the surrogate in the 'wife' class rather than in the 'prostitute' class, if *wife* is defined broadly and *prostitute* narrowly. (The word *legitimate* was used twice in this paragraph. How legitimate is it?)

Throughout our lives, most naming is of this kind – coming upon something new and trying to fit it to our previous experiences, deciding whether it belongs under Label A or Label B. (But first deciding whether we like it or not. Attraction-repulsion is probably biological.)[3] We learn hundreds of new names for new experiences, of course; but for every new one we make a thousand adjustments among the old ones as experiences expand. And new names are not merely learned, but must be fitted in along with what they mean, most often as a subcategory of something for which a name already exists. A *weimaraner* or a *keeshond* or a *papillon* is a *dog*. A *jacaranda* or a *baobab* or a *divi-divi* is a *tree*. *Curling*, *fives*, and *jai alai* are *sports*. As each of these names with its meaning is fitted into place, slight alterations occur in the categories that absorb them – the more trees one knows, the better one understands the difference between a *tree* and a *shrub*; the more sports one is familiar with, the more precise the frontiers grow between *sports* and *games*, *sports* and *avocations*, *sports* and *occupations*. Sometimes a radical refitting takes place – most persons at some time in their lives are surprised to discover that *dolphins* are *mammals* and *tomatoes* are *fruit*. Not that they 'are' one or the other in any absolute sense, but the criteria by which dogs-and-cats go together put dolphins in the same class better than with *fishes*, and high sweetness and being-served-as-dessert are not always the best way to define a *fruit*. Charles Darwin caused a scandal that still reverberates when he placed human life in biological relation to all other life on earth, saying yes to the question, Is a man or a woman an animal?

   This seeing of like and unlike, of putting together and classifying apart, is more than a casual though daily occurrence. It is the mechanism through which reality is organized and the whole construct of language is built, in all its forms, rules, and applications. The world is a vast elaborated METAPHOR. Its beginnings go back to the roots of perception in earliest childhood. Nature does not come to the child in ordered fashion, but the child is equipped to perceive parts of it, and is born with one intellectual capacity that surpasses all others: the ability to see resemblances – which may, to begin with, be the same as the inability to see differences. The psychologists Eve and Herbert Clark have described the sorts of things that a child cannot help noticing, and have related them to universals of language.[4] There are certain 'best' colors for the human visual system; these are noted first, and all languages are found to have names for them in proportion to how good the human eye is in perceiving them. Other colors may or may not be named, depending on how important color is in the culture – and when named, the names tend to be by comparison with those basic colors – a *light* yellow, a *deep* green, a *greenish* blue. There are also 'best' shapes – the open shapes of line and curve, and the closed shapes of square and circle. A child misusing the name of something is apt to do it on the basis of one of these shapes – some other round thing will be called a *moon* or some other long thing will be called a *stick* – and these shapes are exactly the ones that many languages use to classify all objects. (English does this occasionally – a *stick* of candy, a *round* of applause, a *length* of rope.) And there are natural dimensions. Verticality is one, which the child perceives as the pull of gravity, the sensation of falling, and the maintenance of equilibrium in walking; verticality in turn defines the directions of *up* and *down*. Other spatial perceptions include *here* and *there*, where hereness readily involves contact – with the mother, for example – and thereness involves the opposite. There is probably a primitive notion of *thingness* – of constancy in an object that approaches and withdraws, is picked up, held, and laid down, has contours, warmth, and coldness – and this in turn defines oneness and is the basis of number. Further, as two things or happenings occur regularly in close succession, a basis is laid for *cause* and *effect*. All languages reflect these perceptions in their most basic categories. And this is simply to say that as children learn to speak they learn at the same time to draw comparisons, to cast the net of their language wide enough to bring in new experiences and class them under old rubrics. A thing is only what it is; when we classify it with other things we draw a comparison. As Kenneth Burke puts it, 'every perspective requires a metaphor, implicit or explicit, for its organizational base'.[5] In laying hold of new experience the child must use what is already held in mind. Metaphor involves 'pretending, imagining, reasoning by analogy.'[6] An unfamiliar quadruped presents itself; one cannot know that it is a dog, but it looks like one; so we imagine or pretend, and call it a dog. One of the most sweeping of the imaginings inherited from the childhood of the race is the metaphor of space applied to time: we measure it (*more time*, *less time*), locate events IN it (*within ten days*), enumerate segments of it (*first time*, *next time* – literally 'nighest time, nearest time'), describe it in terms of dimensions (*long time*, *short time*) – stamping on it the impressions of body space from childhood.[7] And this extended metaphor is as much alive today as ever – a flight attendant informs the passengers of an interesting sight about to come into view – it will be visible *in about three or four miles' time*.[8] (As speeds increase and people travel more, the metaphor is reversed – it is less cumbersome to mention units of time than conventional units of distance. *Dover is two hours from London. The Andromeda nebula is two million light years from earth* – to express this in miles would require muliplying two million by almost six trillion.) The abstract relations shown by prepositions are also spatial metaphors. A present *from* John is one that was *in* John's possession but now is somewhere else. A lecture *on* anatomy 'covers' the subject. To be *under* the control of someone is to be in a position of subjection. The adjectives that stem from this – *upper* class, *superior* strength, *low* mentality, *base* instinct, *high* fidelity – are matched only by the metaphors of size and weight: *big-hearted*, *small-minded*, *pin-headed*, *heavy-handed*, *light-footed*, *featherbrained*. The same spatial symbolism is quite regularly stage-managed – at court, for example, where the judge is seated *above* everyone else. As Judge Bean said in the film,[9] speaking to a culprit who had just been corralled and brought to his outdoor courtroom, *Get down off that horse; I don't want to have to look up to the likes of you.*

Related to space and motion is the metaphor of *power*. It is the early experience of *moving* unimpeded *over* or *through* obstacles, and the sensation of *exertion* that accompanies it. As the child grows into an adult, the metaphor grows with the addition of tools, alliances, and above all, weapons. It is largely a destructive metaphor – the fantasy we unconsciously invoke when we spray residual poisons on a field instead of planting resistant crops, dig wells on a scenic coastline instead of reducing the size of automobiles, dispatch armies instead of diplomats, and whenever we sit in a seat prearranged for us and pull a switch or push a button. It has numerous synonyms – *controlling*, *compelling*, *ruling* – besides close ties with the *dirt* metaphor with its *cleaning up* and *getting rid of* (see below).

Related to the primitives of *attraction* and *measure* is the single most influential metaphor in all elaborated societies – that of *value*, which is the basis of trade. It says that A is like B in terms of desirability – if I give you my pocket knife for your bubble gum plus your cowboy hat it is because we agree to that kind of metaphor. We extend it from material objects to abstractions such as services, rents, and usury. The metaphors of measurement enter the picture where amounts of value must be accounted for – two things for one, five pounds of this for three yards of that. And this leads ultimately to the standard measurement of value based on the coinage of something highly esteemed such as gold. No other metaphor affects our lives so profoundly – in large degree because of its tremendous oversimplification and hence high degree of manageability. A crust of bread, a wife, a year of bondage, the services of a high-class lawyer, even a life, can be *bought* by the simplistic possession of money. Its level of idiocy is one degree higher than that of the commonest means of acquiring it, the *job*, which can exist for any purpose, from playing the alto horn to smuggling cocaine. Both are temperamentally suited to the robot mind of the computer.

Criticizing the physicist Niels Bohr's hope that the framework of logic might in time lead to wider conceptions that would remove all present paradoxes and 'apparent disharmonies', Hannah Arendt wrote,

> [T]his hope, I am afraid, will be disappointed. The categories and ideas of human reason have their ultimate source in the human senses, and all conceptual or metaphysical language is actually and strictly metaphorical. Moreover, the human brain which supposedly does our thinking is as terrestrial, earthbound, as any other part of the human body. It was precisely by abstracting from these terrestrial conditions, by appealing to a power of imagination and abstraction that would, as it were, lift the human mind out of the gravitational field of the earth and look down upon it from some point in the universe, that modern science reached its most glorious and, at the same time, most baffling achievements.[10]

Metaphor at both extremes – infancy and the pinnacles of science. In between, it should come as no surprise that every thought and utterance is charged with it. When an idea strikes us as new and original, the chances are that it has been conveyed by a metaphor, that some old word with an old meaning has taken a leap in the imagination. The skill is shared by every user of the language – necessarily, for it is indispensable to saying anything that is not routine. Peter Collier captures our mind's eye with a description that is a tracery of metaphor:

> Linus Pauling has one of those faces that photographers love because it does their work for them. In moments of repose, it has that dreamy quality that Einstein's had, hair rising in eccentric silver wisps, periwinkle eyes that often glance inward during the conversation at some abstract law of motion or of matter. It would be tempting to see it as the Face of Science . . . .[11]

What a word *periwinkle* is in this context, a double-barreled metaphor that brings down both the color of the eyes and their twinkle! But the talent is no less manifest in the words of the caller on a radio talk show who remarked, *If you drive around on bald tires, the police will give you a ticket in a hurry.*[12] The imagery of a tread worn smooth could not be better expressed. Imaginative metaphors are highly in evidence in the tools that ordinary people invent and use, because old terms are constantly pressed into use by analogy. Suppose you have a stapling machine that is leaving the points of the staples unclinched so that there is danger of pricking a finger. You want to refer to the part of the machine that does the clinching – and almost without realizing it you have seized on the word *anvil*. Anyone familiar with the situation will know immediately what you mean, whether or not *anvil* has already acquired that technical sense. The metaphor is actually a mixed metaphor, because the 'hammer' is being used to DRIVE a nail-like object, whereas the hammer that goes with an anvil is mainly for shaping; but no matter – our metaphorizing minds dart in every direction.

If all metaphors were as colorful as these, we might be too busy appreciating them to follow the sense of an ordinary message. Once created, an apt metaphor sinks back and loses itself among all the other resources of the language that we learn and constantly reuse. *John is a chimney*, said in the proper circumstances, will be understood to mean that John smokes excessively. But *John is a chain-smoker*, with its old metaphor of *chain*, will be understood regardless; *chain-smoker* is part of the standard lexicon. But even the reuse of second-hand metaphors calls for stretching meanings. When *bald* was applied to tires, it had already been applied to things with a nap, such as rugs and carpets; the new extension may not have been directly from baldness of the head but from baldness of something worn down by friction. Extensions of the word *dry* show increasing abstraction by gradually extending metaphorical steps. A thing that is dry lacks wetness, and wetness can be metaphorized in various ways. A *dry blow* is one that does not draw blood. A *dry run* is a military exercise that does not draw blood because there is no ammunition. A *dry raise* is one that lacks the essentials of a raise – more money; it is a promotion in rank without an increase in salary. *Dry* has become so elastic that we are ready for it in almost any new sense, so long as there is a hint of one of the senses we already know, and the context gives the other clues we need. The change is not always in the direction of a wider leap – it may jump backward to a more restricted meaning. The speaker who said *White glue is different from epoxy in that it has to dry instead of harden* was not suggesting that epoxy glue in curing does not pass from a wet to a dry state, but that white glue cures by literally losing water. Either way, the curing process results in hardening; the context temporarily defines *harden* as 'to cure without losing water' – *hard*, too, is metaphorized.

How a word can leap within a context is illustrated by these lines from a Harold Pinter play:

BEN. Go and light it.
GUS. Light what?
BEN. The kettle.
GUS. You mean the gas.
BEN. Who does.
GUS. You do.
BEN. (His eyes narrowing). What do you mean, I mean the gas?

GUS. Well, that's what you mean, don't you? The gas.

BEN. (powerfully). If I say go and light the kettle I mean go and light the kettle.

GUS. How can you light a kettle?

BEN. It's a figure of speech! Light the kettle. It's a figure of speech!

GUS. I've never heard of it.

BEN. Light the kettle! It's common usage!

GUS. I think you've got it wrong.

BEN. (menacing). What do you mean?

GUS. They say put on the kettle.

BEN. (taut). Who says?

[They stare at each other, breathing hard.]

[Deliberately.] I have never in my life heard anyone say put on the kettle.

GUS. I bet my mother used to say it.

BEN. Your mother? When did you last see your mother?[13]

Told to light the kettle, most speakers of English would know what to do – as they would also probably know if told to *turn the soup off* – to turn to 'off' the knob that controls the valve that releases the gas that feeds the fire that heats the kettle that contains the soup: the figure of speech[14] takes the line of least resistance, hopping from one connection to another along a natural causal chain. A news report speaks of a *westbound accident*, surely a strange thing for an accident to be, but the figurative terminus of another chain: *westbound commuter* → *westbound car* → *westbound traffic* → *westbound lane* → *westbound lane accident* → *westbound accident*.

If all that we can know and talk about is ultimately in terms of something else, and that in turn is shaped by childhood gropings for connections grounded firmly enough in impressions of space, touch, size, motion, direction, and balance to hold them steady and enable an uncertain mind to grasp them, then our assurances come more from finding that our reality is shared by others than from the security of its own anchors. Metaphor is at work, but it has been at work in the past and brings to us a world to some extent prefabricated in our language. We do not have to learn for ourselves that an *aspen* is a *tree* – we can be told so by someone who has seen a hundred-foot specimen in the lowlands, unlike the stunted shrub-like growth of a Colorado altitude. Most of our learning of the terms in our language is learning WHAT metaphor to apply: X is Y – every equation that does not express identity (a dog is a dog) is an extension, but most extensions come ready-made. They are compact, agreed-upon, and relatively harmless. A *hammer* is a *tool*, a *gun* is a *weapon*, a *house* is a *dwelling*, a *confidante* is a *friend*. But what does one make of the advertiser who says *Your friends at Bayview Motors are waiting to serve you* – speaking of people who are not even acquaintances? This is not a *friend* from the dried-out store of word meanings that preserve the metaphors of long ago, but a fresh start – you are invited to regard a stranger as a friend. If all thinking is metaphorical, there is always someone willing to help us think by providing us with a metaphor that accords with HIS views – his permanent views of the world, or his temporary views of his advantage here and now. It would be hard to abolish the latter, given the natural egoism of human nature, and anyway, we synthesize our own antibodies: no one can live long without inventing defenses against it. But world views are more serious, because the imagery is so complex that one can never be quite sure how much of it is relevant and how much is humbug.

This brings us to politics, where large views are everything and metaphors sweep from horizon to horizon. A single decision, guided by a metaphor that has become a rallying cry, can affect the lives of millions. The very structure of government shows the mental picture of society that leaders carry in their heads. In the United States there are fifteen adminstrative departments that incorporate the infinitely varied activities and interests of a large and complex state: Agriculture, Air Force, Army, Commerce, Defense, Energy, Health-Education-and-Welfare, Housing and Urban Development, Interior, Justice, Labor, Navy, State, Transportation, and Treasury. What picture of the political world do they convey?

To begin with, the proportions are significant. The Department of Defense is the only Department that embraces three other Departments, Army, Navy, and Air Force, which gives the military a quadruple representation on the President's Cabinet. By contrast, until 1979 Education existed only as a Division, crowded into the same Department as Health and Welfare. The budget reflected the same order of importance. Of an estimated total national budget for 1978 of 440 billion dollars (that is, 440 thousand million), Defense was to receive more than a fourth – not counting payments to and for veterans of former wars. Education – elementary through higher – was allotted about one-tenth that amount. From these priorities it follows that many programs and policies that might be seen in another light are going to be construed as 'military', since – if related services are to be offered – the military will have to pay for them. Not that this will be done in a militaristic manner, necessarily – much of it will be simple patronage, the beneficent seigneur pensioning an architect or a sculptor and giving him a free hand. During the 1960s it became almost a joke among linguists to read the first footnote to a publication and discover that the work had been subsidized by the Air Force, the Army Signal Corps, or the Office of Naval Research. (What sort of society would it be that allocated the fourth to education and the fortieth to the military, with military programs dependent in part on largess from education?) In social matters the relationship has sometimes been less philanthropic. How the choice of metaphoric label affects the solution is discussed by Murray Edelman:

. . . Urban planning is for urban planners, not for the people who live in cities, and especially not for those who live in central cities, rather than suburbs.

The categorization of these problems legitimizes the power of specialized authorities to deal with them, even though their decisions systematically affect many other aspects of people's lives. Military planners create employment in some places, unemployment in others, inflation everywhere and moral dilemmas for many, but the problem is labeled 'military'. Psychiatrists reinforce the norm that cheerful adjustment to poverty or war is healthy, while despondency or anger in the face of these pathologies is sick, but their decisions are labeled 'medical'.

In the contemporary world, a governmental decision can have severe effects upon many aspects of our lives. For this reason, labeling policies as military or medical is both metaphoric and metonymic. It stands for a larger pattern of cognitions, or it highlights a similarity to something familiar while masking other critical features. In doing so it legitimizes a specific kind of political authority while degrading the claim of mass publics to participate in policymaking. Because anxiety about foreign enemies, internal subversion and deviant behavior is frequently reinforced by government officials and is especially widespread, military, police and psychiatric authorities benefit most consistently from this form of linguistic structuring. Anxiety about economic survival and social problems is limited to particular groups, is far more sporadic and is constantly deflated by governmental claims that the outlook is good.[15]

'Though symbolic cues are not omnipotent,' Edelman concludes, 'they define the geography and topography of everyone's political world.' As with national politics, so with international:

The words of international power politics are typically analogic. There are analogies from interpersonal relations: nation states become *We*'s and *They*'s who assume military *postures*, who glare at each other *eye-ball to eye-ball*, who *harass* or *intimidate* each other, who *trust* or are *suspicious* of each other. There are analogies from nineteenth-century physics, with *balances* of power or power *vacuums*, with *slippery slopes* or *rows of dominos* along which vague forces operate with some natural inevitability, with *attractions* and *repulsions*, and centers toward which power *gravitates*. Analogies have the same sharpening and blurring effects upon thinking that ordinary words do, only more so; they raise the feature analogized to a dazzling prominence which obscures other, often more relevant features.[16]

Governments control their subjects – a better term in this context than *citizenry* – by organizing their reality for them. Some metaphors are approved, others slighted. The individual is prevented from forming his own reality not only by indoctrination but also by impoverishment, which takes two forms, one extreme, the other mild but equally effective. The first is censorship. When information is withheld, the individual cannot categorize that part of experience; pieces are missing, comparisons cannot be made, concepts are left unformed. The censorship may be of current news, or older books containing subversive ideas, or speakers voicing a protest or criticism. In most Western industrial societies there is little or no official damming of the flow of information, but there is frequent exercise of the second form of deprivation, which can be likened to the scrambling of transmissions used by cryptographers. To keep a message from being understood it is not necessary to put it in code: instead, it can be chopped into fragments of less than word size and then randomized – with a machine at the other end to reassemble it. An eavesdropper finds it meaningless. Much of our published information has been fragmented. For example: On three successive weeks, rear-end collisions on the highways result in exploding gas tanks. In one accident, the driver is burned to death. A month or two later the family of the victim files suit against the manufacturer of the car. If there is a pattern in these events, the average reader of a newspaper may be unable to form it in his mind because: (*a*) the paper reports one of the events but not the others; or (*b*) it reports all four events but omits the make of the car: or (*c*) it reports all three accidents and the make of the car but at the time of the third accident it does not refer again to the earlier ones, and meanwhile the reader has forgotten; or (*d*) it reports the lawsuit under the headline 'X Company Says Gas Tank Perfectly Safe', which misdirects the reader's attention. There are many other possible permutations and modifications in this filtering of information through the indifference, forgetfulness, overcaution, prejudice, selectiveness, incompetence, vested interest, or sensationalism of the reporting medium. When a second filter is added, such as a government source with its own overcaution, selectiveness, vested interest, etc, the underlying pattern may be quite inaccessible to all but the most astute and attentive reader scanning a wide variety of publications. The critic I. F. Stone, credited with exposing more than one government scandal, often disclaimed any special contacts or sources – he went to the news as a jigsaw puzzle and put the pieces together, assigning the meanings and relevant metaphors to what had been presented as random events. At least some of the scrambling of the news is probably deliberate – to defend a government policy, to shield a powerful advertiser, to avoid public alarm, or whatever – and though it is not censorship in the crude sense, it suffices to keep reality out of focus if not entirely out of mind; 'our political worlds are segmented and disjoined,' says Edelman, though their parts, if we could see them together, form 'an increasingly integrated whole. . . . In place of the ability to deal with issues in terms of their logical and empirical ties with each other, the language of politics encourages us to see and to feel them as separate.'[17]

A third means of control is fully conspirational. If to the disassembled bits a piece or two can be added that seem as if they might fit but in fact do not, the puzzle may never be solved. This is the domain of rumor. Suppose that the critics of the Warren Commission are right, and John F. Kennedy was the victim of a plot. If the conspirators felt the net closing in, one of the surest ways of escaping it would be to set afoot a theory agreeing with the critics but providing false clues. When true leads are themselves insecure, they are scarcely distinguishable from false ones.

Against the metaphors by which we do our own organizing are arrayed those staid and stale metaphors that evoke predictable reactions. Take the *sea* metaphor and the *ship of state*:

> Speakers can say that society is launched upon a troubled, uncertain ocean. Now picturing society as a storm-tossed ship, they can extend the metaphor . . . [:] citizens ought to buckle down and do their duties like good crewmen. Such a metaphoric conception is not favorable to civil liberties, to rebels and other misfits who don't like to row along with others. Freedom of speech is rarely practiced on board a ship. And . . . nowhere is there a more authoritarian image than that of the sea captain. . . .

Countering this is the *disease-and-remedy* metaphor:

> The speaker sees society as sick and diseased, the illness may appear terminal, radical surgery is called for. The image is decidedly revolutionary. The implied image . . . links the power of metaphor with the appeal of one of the most favored symbols of our culture, that of the physician.[18]

The *war-and-peace* metaphor served President Lyndon Johnson in his *war on poverty* – as it has served successive administrations and local agencies in their *war on crime*; but it is a risky image because it promises too much – a war has to be won fast (and a war on *crime* – itself a metaphorical complex of vast proportions – can never be won). Harry Truman showed more cunning in calling a real war a *police action* – an obvious euphemism but it 'reduced the pressure on old Harry to win at all costs and by any means'.[19]

The euphemistic and dysphemistic metaphors are the ones with widest appeal, for they mask their partisan nature through a connection with something that is NATURALLY good or bad. The metaphor of *dirt* incorporates a wide range of terms that compel a listener without alerting him to the actual image he may be tricked into accepting. Its subtlety harks back to the perhaps instinctive attraction-repulsion mentioned earlier plus early training in avoidance, the infant's rejection of anything *nasty* or *icky*, carefully nurtured by parents. The sentence *We've got to clean up the police force in this city* implies, without saying it in so many words, that the police force is dirty. Most of the synonyms of *dirt* and *dirty* have figurative uses: *smut, filth, mire, soiled, spattered, tarnished*. On the other side are *clean, pure, immaculate, spotless – a clean bill of health, a spotless reputation, a pure friendship*. Until recently the commonest way of denigrating sex was through the *dirt* metaphor – and an old man who has the misfortune of retaining his drives is still a *dirty old man* (also *denigrate* is literally 'to blacken'). Diseases were long metaphorized as *unclean*. And the racial overtones of *dirty* and *unclean, black* and *white*, are obvious. Related metaphoric terms are *riddance, clearing the decks*, expressions connected with bad tastes and smells, and formatives like the compounding element *free* in *germ-free, dust-free, lint-free, pest-free, weed-free* – handy for products that want to insinuate that an ingredient they don't contain would only be undesirable anyway: *fat-free milk* (lots of people like cream, but who wants fat?), *sugar-free gum*. The metaphorical associations of *free* itself would fill a volume.

Societies differ of course in the metaphors that serve them, and between two widely separated cultures the differences may go all the way back to the perceptual metaphors that start the process in infancy. Take the metaphor of *possession*. The infant begins with the inalienable possession of its own body. Trading on the associated metaphor of nearness, ownership is extended to what is intimately associated with the body and continues to reach out till it embraces a set of tools, a tent, and a family, all MOVABLES that do not violate the condition of nearness. A nomadic society may push the metaphor no farther; a settled agricultural one may extend it to the ownership of land, and with that step the earth is the limit, long after the agricultural beginnings are forgotten. And the symbolism of ownership is attached to that of value and institutionalized in systems of exchange or money, whose purpose is the acquiring and transfer of property. The concept of property has a long history in the relationship between white settlers and Indian aborigines in North America. It continues to the present in the collision of white and Eskimo cultures in Alaska. By provision of the 1971 Native Claim Settlement Act, the Eskimos and Aleuts were to receive 962 million dollars and permanent title to ten per cent of the state, or forty-four million acres. From the white standpoint, this was the most generous treaty ever concluded.

> To receive the land and money, the natives had to set up regional corporations in 12 areas and village corporations in 200 settlements. Each corporation would be wholly owned by native stockholders. Acreage and revenues were to be divided under complex formulas.
>
> Today . . . the natives are tangled in a nightmare of lawsuits, government red tape and financial difficulties. . . .
>
> Village corporations are impoverished. Several regional corporations have lost millions of dollars. Native stockholders are fighting native administrators, and the corporations are suing each other.[20]

The consultant to several of the villages, Paul Gaskin, observes that 'These villages have never known private property before. All they've gotten under the act is the privilege of paying taxes. Why should they own the land when they can get the game from it anyway?'

In our own society, most of the metaphorical constructs that remain intact do so partly because they go unquestioned. Our picture of our society is so deeply planted that it merges with the landmarks and phenomena of nature – streams and cliffs, forests and raindrops. No conspiracy is needed to appeal to the parts of it, only a quick wit and an instinct for self-promotion or self-preservation. But there are times when the way things appear is seized upon and deliberately passed off as reality. This happens more and more in a culture where 'public relations' competes with the dissemination of information. Curiously, the vocabulary used for the fabrication admits to it by employing the word *image*: *image-making*, *image-building*, *improving the image*. A public figure is criticized for his policies. His response is not to change them but to give his public relations department the task of making him LOOK better. HE is not in the wrong; WE are incapable of judging a person's true character and must be given a stage presence instead. Truth gives way to appearance, substance to style. 'That's the trouble with us,' says Malcolm MacDougall. 'We say we want an honest President. But do we really want an honest President? Or do we want a terrific actor who can PLAY an honest President?'[21] And this takes place to the drumbeat of jargon behind the symbolic façade. It is an ancient ploy. Machiavelli writes,

> A prince . . . should seem to be all mercy, faith, integrity, humanity, and religion. And nothing is more necessary than to seem to have this last quality, for men in general judge more by the eyes than by the hands, for every one can see, but very few have to feel. Everybody sees what you appear to be, few feel what you are, and those few will not dare to oppose themselves to the many, who have the majesty of the state to defend them; and in the actions of men, and especially of princes, from which there is no appeal, the end justifies the means. Let a prince therefore aim at conquering and maintaining the state, and the means will always be judged honorable and praised by every one, for the vulgar is always taken by appearances and the issue of the event; and the world consists only of the vulgar, and the few who are not vulgar are isolated when the many have a rallying point in the prince.[22]

The politician is not the only person who believes that if reality is going to be confected anyway it might as well be confected to one's own advantage. In a society that views itself as fundamentally an *economy*, economic beliefs and practices guide the metaphoric structuring of reality. The naming practices of commerce reflect the metaphor of thingness. Real objects have names, so names become the guarantors of objecthood. Where the 'objects' are cultural artifacts in the first place, it is easy to substitute others for them that may be more advantageous to some commercial interest. Measurements, for example. In Britain and some of her former colonies, the pre-metric liquid standard is the *gallon*. This unit is already suspect, because in the United States the standard gallon is the old British *wine gallon*, about 17 per cent smaller than the imperial gallon. What was doubtless the practice of British wine merchants continues in the trade. In place of *quarts*, most wines are sold in *fifths*, a confected unit without justification except for its resemblance to a quart. A size smaller than the gallon is the *so-called gallon*, standardized as the number-10 tin or can, used for packing fruits and vegetables for heavy users such as restaurants and institutions, and varying in weight of contents from about 6 pounds 8 ounces to about 7 pounds 2 ounces. Imitations of standard units continue down the line of size, with tins and packages chiseled off a degree from some standard unit or major fraction or multiple thereof, and then, when the public has got used to the smaller size, chiseled again: salmon in $15\frac{1}{2}$ ounce tins, raisins in 15-ounce packages, tuna in 7-ounce tins, fruits (large size) in 1-pound 14-ounce tins, and of course the famous chocolate bar which evolves periodically from eight ounces down through various 'giant sizes' to four – but now, to 'We reduced the size in order not to increase the price' must be added 'but we planned our metaphor hoping you wouldn't notice'. 'Creation, existence, and naming are inseparable,' declared Edith Kern in her presidential address to the Modern Language Association,[23] and nowhere is this more evident than in the Alice-in-Wonderland heaven of the merchant, where things grow smaller but seem to stay the same as the eye diminishes.

The result of successive reductions has been a profusion of fractions and odd sizes so baffling, especially when multiplied by the enormous VARIETY of merchandise lavished on supermarket shelves, that comparison with standard weights and measures is no longer practical for the average shopper. This suits the merchant just fine, because the package is now sui generis – it is its own reality, and can be expanded and contracted at will. Not all shoppers have accepted this sharp practice quietly, and in some places the competing reality of the standard reasserts itself as *unit pricing*: packages are required to carry not only net weight, but price per pound or other standard unit. The Prince is sometimes a buyer too, and has a stake in the reality of the standard. But the battle between standard and imitation goes on, and will go on forever. The sharpies also include buyers, who have been known to print imitation money and put slugs in vending machines.

While the state decrees a standard of measurement and merchants prefer a fluctuation, the retail marketplace decrees a fluctuation in prices, but merchants would prefer a standard. In the real world of action this may lead to price-fixing. In the world of symbol it leads to the metaphor of regularity, bodied forth in the *regular price*. A regular price goes up as wholesale prices advance, but does not necessarily go down when they fall. Price competition is usually resisted, and various artificial entities have been created to avoid it. One is the *trading stamp*, by which a small return is given in the form of merchandise, called *premiums* – nothing so prosaic as getting back what you have already paid for, but a *reward*. This has fallen into disfavor as consumers became less enamored of small gadgets and had less time for licking and sticking. The current preference is for an old-time favorite, the *discount coupon*, which has the advantage that the producer can tie it to his product and maintain the fiction of a *regular price* while still selling now and then for less. In the wildly fluctuating coffee market of 1977–8 most of the major brands offered reductions – up to 10 per cent – to the diligent coupon-clippers. Rather than stamps or coupons, which have some real though slight value, the more common type of entity is the mythical one – price competition is avoided by distracting attention from it to something ephemeral or imaginary. In the product advertising of radio and television, the emphasis is on some pretended quality, service, or convenience. It is the rare advertisement that mentions price except in general terms.

If price and package have their fictive realities, so do the products themselves. Here the war is between brand and generic. In the naive view, a real thing should have a real and unique name, and the clearest manifestation of this honest relationship is in the drug industry. Most drugs make their debut as patented formulas with trade name attached. The drug *chlordiazepoxide hydrochloride*, a tranquilizer, was patented and marketed as *Librium*. When the patent expired, in 1976, competitors were free to sell the product under its generic or 'real' name. (But the brand name remains private property and continues to help the original manufacturer sell his product at a higher price. Librium still has 95 per cent of the United States market, in spite of costing from two to five times as much as the generic equivalent.)[24] With chemicals the real or generic name is somewhat predetermined by the nature of chemical synthesis, which gives us what comes as close as anything can come to being genuinely new things in the material world, named according to their chemical composition. Using generic names makes drugs so much more economical that by 1976 nineteen states in the United States and the District of Columbia had passed laws encouraging or requiring physicians to prescribe generic equivalents of brand-name drugs whenever they were available. The brand name does sometimes offer the convenience of being easy to remember, though not when – as in the case of the hideous *thalidomide* – a drug is marketed under twenty-seven different names.[25]

Where chemical formulation is not involved, the war between the brand and the generic becomes a thing of makebelieve. In place of syntheses there are RECIPES. A puffed cereal is coated with sugar and marketed as *Sugar Puffs*. Instant coffee (a little) is combined with artificial milk (a lot), sugar, and artificial flavoring, labeled *Café au Lait*, touted as one of a line of *International Coffees* – and sold at three times the cost per serving as pure coffee.[26] There is nothing to stop the consumer from buying generic coffee, generic sugar, and generic cream, and mixing them himself; so the recipe is worthless except as the user can be made to believe he is getting a genuinely new entity.

Now imagine the profits for the coffee industry if it could remove generic instant coffee from the market, making it impossible to buy anything but the *International Coffees*. Hardly thinkable, of course, because with coffee the public would know enough to raise an outcry. With certain other products, especially those that have to be used in a gingerly way – medicines, detergents, insecticides – concealment and secrecy dampen protest. The demand for the generic falls off and it may be to some extent forgotten. Probably more people shop today for cans of *Drano* than for cans of *lye*. Thirty or forty years ago one could go into almost any pharmacy in the United States, ask for *insect flowers*, the popular name for the natural insecticide *pyrethrum*, and be sure of being served. Nowadays the only response is a blank look. Generic pyrethrum cannot be bought even from merchants who specialize in farm and garden supplies. Despite the fact that it is probably the safest of all insecticides and is easy to handle as a powder or infusion, it is available today only in brand-name conglomerations some of whose ingredients are anything but harmless.

So we have a metaphor of reality in which the main function of entities is to support the verbal illusions attached to them. They are sufficiently thing-like to be accepted as genuine by an uninformed public, though many of them deserve to be taken no more seriously than the feather that Yankee Doodle stuck in his hat and called macaroni.

Not that all recipes are deceptive or even that some of the deceptive ones are totally without value. It is possible to take generic flour and yeast, generic water, generic diastatic malt, and one or two other generic ingredients, make them into a loaf, bake it, crumble it, and toast the crumbs, and come out with a superior-tasting equivalent of *Grape Nuts*. Most would rather buy the brand-name product than go to the bother. As for generic water – the one true thirst-quencher – it masquerades as countless elixirs containing sweeteners, mysterious flavors, and carbon dioxide, commanding a magisterial price for a tingle on the tongue. Everywhere the aura of secrecy makes it more difficult to detect the true frauds. In a complex society that needs information about its realities above all else, the subservience of fact to proprietary interest is appalling.

Perhaps it is pushing the analogy too far, but corporate industry itself seems as if it were on the way to becoming a collection of incongruous recipes, as mutually irrelevant enterprises merge into conglomerates. There is no organizing principle behind a conglomerate except profit. Tobacco companies go into food processing; railroad companies publish textbooks and publishers build condominiums—business activities that belong together as much as ice cream and pickle relish. With generic things lost in a welter of random combinations, the public is stripped of the power to make rational decisions about them. Our metaphors are frozen before we can reach out to them.

It is important for us to have a voice in urban planning, health services, taxation, environmental protection, and all the other things that affect us daily and so dearly, as Murray Edelman implies. But the concepts we form, the images accessible to our minds, the judgments on which we base our decisions – to what extent is it our voice that speaks in THEM?

Chapter 13

A last case in point: bluenoses and coffin nails

The late summer and early fall of 1978 was a time of heavy politics in California. Two of the ballot proposals for the November election drew national attention. One would have singled out school employees who happened to be homosexual for special punitive action. The other would have placed restrictions on smoking in enclosed public areas. Both lost. The campaign on the smoking initiative was the most expensive in California history. Its backers spent about half a million dollars, its opponents about five million, contributed mainly by the tobacco industry. Most of the money went for advertising on a huge scale, by radio, television, newspaper, and billboard. The outcome was to ride on which side was more successful in manipulating its metaphors by every means that could reach the public eye and ear. The opponents had to overcome an initial handicap. A poll earlier in the year had shown a majority in favor of restrictions on smoking.

The tobacco industry is an old hand at fending off attacks from reformers and religious groups, and some of its weapons only needed refurbishing. Others had to be fashioned to deal with a new adversary, the medical profession, which for the first time was coordinating its attack through the major medical associations. The battle with the doctors began in the 1960s, when the governments of Britain and the United States were compelled, by mounting evidence of disease, to require a warning on cigaret packages and in cigaret advertising: smoking was potentially harmful to the smoker. But now the doctors were making an additional claim, that called for new countermeasures: non-smokers could be injured too, by tobacco smoke in confined areas.

Metaphors never come singly, as we saw with the childhood complexes of space, time, possession, etc. When put to the service of propaganda, they cluster in what might be called THEMES. This is only to say that some metaphors are more inclusive than others, and that together they form a infinitely overlapping hierarchy. Two metaphoric complexes, or themes, served the defenders of the California initiative: *freedom* and *health*. Freedom embraced both not being imposed upon by smokers and not being exposed to pollutants. The latter tied in with the health theme, which embraced the *clean* metaphor as well as the more obvious threat of *disease* – the measure was called the *Clean Indoor Air Initiative* by its proponents.

Health has been a hotly debated issue ever since the use of tobacco spread across Europe in the sixteenth century. Tobacco was thought by the American Indians to have curative powers, and this notion was imported with the product; but it was also used for gratification, which put it in the category that is occupied by the term *drug* today. According to one's views, it could be praised as a boon or denounced as a bane. An instance of the *drug* theme was a story published in the *Anti-Tobacco Journal* after the assassination of President Lincoln, claiming that 'one of the assassins . . . confessed to having smoked a cigar a short time before the deed was committed'.[1] The *drug* theme was the chief weapon against tobacco in the nineteenth century as it has been more recently against marijuana, with one difference in the associated themes: besides *health*, it was then connected to *sinful pleasure*, whereas now the connection is with *antisocial behavior*. Tobacco no longer qualifies as sinful or as seriously antisocial, which exempts it from the *drug* theme (and the exemption is also official – tobacco is no longer listed as a drug in the US Pharmacopoeia); but the health question remains.

Up to the 1950s, one could find doctors arrayed on both sides. But the positive pole gradually shifted to neutral; tobacco was no longer a health aid, it was merely harmless: *Not a cough in a carload, Reach for a Lucky instead of a sweet* – essentially neutral claims. When clinical and population studies began to show the effects of increased cigaret smoking – after and partly as a result of the First World War – the polarities were reversed, and the tobacco industry no longer found it advantageous to mention health in any context at all. Tobacco advertising had a supply of safer themes, and their use was stepped up, with the assistance of motivational research. But the health issue nevertheless had to be met when it was pressed by government and other agencies, and here the industry countered with an astute manipulation of the metaphor of *cause*, which harks back to the spatial perceptions of childhood – movement, direction, nearness, sequence. A child pushes a pile of blocks and it falls. This can be repeated indefinitely, almost always with the same result. The merely temporal sequence of push plus fall is cemented into a causer-causee one, in which an animate mover PRODUCES an effect. The causer, being animate, is felt to be unique, and we begin to speak of THE cause of something (as we do of THE truth and THE law), ignoring all the other antecedents of an event that do not possess animate power – the shakiness of the pile of blocks, the pull of gravity. This childish view of cause becomes the folk view, and persists in a way that enables it to be played against the scientific view of causation, where cause is always multiple and depends not on single-handed power but on statistical probabilities. To every new bit of evidence that smoking was linked to cancer and other diseases, the tobacco industry was able to respond that no causal relation had been proved, that more research was needed – and to underscore its devotion to the search for THE cause by subsidizing its own program of research and contributing generously to other programs.

Eventually this argument wore thin where smokers were concerned – the proofs became too numerous; but it was revived against the claim that smoking is harmful to non-smokers. In 1978 the medical evidence was still tenuous enough for the opponents of the California initiative to be able to quote – and misinterpret – a past president of the American Cancer Society who had said that he did 'not have any hard evidence' to show that non-smokers are harmed.[2] Even the harm to smokers continues to be played down. After the release of the US Surgeon General's new report on smoking, 11 January 1979, the Medical Director of the Tobacco Institute, Dr Charles Waite, revived the causal metaphor. 'Risks are not causes,' he said, and added that he saw no reason to oppose smoking in general, because of 'an absence of total scientific facts'[3] – which is either nonsense, or is meant to suggest, without assuming the responsibility of saying, 'a total absence of scientific facts'. (Hearers unconsciously rise to this kind of bait because they must be ready to adjust for unintended nonsense – for example, *She is critical*, for *She is critically ill*, or *The severest group hit by unemployment*, for *The group most severely hit by unemployment*.)

Up front, in the promotional advertising for cigarets, the theme of cause-and-proof was absent. Here the strategy was to deflect the health issue by indirect appeals. The first was the metaphor of *newness*, which is a perennial one in advertising (*the new, improved model*), but had a special value here because it implied an escape from the old – and maybe dangerous – model. To every charge that cigarets are harmful, the tobacco industry has responded – without emphasizing the connection – with 'We are doing something about it' – lengthening the tube, lowering tar, lowering nicotine, attaching filters, recessing the filters to prevent 'filter feedback', adding synthetic tobacco, and so on. Though these measures were mostly useless and some led to further dangers (as when farmers switched to a darker leaf to make up for the weakening of the smoke as it was filtered), the smoker felt reassured – the causal connections if any were with the old model, the new model was safer.

The other indirect appeal was nonverbal – images of sun and sand, of hardhat worker and plaid-shirted sportsman – suggesting a link between cigarets and healthy people. Earlier visuals of this kind had contained outright testimonials by sports figures, and merely had to be adapted to a more subtle technique. Tobacco advertising was part of the general shift to nonverbal communication, as we noted earlier – it is hard to prove misrepresentation when a claim is not expressed in propositional language.

But the approach was more intricate than this, and embodied themes that are conduits to some of our innermost – and least questioned – desires and allegiances. The three that stand out are *fashion, freedom,* and *fun.*

Fashion at one and the same time asserts most of what is good about a social practice and most of what is bad about the opposition to it. On the one side its associated metaphors include *youth, unconventionality,* and *daring*; on the other, the *frowzy,* the *intolerant,* and the *fuddyduddy.*

The tie to *youth* is evident in the words that cohere with *fashion* and *fashionable.* We readily say *a fashionable young woman* or *a fashionable young man*; but *a fashionable child* is odd and *a fashionable old man* is almost a contradiction in terms. To the extent that cigaret smoking can be presented as fashionable, it appeals both to youthfulness – to the desire on everyone's part to appear young – and to youth. The latter is important to an industry that must persuade young non-users to become users if it is to survive. The advertising that employs visual metaphors to emphasize health also purveys youth – the robust types in the ads are young and highly presentable.

Unconventionality and *daring* are the growing end of fashion. They are also fully shared with the theme of *freedom.* They appeal to those who want not only to be in the swim but to be the leading swimmers. Fashion bestows in this way the illusion of exclusiveness without actually excluding anyone who accepts the point of view. It is enough to be ahead of all those whose ideas and tastes are circumscribed by traditional authority. It was daring that induced French ladies to begin to smoke cigarets, as Louisa Stuart Costello noted in 1842,[4] that carried the fashion to women of the smart set in other countries within a few years, and has now extended its swing through all social classes by spreading downward through age groups – very early for boys, with whom it was an initiation into manhood and was held in check only by the inhibition of 'Children should not smoke', much later for girls, who had to contend in addition with 'Females should not smoke'. And here daring incorporates itself in the theme of *freedom* under the guise of women's liberation. If it had not been for this century-long struggle, daring would have burnt itself out long since, because smoking would simply have become customary and noncomformity would have taken other forms; but the right of women to smoke has been continuously challenged, and feminists have responded by daring to smoke. And even in their feminist stand there was a further challenge that kept the issue alive. The feminists themselves were divided – many were active in the temperance movement which on the whole opposed tobacco as it did alcohol – and this increased the social risk for women who smoked. A famous cigaret ad of the 1920s – one of the earliest aimed at women – coupled boldness with style: *Women, when they smoke at all, quickly develop discriminating taste.*

The addition of physical to social risk has – for many of the young especially – enhanced the *daring* metaphor in a way obviously not intended by the medical authorities who were intent on publicizing it. The warning on cigaret packages is a dare: *The Surgeon General Has Determined that Cigarette Smoking Is Dangerous to Your Health.* The word *dangerous,* along with *wicked* and *naughty,* forms a set that interacts in a very special way with intonation. One pronounces

It's d a a a a a n ger o u s !

with a glint in the eye that says 'Let's try it!' This is hardly possible with synonyms of *dangerous* such as *risky, harmful, chancy, injurious, damaging*, etc.[5] People who avoid what is harmful are merely prudent, but people who defy danger are *brave*. And so *bravery* receives a ticket to *fashion*.

The upshot of the multiple inhibitions was that the *daring* metaphor, plus all that goes with style, chic, youthfulness, unconventionality, and social protest, has been good for prolonged exploitation.

The *fashion* theme has been just as useful in stigmatizing the opposition. The mainspring of fashion is a constant break with tradition, and the anti-cigaret forces were from the beginning aligned with the crusading arm of traditional religious groups. These same forces were responsible for the prohibition of alcohol, and their rigidity made it easy to caricature them as moral busybodies, concerned more with sin than with hygiene. Hence the bluenose – the anti-tobacconist was everything that the fashionable person was not: old-fashioned, moralistic, prating, a meddler and a killjoy. There was also more than a little anti-feminism in the construction of the bluenose image: in the beginning it was chiefly MALE smokers and drinkers whose pleasures were being interfered with and the crusaders were mostly women. Making the cigaret fashionable had the effect not only of spreading its use but of depriving the opposition of its troops.

The *bluenose* theme was revived in the California campaign, but since the temperance movement had been dead for half a century, it needed a new face. The twin themes of *Big Brother* and *Big Government* supplied it. In the past, reformers have drawn authority from religion; now they draw it from government, and government is interfering in our lives more and more. 'You will be voting on whether you want a BIG BROTHER GOVERNMENT,' declares the California Voters Pamphlet, 'making personal decisions and controlling private property.' The authors of the statement, the coalition that successfully opposed the California initiative, called themselves *Californians for Common Sense*. The power of this lay in the imputation of its antonym: the proponents of the measure were extremists who lacked common sense – today's version of the bluenose. And the campaign advertising revived the associations: *They're at it again! Vote NO on 5* was blazoned on billboards across the state – the vaguely ominous pronoun coupled today's reformers with the busybodies of old.

Fun is the sister of *fashion*. Smoking is pleasurable, and daring to smoke is pleasant as well as fashionable. The sexual emphasis of modern advertising provided an obvious link: sexual *freedom* involved the same rejection of moral authority as smoking. Much cigaret advertising is sexually suggestive both visually and verbally – the innocently lascivious disembodied lips embracing a cigaret, the wording *Don't filter your fun – like your pleasures big*, which the Institute for Motivational Research called 'a conscious attempt to send a latent sexual message enclosed in the language of manifest innocence'.[6] *Fun* is a theme that holds its own against the health scares: 'The friendly faces with their test tubes have been replaced mainly by lean, leather-faced macho figures in workshirts and Levi's who gamely, if a bit defensively, proclaim that they smoke because they like it. Mortality statistics be damned, they seem to imply.'[7]

Most tobacco advertising plays up the satisfactions of smoking, leaning on the themes of fashion, freedom, and fun. But various industries of late have begun to publicize a line of argument that used to be limited to board meetings and congressional hearing rooms: the practical advantages and services offered by the product and the producer. Industry groups generate good will by making known their contributions to society through institutional ads: dairy associations speaking of nutrition, power companies extolling the cheapness of electricity, oil companies advising the public on how to conserve energy. The tobacco industry has two metaphors that are useful for this, and for blunting any hostile moves on the part of government: *revenue* and *jobs*, both attached to the theme of *business* (*the economy*, etc).

Revenue is a manifestation of the *value* metaphor mentioned in the last chapter. It came on the scene when cardinals and princes tried to stamp out the use of tobacco by taxing it. They failed, but succeeded in enriching their treasuries, and tobacco sales and taxes have been a main support of governments ever since. Tobacco taxes in the United States are approximately six billion dollars a year. A number of countries – France and Italy, for example – have monopolies that bring them income from sales. The effect of this on opposition to tobacco was recently seen in France, where the Minister of Health found her hands partly tied by the fact that she had to contend with other departments of her own government.

The *job* metaphor parallels that of *value* in that it brings all occupations down to a single level, without distinctions of worth in product or service: *to have a job* is an economic common denominator. The tobacco industry employs about four million persons in agriculture, advertising, research, and marketing in the United States. The appeal to jobs is a powerful one.

The diagram below shows the network of themes and metaphors that have served the tobacco industry in its fight to preserve the use of tobacco as an institution in Western society, one that became fully ritualized at about the point where a normally considerate person no longer felt it necessary to request permission to smoke in someone else's presence. Only an apparatus capable of molding our reality for us, shielding tobacco from the misgivings that were attached to drugs in general, could have made it possible for government to subsidize that product while moving swiftly to ban the use of such things as colorings and sweeteners, on much less evidence of potential harm.

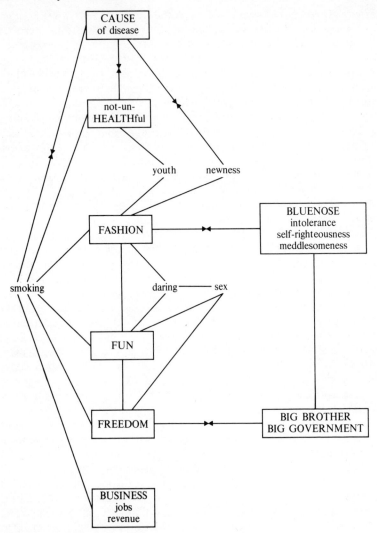

(The lines with the opposed arrows signify 'opposed to'.)

Still, one need not be unduly impressed by the apparatus alone. To succeed, it required lavish promotion. The millions spent on cigaret advertising have had the double effect of spreading the industry's message and inhibiting the opposition – where possible, silencing it altogether. Something approaching this was managed in 1969 when the tobacco companies, in what looked at the time to be a burst of altruism, agreed to give up their television advertising. Two years earlier, in response to a lawsuit under the 'fairness' doctrine whereby controversial matters require presentation of both sides, the Federal Trade Commission had ruled that television stations must carry anti-smoking messages without charge. They complied, and though the anti messages never amounted to more than a fourth of the pros, by 1969 cigaret sales in the United States were down by twelve billion. But as soon as the pro ads were withdrawn, the television stations dropped the anti-smoking ads as well. The debate on the air was silenced, and cigaret sales were soon on their way to the moon. Advertising that could no longer be carried on television was returned to print, where the fairness doctrine did not apply. Between 1970 and 1976, the magazine advertising budget for tobacco in the United States jumped from some 62 million dollars a year to almost 152 million. In that same period, a survey of leading national magazines that accept cigaret advertising showed that not one article appeared that 'would have given readers any clear notion of the nature and extent of the medical and social havoc being wreaked by the cigaret-smoking habit'.[8]

In today's society, the Second Coming will come and go unnoticed, if it is kept away from the media.

Chapter 14

School for shamans

Shamanism lives.

When a popular discussion program on Public Television gets around to language, who are the people invited and what do they talk about? The guests on one such program[1] were all notables in various fields: Agnes de Mille, choreographer, John Kenneth Galbraith, Harvard University economist and former ambassador to India, Edwin Newman, newsman with the National Broadcasting Company, and John Simon, columnist for *Esquire* magazine. No linguist – structural, generative, historical, descriptive, socio–, or psycho– – was present. There were no garbage collectors either, though their presence might have been justified by the views of one of the panelists: 'I can sympathize with people who dislike being called garbage collectors, though that is a perfectly useful and honorable calling – certainly better than that of structural linguist, semiologist, or punk-rock superstar.'[2] The same panelist drove his point home during the program:

> The idea that anything and everything goes, and what's behind it is these either disaffected or very esoteric or very sterile intellectuals in the academy . . . who have to have a profession, a profession that has not been in existence before, so things like sociology get invented. . . . But finally they invent structural linguistics and descriptive linguistics, and this means you go out into the field and you find the obscurest and the most benighted group of speakers or non-speakers and record every one of their miserable grunts and introduce it in the next edition of the Webster's dictionary. So you have the Webster's *Third* where twenty pronunciations are listed as possible, any kind of solecism and ungrammatical usage is considered all right because somebody somewhere uses it, and the result is chaos. And then you get some joker who says, 'But look, here's Shakespeare who used English badly . . .'; but poor Shakespeare, he did not have the benefit of these good dictionaries and these good grammars – grammars which we have since evolved. Now that we have those good dictionaries and those good grammars, for God's sake let us use them!

The panel of five spent a good part of the hour tending the familiar scapegoats: *hopefully, averse-adverse, imply-infer, flout-flaunt, nauseated-nauseous, comprised of-composed of, concur-agree, can't seem*. The schools were to blame, there was not enough silence, youth was rebellious, the Merriam dictionary was an obscenity.

An informed listener could be forgiven for concluding from this that shamanism is opinionated rubbish beyond saving. It would be a pity, because shamanite values are those of a majority of writers, critics, editors, and other members of the literary community, who certainly deserve to be heard – but desperately need to be jockeyed back from the extreme position they have allowed themselves to be pushed into. Fortunately there are shamans not so strident as the ones who get the most public attention. It is time to make the acquaintance of one who believes that linguists have something worth while to say, and ask whether a little more of the same might help him and his fellow shamans to improve their aim.

Our example is the author and historian Jacques Barzun, a shaman in his spare time who hates pedantry as much as he hates error. Like a number of other shamans he learned English as a second language. His book *Simple and Direct*[3] is a gem of its kind: the genre of writing and speaking well.

Barzun is at his best where linguists were for a long time at their worst in both theory and practice: language above the sentence, composition, discourse. In these higher levels, language is hardest to analyze and closest to thought, and one who has toiled for a lifetime at putting complex ideas into well-ordered paragraphs has the best right to tell us how to design with words. Here is a sample exercise, a long sentence from George Bernard Shaw which he tells us to 'scan and parse' until we 'appreciate how cunningly it tells its tale'. His comments follow the citation:

> Stranger still [Shaw writes], though Jaques-Dalcroze, like all these great teachers, is the completest of tyrants, knowing what is right and that he must and will have the lesson just so or else break his heart (not somebody else's, observe), yet his school is so fascinating that every woman who sees it exclaims: 'Oh why was I not taught like this!' and elderly gentlemen excitedly enroll themselves as students and distract classes of infants by their desperate endeavours to beat two in a bar with one hand and three with the other, and start off on earnest walks round the room, taking two steps backward whenever M. Dalcroze calls out 'Hop!'

I am not recommending that you write sentences like this – until you can do it; and even then, so long a pull at the complex form must be justified by a scene or mood to be conveyed, as it was in Shaw's sentence about Dalcroze. Its clear complexity illustrates a number of new points about structure. By the placing of its details as much as by their contents, it creates a storylike effect that cannot be obtained from the purely declarative style: 'John hit the ball. The ball hit the window. The noise brought the owner to the door. The owner scolded John.' The complex form gives and withholds information, subordinates some ideas to others more important, co-ordinates those of equal weight, and ties into a neat package as many suggestions, modifiers, and asides as the mind can attend to at one stretch.

A second point to note in Shaw's 110-word sentence is that it presents no barriers to consecutive thought. It may indeed require you to store up impressions before their full bearing can be seen, but it gives no false leads, it never compels you to return and reread. You will remember the likeness to a skeleton, which I suggested was truer of sentence structure than the analogy with a house of bricks. We feel in our long sentence the force of the better image: the sentence runs, it virtually flies, because it is not rigid but has joints; it is always on its feet and never thrown off balance by the continual insertion of fresh ideas.

Let us now ask ... what gives the necessary push to this remarkable composition of Shaw's: The first two words, 'Stranger still,' arouse curiosity and the assertion 'J.-D . . . is the completest of tyrants' makes us want to know in what ways this 'great teacher' imposes his will. But it is not only fact or substance that impels us forward; it is the third word in the sentence, 'though.' The *periodic style*, in short, is always good for creating suspense. That is why it should be reserved for matter interesting in itself and not wasted on trivial details or 'bridge passages' between important subjects.

Come now to the place where the sentence, after offering six distinct ideas, takes a turn and (so to speak) lets out its suspended breath over the remainder of its course. That turning point is YET; and we might suppose the momentum was spent, but no: by including the word *so* in the predicate – 'a school so fascinating that' – we are shoved forward again and willingly pass in review the picturesque features of the school.

The last lesson to be drawn from the example is the most valuable: what makes for smooth reading is the continuous presence and *activity* of the original subject – one only – until the comments to be made about it are exhausted. Violating this simple law produces the catchall, nonstop sentence, invertebrate and mindless: 'Soon the ruins came into sight and the porters threw down their packs, when Dr Benvoglio said: "This is a great moment;" some of us started looking for tent sites and others went searching for water, wells being said to be not far off, and even the map indicated a number, though drought of course might have dried them up.' There is no reason for that sentence to cease and desist; it pursues one like a stream of lava down a hillside.

Be warned, then: follow through! Grasp the subject and do not let go. You may, incidentally, look upon this principle as another application of right linking, and one that shows how the same uses of the mind recur in the several duties of the writer.

But you will not be able to maintain your hold unless what you begin with is the true subject of your thought, the subject that organizes everything in sight around its central importance. In our instance, that subject is 'Dalcroze,' equated with 'great teacher.' All other ideas are *predicated of it*, are its predicates – that he is a tyrant / knowing what is right / having the lesson just so / breaking his heart (not somebody else's) – YET (the turn by which we temporarily leave Mr D behind and attend to the closely related subject no 2) 'his school' / so fascinating that / 'every woman' (first subordinate subject) exclaims about it / and gentlemen enroll in it who . . . ; 'gentlemen' (a subordinate subject, like 'every woman') explains the sort of school in question, until it adroitly and logically carries us back to Mr D shouting 'Hop!' At every point the cluster of fresh facts is attached to the subject continuously in our grasp.

This faithfulness to one subject till justice has been done to it is the rule of clear thought. It governs not only the good sentence of whatever type, but also . . . the good paragraph.[4]

No linguist could improve on this tour of a Shavian sentence, and most linguists – not to mention sociologists, educationists, and other writers of heavy prose – need to take a lesson from it. But let us turn now to other parts of Barzun's instruction, covering smaller units of language – words, phrases, and sentences – where linguists are more at home. The object is to show that the shaman needs the linguist even in the limited sphere of Correct Usage.

Now the scapegoats are back in evidence. 'If you think about transitive and intransitive verbs,' Barzun writes,

you will never again mix up the common little words that a teacher once called catchfools: *sit* and *set, lie* and *lay, rise* and *raise*. Their misuse is a sure mark of illiteracy, not because the mistake is in itself more damaging than others, but because the failure to master the difference in direction argues a general inattention to the details that make the conventions of writing almost as important as those of bridge.[5]

No, they are not the mark of illiteracy because of a failure to master the feature of transitivity. They are a mark of illiteracy because they are a mark of illiteracy – they are carriers of the Stigma, shibboleths of verbal caste. If using *lay* as an intransitive verb were a mark of illiteracy because an intransitive, *lie*, is already available for that meaning, then the same should be true of *stop* because the intransitive *desist* is available. The relevant patterns are the same:

Now I lay me (lay myself) down to sleep.
*Now I lay down to sleep.
Now I lie down to sleep.
I stopped myself just in time.

I stopped just in time.
I desisted just in time.

The *lay-lie* pair belongs to a disintegrating set that includes *set-sit* and *raise-rise*, where the same confusion is found to a greater or lesser degree. (We have solved it for *raise-rise* by substituting *get up* for *rise*.) Other reflexive actions simply ignore the distinction:

He shaved himself, he shaved.
They washed themselves, they washed.
She dressed herself, she dressed.

There is no logic in *lay-lie* except the inexorable logic of linguistic change where conditions for maintaining something are highly unfavorable. Not only is the distinction semantically useless, it has other strikes against it. The importance of CONTRAST has been stressed again and again in this book, and *lie*-versus-*lay* violates it in at least three ways:

1   The two verbs share an identical form, *lay*, as present of one and past of the other: *Lay it down; I lie in bed for an hour, I lay in bed for an hour.*
2   *To lie* also means 'to tell a falsehood', and in part to avoid this meaning we add *down*. Thus *I'm tired – I think I'll sit for a while* is normal, but **I think I'll lie for a while* is not – we say *lie down*.
3   When we put *lie down* in the past tense, we get *lay down*. The *d* of *down* is easily transferred, producing *laid down*. Result: to a child learner's ear the verbs in *He laid down the load* and *He lay down* become identical.

The *lie-lay* distinction is fragile and impractical, and the price of maintaining it is too high. But that is exactly what makes it so useful as a social password: without the advantage of a proper background or proper schooling, you fail. (And if it has cost you an effort and you have mastered it, you do not want to admit that you have wasted your time.)

  PRESCRIPTION A good linguistic lesson on the conflict of closely related forms. The *lie-lay* pair is a lost cause, and others are too, or soon will be – *disinterested-uninterested, labor-belabor, hung-hanged*. The very fact of their being so constantly harped on calls the bastard brother to mind even when one has always used the forms correctly.

  How should a shaman advise his patients in a case like this? It is best to acknowledge defeat, and to say to those who seek advice, 'Many people use *lay* for *lie*, but certain others will judge you uncultured if you do. Decide for yourself what is best for you.'

  Barzun has the traditional scholar's admiration for etymology as a help in making distinctions – as indeed it is, especially for those who know enough Latin or Greek to peg derivative words to their origins.[6] But it easily leads to the etymological fallacy: *burgle* and *sculpt*, he says, are 'not bona-fide words'[7] because they are improperly derived from the noun (the noun should come from the verb: *to view, a viewer*). But if etymological pedigrees were required, much of the most colorful vocabulary in the language would go by the board – 'irregular' derivatives are almost as numerous as regular ones.

PRESCRIPTION Two lessons, one on etymology in general looking at native sources as well as Latin and Greek, and one on back-formations in particular (*sedate* from *sedation, televise* from *television, typewrite* from *typewriter* – and *burgle* from *burglar*). The genuineness of a word never depends on its etymology, though knowing an etymology gives depth and is a great aid to memory. The rules of Latin are not the rules of English, and it is foolish to impose one on the other. (Needless to say, these examples from Barzun are plucked from a context rich in practical advice. We are concerned here only with how linguistics can improve it.)

A rather common fault among shamans is to let the grammatical tail wag the usage dog. A rule – learned too well from a sixth- or seventh-grade grammar lesson – gets stuck in the head and influences judgments of right and wrong. Take the following, which Barzun identifies as the problem of the possessive case of a proper name serving as antecedent of a pronoun:

> 'Wellington's victory at Waterloo made him the greatest name in Europe' is all askew, because there is in fact no person named for the *him* to refer to. *Wellington's* is not a noun but an adjective; it corresponds to 'the *Wellingtonian* (victory)' and the only subject word is that same *victory*, with which *him* obviously doesn't go.[8]

Assume that Barzun is right, and the example sentence is a bad one. Is it bad because *Wellington's* is an 'adjective'? Barzun himself identifies it earlier as the possessive case of a proper NAME, which makes it the possessive case of a NOUN. If it is a noun, it can readily enough serve as antecedent of a pronoun. One of the two grammatical tags applied to *Wellington's* has been allowed to DEFINE the sentence as wrong. If it is wrong, the main trouble lies elsewhere, and is too tedious to unravel here. The reader may consider whether the following sound better, and try to work the problem out for himself:

> This is delicious – I would say your *mother's* pies are the things *she* does best.
> The *carpet's* deep pile is what makes *it* pleasant to walk on.[9]
> *Wellington's* victory at Waterloo made *him* the most famous man in Europe.

(One might also ask if *The victory of Wellington at Waterloo made him the greatest name in Europe* is not just as bad as the original.)

PRESCRIPTION A lesson on discourse analysis, to find out about topics and comments, subjects and predicates, and their relations. Also a lesson on comparative grammar, to get a better appreciation of grammatical categories and their relativity.

Two more examples, just to make it clear that the misjudged possessive is not an isolated instance of a poorly conceived grammar rule getting in the way of better judgment.

First, Barzun on *and* and *but*:

The first pursues and adds to the thought just preceding; the second takes away from it a part of its force or truth, modifies it by reduction: 'He was penniless, *but* he still had his violin and his grim determination to succeed.' I have chosen on purpose a *but* sentence that seems to add rather than subtract, in order to show that the seeming addition actually reduces the scope or effect of the pennilessness. Consequently, *but* is illogical whenever a true addition is made to an idea, even and especially an idea stated in the negative: 'The picked guard had never surrendered or so much as retreated, but had always carried the war into the enemy's territory.' The *but* must be *and*, because the facts about the guard form a straight addition: no surrender, no retreat, and *what is more*, carrying the war to the enemy. The temptation to use the illogical *but* comes from the frequency with which a negative sentence is followed by a true *reductive* idea. Go back to the man with the violin, changing *penniless* to *he had no money left*, and see how naturally the still correct *but* increases your certainty that it is right. We are always saying *No, but*, whence the too hasty *but* after negative wordings that are being amplified, not reduced.[10]

If we follow this advice and substitute *and* for *but*, we change the point of view. Compare the following sentence with the original:

The picked guard had never surrendered or so much as retreated, but had always stood their ground.

This, like the other one, does not express a 'what is more' but a 'but rather', 'but instead'. (In fact, the *but* in this very sentence does the same.) After a negative, it is possible for a *but* to convey not something additional but an alternative to what has gone before. Rather than surrender, the guard in the original sentence go on the offensive. In the new sentence, rather than surrender they merely hold out. To put an *and* here would be anticlimactic – holding out is the minimal way of not surrendering, and saying it at all is probably to say they did no more. But the grammar in both sentences is the same. The general function of *but* is to controvert, not to subtract. When it controverts an old idea, we have the 'alternative' or 'but rather' meaning we find here. When it controverts a new idea, it adds: Barzun's first sentence is to be interpreted 'He was penniless, but don't get the wrong idea – he still had etc'. There are languages in which the two uses of English *but* are conveyed by different words. In Spanish, the 'new idea' *but* is *pero*, the 'rather' *but* is 'sino'. English usually makes the distinction fairly clear in the rhythm of the sentence. The 'but rather' sense, where the speaker plans ahead, calls for little or no pause at the *but*; and the pitch tends to run down. Also other signs of a break between the clauses may be missing, such as a repeated subject: *I didn't wait to say good-bye, but left hurriedly. But I* would be rather out of place here. On the other hand, in *I*

didn't wait to say good-bye, but I did leave a note to explain things we find
not only the repeated *I* at the break, but the added affirmative *did* to
emphasize the unexpectedness of what follows. The kind of context
where the 'but rather' sense is easiest to see is the one in which single
words rather than clauses are counterbalanced: *He didn't drink beer but
wine.*

Barzun's misunderstanding of the grammar does not detract from his
good advice. The 'but rather' alternative is often obvious from the
context – *They didn't eat for ten days but went without food for all that
time* – and then *but* and all its works had better be avoided. The true
message is simply *Don't waste words.* A sentence like *She didn't utter a
sound but only bowed her head* wastes no words.

PRESCRIPTION An ear tuned to contrasts of rhythm and not just to
grammar and the meanings of words.

The third example of grammar as a stumblingblock is one where
Barzun realizes that the rule causes trouble but ignores his own good
advice on another point. The supposed rule is on *that* as the relative for
restrictive clauses and *which* for nonrestrictive ones:

The first house that I bought in 1960 was a duplex.
The first house, which I bought in 1960, was a duplex.

The nonrestrictive clause is sometimes called parenthetical, for the
obvious reason that it can be set off as a parenthesis rather than by
commas: *The first house (which I bought in 1960) was a duplex.* The first
sentence, with its restrictive or 'limiting' clause, implies that I bought
more than one house in 1960. Barzun points out that his own statement
introducing the topic of *which* is itself a violation of the rule:

In numerous works on grammar you will find a rule which
    appeals to those who like their guidance cut-and-dried.[11]

– obviously a restrictive clause because it defines the rule. 'The reason I
broke the supposed rule,' he says, 'is stylistic: I do not like to put close
together two *that's* of different meaning, the one a conjunction before a
subordinate clause [*that*], the other a relative pronoun before another
clause [*those*, the plural of *that*], nor do I favor the repeated sound.'[12]
This is a typical case of having a toothache in one jaw and mentally
transferring the pain to the other. Suppose we keep the word *those* where
Barzun has it, but make other changes in his sentence:

I couldn't find the rule that referred to those previously cited
    cases.

The two *th-* words, both forms of *that*, are still there, but a *which* in this
context would be less appropriate than in the other one. Why? Because
the real reason for Barzun's correct preference for *which* in his sentence
is simply the meaning of *which* in contrast with the meaning of *that*. One
of the most valuable points of *Simple and Direct* is the insistence that
becoming word-conscious is the first law of good writing. Here is a place

to apply the precept. *Which* is fundamentally interrogative – its primary use is in questions: *Which story shall I tell? That* is fundamentally demonstrative: it points to something already on the scene.[13] In the 'relative' uses of the two words these functions are still alive, though our preoccupation with the grammar of restrictive and nonrestrictive clauses blinds us to them. Notice that Barzun in his original sentence is introducing something: '*you will find* a rule' – he is drawing attention to a new QUESTION. In the substitute sentence the rule is already there, and *that* merely points back to it. When a writer – or speaker – wants to perk up his reader's – or hearer's – attention, he has *which* at his disposal. When he wants to suggest what-is-already-familiar, he uses *that*. This is indeed stylistic, but it is founded on a true semantic fact and not a foolish phonetic one – beware of rules that proscribe something because it sounds bad; there is usually a deeper reason. The story of *that, which, who,* and zero (*the dog he bought, the man he saw*) runs on to more chapters, but this is the gist of it. *Which* is used in nonrestrictive clauses not because of any rule about nonrestrictive clauses, but because such clauses are outside the flow of the sentence and call for a relative that will put the hearer on notice. If the content is presented as something already familiar, a *that* is normal even when the clause is nonrestrictive:

> The paper I handed in last week, that you liked so well, remember? – was the first one I had done entirely on my own.

As for 'cutting out the *which*'s', a trick that good stylists urge on beginning writers, its effect is not to create a grammatically better sentence but to give the reader a chance to relax, not to be constantly prodded into wide-awakeness about unimportant things – a simple matter of stylistic courtesy. Beginning writers are so intent on dotting every *i* and crossing every *t* that they tend to overtax the reader by overdoing the *which*'s.

PRESCRIPTION 'Be word-conscious!'

'Logic' is a favorite among the justifications given for shamanite rules. Generally what the shaman really means is CONSISTENCY: there is some more general fact about the language that can be elevated into a rule, with which the doubtful usage conflicts. But most apparently exceptional constructions are simply what they are, and one can either accept them as idiomatic – that is, inconsistent with major patterns in the language – or look at them as setting their own norms of consistency. One of Barzun's examples of 'errors of logic' [14] is tautology, saying again what one has already said. (Things like *sufficiently enough, at 10 am in the morning.* The third sentence in this chapter was originally worded *The invited guests were. . . .* As guests, however, they had not crashed the party or been dragged in off the street, so the tautological *invited* was dropped.) Barzun gives a number of examples, among them the venerable scapegoat *the reason is because*, corrected to *the reason is that*.[15] Presumably what makes it tautological is the fact that *reason* already includes the meaning of *because*. Curiously, those who object to *the reason is because* seldom if ever object to *the time is when* or *the place is where*, which contain the same tautology:

> The reason I did it was because I was mad.
> The place I live now is where there used to be a Congregational church.
> The time I made my worst mistake was when I had gone without sleep the night before.

With manner clauses, the construction is marginal, though possible:

> The way I did it was as (how) I had been taught to do it.

If *the reason is because* is objectionable, there must be some other explanation. A clue to the problem can be seen in the difficulty of using the expression with modifiers:

> ?The best reason for refusing is because you don't want to.
> *The reason that occurs to me is because I don't have time.
> *The reason I'm going to mention is because it's getting late.

Time and *place* are normal with modifiers:

> The best time for hunting is when it's a bit overcast.
> The place that occurs to me is where they offer full service.
> The time (place) I'm going to mention is when (where) the meeting is to be held.

The reason is because tends to be used only in a restricted type of context – as an immediate response to a *why* question, under exactly the conditions where a confusion might occur between two other possibilities:

> Why did you do it? – The reason is that I wanted to.
> Why did you do it? – Because I wanted to.

That I wanted to and *because I wanted to* serve an identical purpose – the speaker thinks of them at the same time and unintentionally creates a BLEND: *The reason is because I wanted to*. Such blends occur all the time, some so frequently that they tend to pass unnoticed, and then are imitated by other speakers and no longer are created anew each time we hear them:

> It will take five minutes to get there + It will be five minutes before we get there → It will take five minutes before we get there.
> You'll have to decide between going and staying + You'll have to decide whether to go or stay → You'll have to decide between going or staying.
> This one is just as good + This one is equally good → This one is equally as good.

As a result of this and other influences, the word *reason* is pulled in the direction of the small class of nouns that speakers tend to use adverbially. We can say *He didn't do it that way*, using the adverbialized noun *way* to modify the verb *do* – no preposition such as *in* is necessary. But we can't say **He didn't do it that manner* – the *in* must be added: *He didn't do it in that manner*. The nouns *time* and *place* pattern similarly, and *reason* is so much like them in its syntax (all are tightly related to the basic questions *how, when, where,* and *why*) that it tends to be used in the same way and we get expressions like *That was the reason he did it*, resembling *That was the way (time, place) he did it*, where these nouns contrast with others that have virtually the same meanings but require a preposition: **That was the motive (manner, occasion, location) he did it*. (Compare *That was the motive for which he did it, the occasion on which he did it*, etc.) In other words, *because* is attracted toward the 'logic' of adverbialized nouns, but is also held back by the 'logic' of nouns that have not been adverbialized. It is not a question of logic versus illogic, but of which logic – which pattern – is to prevail.[16] And to be logical, that is, consistent, the shaman who objects to *the reason is because* should also object to *That was the reason he did it*.

One should be as suspicious of the rule that invokes logic to justify a usage as of the one that invokes 'euphony'. Now and then we say something because it is logical, or because it sounds right; but more often it is logical, or sounds right, because we say it.

PRESCRIPTION Again, study the categories of words, the 'parts of speech', to get an understanding of their relativity. There is a point at which nouns and adverbs converge.

Barzun illustrates one more point. To temper one's pronouncements about usage, it is well to know something not only of English structure but of the HISTORY of the language. To say that *'em* is a shortening of *them*[17] is a common misconception that makes *'em* for *them* seem a shade worse than *'im* for *him* and *'er* for *her* (only a pedant will insist on a full-blown *h* in *Give her the money*, unless *her* is accented – see pages 95–6). The fact is that *'em* is the older form, inherited from Old English *heom*, whereas *them* was imported by Scandinavian settlers in Britain. This gives *'em* a better pedigree than *them*. But of course pedigrees are irrelevant, and *them* is now the formal equivalent of *'em* because that is how people see it.

A little history will also help with *disinterested-uninterested*, if one realizes that the *Oxford Dictionary* records as the earliest sense of *disinterested* exactly the sense that is condemned today, and for *uninterested* the sense that purists would like to require for *disinterested*.

We put this little book down tenderly, so as not to bruise the ninety per cent that is precious about it and delightful as well, and go on to cite a moral.

English is the most-analyzed language on earth – a reflection of its universality and of the spread of Anglo-American enterprise and technology around the world. Not only do a majority of linguists, whatever their native language, write and publish IN English, but many in far-flung lands write ABOUT English. Add this to the great volume of work done by British and American scholars and you have a storehouse of knowledge about the language that touches on every question of style and usage; the shaman must draw upon it if he wants to be taken seriously. One cannot speak sensibly about what OUGHT to be until one thoroughly understands what IS.

If that seems obvious, and we wonder why shamans have stayed away in droves, part of the blame must be put on the linguists themselves, and certain of their hangers-on who have climbed each new bandwagon with an eagerness that embarrasses the bandleaders. This has been mortifyingly true in the introduction of new textbooks and new programs in the schools – dressed up in the lingo of the latest theory, with publishers and school administrators sold on concepts drawn from the technical writings of structuralists, transformationists, and case grammarians, and cited because they sound authoritative, not because they are particularly useful. It is not altogether the fault of the theoretical linguist that his abstractions are taken as guides for pedagogy – though goodness knows there is much he could do to make his own language more approachable. The one who does the most mischief is the quickie revolutionary in education who is determined to be ultra-scientific and ends by being unintelligible. The shaman listens to this performance, is justifiably disgusted, and blames the theorists instead of the promoters.

Between the stratospheric theorist and the mucking opportunist is a middle layer occupied by figures whom the shaman could consult with profit. We might call them stylistic technologists and compare them to the medical technologists (developers and testers of techniques of therapy, from drugs and transplants to exercise and diet) who mediate between the sciences related to medicine and the practitioners themselves. Their business is the thoughtful examination of English, not the THEORY of English, and they are in a position to interpret – to layman and educationist – their own findings as well as those of their ivory-tower colleagues: they include lexicographers, dialectologists, grammarians, and editors of middle publications such as *Verbatim* and *American Speech*. No technology of style exists on the scale found in medicine, but such as it is it is vastly better than what the shaman usually depends on. And besides, there is no need of full dependence on middlemen – for some things one can go to the source. There is a rising generation of linguists who have gone back to the comparative study of languages around the world, seeking what they have in common to try to understand not the sideshow variety but the unity of the main attraction – the deep resemblances in the ways in which human beings lay hold of the material forms of languages to express their meanings. Some of this is accessible directly to any shaman who will take the trouble, and without a grasp of its riches most of his rule-giving is mere gesticulation. One way or another, something can be picked up for every rule the shaman can imagine.

Here are five samples – that could easily be multiplied to fifty – all from recent probings of linguists and all relevant to some concern of usage.

1. NEGATION There are two intersecting and sometimes conflicting tendencies in the way languages handle negation. One is logical: two negatives cancel each other (*It is not that I don't like you; It is impossible not to agree*). The other is a sort of 'agreement', like plural verbs agreeing with plural subjects; in a negative sentence, everything is made negative to agree with the negative idea (Spanish *No* dije *nada* a *nadie*). This second tendency has always existed in English – it was the RULE in Old English and Middle English – and is very much alive today: *He didn't do nothing to nobody.* It is considered substandard, but is not to be condemned on account of logic, which is irrelevant, since it obeys a different kind of rule. Nor should it be condemned on account of possible confusion, because the two kinds of negation are usually differentiated quite clearly. The intonation

$$\text{They} \quad \text{did}_{\text{n't say}} \overset{\text{noth}}{} {}_{\text{i}}\text{ng.}$$

with a rising tail at the end is logical negation: 'They did say something.' The same intonation with a falling *-ing*, or the intonation

$$\text{They} \quad \text{didn't say} \quad \text{noth.}_{\text{i}} {}_{\text{n}} {}_{\text{g}}$$

(in both cases the *-ing* falls) is 'agreement' negation: 'They didn't say anything.' It is substandard for reasons of etiquette, no more.

2. RAISING This principle involves such things as shifting a subject or a negative from one clause (a subordinate one) to another (a 'higher' or superordinate one):

It is hard to convince *him*.

He is hard to convince.
I think he does*n't* want it.

I do*n't* think he wants it.
The thing I want to do *first* is this.

The *first* thing I want to do is this.

The 'bad' sentence *I can't seem to do it (It seems that I can't do it)* is part of this complex and cannot be understood in isolation from it. And if this is bad, so is *He is hard to convince*, which seems to say that he, rather than the action, is hard.

3. HIGHER SENTENCES Give a shaman the following sentences at separate times, embedding each in a suitable context so as not to give your intentions away, and which one can you be pretty sure he will pounce on?

Incidentally, I saw your brother last evening.
Confidentially, the firm was about to go into bankruptcy.
Understandably, the poor fellow could only speak in incoherent syllables.
Hopefully, the weather is going to improve.
Parenthetically, it got only lukewarm reviews, though the public seemed to like it.
They are definitely going to make their position known.

You guessed it: the one with *hopefully*. Pressed for a reason, he may say, as one of the television panelists did, that it is ambiguous. And also absurd on one of its readings: how can weather improve hopefully? But the other adverbs are open to the same objection: the firm was not about to go into bankruptcy confidentially, nor could the poor fellow speak incoherently understandably. These are instances of the 'floating adverbs' described in Chapter 4 (page 33). They can be made explicit by adding a 'higher sentence', a main clause that subordinates the sentence in question:

I tell you incidentally (I make the incidental remark) that I saw your brother last evening.
I tell you confidentally that. . . .
It is understandably the case that. . . .
I say (I pray) hopefully that. . . .
I tell you parenthetically that. . . .
It is definitely the case that. . . .

So why is *hopefully* resented? Surely because it is NEW (and maybe also because it is borrowed from German). The others were stereotyped in the long ago and we are used to them.

4 TOPICALIZATION How sentences are linked together is a problem no shaman-stylist can ignore, and to understand it one needs some awareness of what linguists have been learning about topics and comments (see pages 30, 123–4). In a story or essay, each sentence tends to develop the plot or argument by adding successive new material. What has gone before is retained in memory as background. But frequently it is not enough to remember, and some explicit tie with preceding context is added. The natural place for it to go is at the beginning, since that puts it closest to what it refers to. And the natural way to pronounce it is with

relatively low emphasis, since it is already at least partially known. So we get a sequence like

> A healthy suspicion is advisable here. If you are trusting, you will be taken in.

If you are trusting is the topic of the second sentence, referring to the suspicion in the first. But there is another possibility, very common in speech:

> A healthy suspicion is advisable here. You will be taken in, if you are trusting.

Here the topic has been put at the end, and is distinguished as topic by being spoken at a low pitch and probably with a terminal rise. A writer who wants a sentence with punch will generally avoid putting flabby elements at the end, and will prefer the first of these two arrangements, which also fits the reader's expectation (see the next section) of having the main accent at the end. But if a less emphatic ending should be desired, then the other arrangement is available. What matters is knowing how the effects are achieved.

Topics and comments tell us something else about good writing. Since the function of the topic is to get hold of the sentence in the most comfortable and comprehensible way, it needs to fit the hand obviously and comfortably – the looser stuff should come in the comment. Yet many writers behave as if the way to pick up a duster were by the feathers instead of the handle: they insist on packing the bulk of the information in the topic – which is usually the grammatical subject – rather than in the comment. Here is an example of an overloaded subject:

> *Expression of the degree of overt recognition of social class distinctions necessary for correct usage of politeness formulae* changed over the nineteenth century.[18]

This can be turned around, with *century* as the topic – periods of time are obvious and easily grasped:

> During the nineteenth century there were changes in the way politeness formulas were viewed – in how explicitly they depended on the recognition of class distinctions in order to be used correctly.

The reader will notice several other changes, to get away from the sociolinguistic jargon.

5 INTONATION The examples just given show its importance, as do the one with negation above and the one with *only* on page 6. Intonation (not to mention other elements of language 'above the word') is the area least known to people with a letter-bound education, including shamans – despite the fact that it is a rich hunting-ground for mistakes. The most conspicuously freakish thing that great numbers of people are most likely to hear in today's spoken English is probably the

misplaced accents in the speech of radio and television announcers and newscasters. They place accents with a sort of mechanical emphasis, which affects their diction in two ways. First, the emphasis may favor an auxiliary verb or a preposition or some other insignificant element over a substantially meaningful word. Doing this makes you sound forceful without committing you to anything:

> It was for someone ELSE *becomes*
>> It was FOR someone else.
> In the afternoon we can expect local SHOWers *becomes*
>> In the afternoon we CAN expect local showers.
> The debate will be held as PLANNED *becomes*
>> The debate WILL be held as planned.

Accent on an auxiliary verb is normal, of course, when the speaker wants to put someone right who has made a false statement; the radio announcer sounds as if he were perpetually disagreeing with someone.

The second effect is one of overdoing climax. As we saw in the preceding section, a sentence can be given a bigger bang by putting the accent closer to the end. Speakers often do this unconsciously when they get carried away by the force of what they are saying. A radio report of a newspaper interview with President Jimmy Carter quoted him as saying

> The reason for the increase [in the number of persons on the White House staff] is tempoRARy.[19]

A radio announcer said

> She was so weak that she could not keep her head upRIGHT.[20]

The normal accents of course are *TEMporary* and *UPright*. Announcers do this constantly without regard for the normal pronunciation of compounds or for whether the accented word is entitled to any semantic prominence. For example, the word *matter* belongs to a class of compounding elements that should not be accented, yet we hear

> What they need is some reading MATter.

in place of

> What they need is some READing matter.

Other examples heard on radio:

> Blanche is expected to reach hurricane STAtus today.
> It melted telephone lines in the ARea.
> It went into efFECT today.
> I'm a professional WOMan.

The same tendency can be observed when people read aloud, which may be one reason why announcers do it so much. The shaman who knows this can give an important bit of advice to writers. The reader will always impose an intonation contour on what he reads, so it is well to arrange

the written words to agree with the contour most likely to be imposed.
Here is a sentence that disregards this rule:

> The Journal of the American Medical Association . . . adds, 'Instead
> of measles, vaccination will be considered essential.'[21]

The reader wants to put the accent on the last substantially meaningful
word, *essential*. But the important word – the one that contrasts with
measles – is *vaccination*. It should be maneuvered to where the reader
expects the accent to go: *Instead of measles, we must have vaccination.*[22]

In the end, shamans and linguists share a desire: that people learn to
be more interested in, and to care more about, their language. The
shaman tends to view the common object as an art form – to be
cherished for good taste and fine distinctions. The linguist is more apt to
see it as a social phenomenon, with practical means adjusted to practical
ends. But it is the same language; there is no real separation. The linguist
would have to concede that if, say, such distinctions as those between
infer and *imply* and between *substitute* and *replace* could be maintained
without neglecting more important things and without creating a hypercorrect reaction, the effort would be worth while: distinctions are what
language is about, and the careless or hasty speaker or writer who
initiates a chain of confusions does not help us when we need to convey
precise meanings. There are countless occasions when a writer or
speaker STRIVES to be precise, and will censor his own production if he
has time: 'No, I guess I didn't mean X, I meant Y.' And will accept the
editing of others: 'That IS better: I recognize it now.' Take the current
tendency to allow the word *minimal* to absorb the meaning of *at least*,
resulting in contradictory senses. A social anthropologist wrote this
sentence: *The channels are organized so that minimal accuracy is
maintained.* Did he mean 'the least possible accuracy' or 'at least some
accuracy'? If there is any justification for a list of errors – list of TRAPS
would be a better notion – *minimal* belongs on it.

The fact that many normative statements are foolish does not mean
that as many more are not welcomed for their usefulness by speakers
and writers who might otherwise do something contrary to their
intentions. We are constantly correcting one another, if not directly,
then by example. We need our shamans, if they will stay within the realm
of the possible and the practical, and will accept help in mapping that
realm.

As for the linguists, they are by no means blameless in the running
shaman-linguist dispute. One fallacy is peculiarly theirs when they press
their case too hard, the hindsight fallacy – a bit of perverted reasoning
that runs along the lines of a familiar domestic game:

> 'Dear, aren't you glad now that you didn't marry Thelma Lutz?' (or,
> decide to be a chemical engineer; or, join the Marines; or, run away
> from home when you were twelve, as you were thinking of doing.)

'Yes, I'm lucky I married you.' (decided to be a CPA, joined the
Navy, stayed home with Mom and Dad.)

Using Korzybsky's indexes, the gladness of you $_{1980}$ has nothing to do
with the prospects for gladness of you $_{1934}$ – you are what you have
become, and the other term of the comparison, what you MIGHT have
been had you taken that other road, is simply absent. The linguist with
historical training is wise after the fact. He looks at a form such as *want*
meaning 'desire' and remarks how wasted the efforts were (assuming
there were any, in the early part of the eighteenth century) to preserve it
in its original sense of 'lack'. It was 'inevitable' that *want* should come to
mean 'desire'. History decreed it. But who knows? There was no real
need for it – the language has *wish, desire*, and *crave* in much the same
sense (with delicate distinctions) and might as well have kept *want* as a
synonym of *lack* (with delicate distinctions). There must have been a
period of confusion, when people were unsure of your meaning if you
said *I want ten shillings* – do you desire ten shillings or are you ten
shillings short? – certainly no advantage to communication. A little
more insistence at the time, a little more self-correcting or correcting of
others, might have preserved the distinction and perhaps did postpone
the reckoning. History is not an irresistible force. The linguist is as
wrong to personify it as the shaman is to ignore it. Which points us to a
moral that lies squarely in the middle of the road: at any moment in the
history of a language, it is the speaker's duty to cater to the need and
comfort of the hearer. We might call this the law of communicative
responsibility. Like all other laws, it requires constant reinterpretation,
as attitudes change and language evolves.

Chapter 15

An ecology of language

Fifty years ago you could drink from that stream. And every dark cranny under the submerged stones hid a crayfish that would goggle at you and back hurriedly away toward the next hiding place if you exposed his lair. The sycamore held its leaves till late autumn, and the spring near the road was cold and clear in mid-August.

Now the crayfish and the sycamore are gone, and the barbed wire dipping into the water below the crossing snags a perpetual beard of algae. The spring is a muddy leak and a brown trickle as it joins the current. For a generation, phosphate and nitrogen fertilizers have drained into the basin from the farms upstream.

Pollution. All streams carry it – water, air, light, sound, language. A beach is declared unsafe, a smog alert is issued for people to stay indoors, a stargazer sells his telescope because of the city glare, a community protests the siting of a new airport. What then are we to do with channels of communication reduced to a state of permanent aneurysm? What happens to a reality seen only through representations of it when those representations are permanently dimmed – or, worse, when some of them, under a control beyond our reach, come through with crystal clarity, and the rest are blacked out?

The first line of defense is knowing that there is no ultimate defense. Conscious and unconscious deception is all around us, an unavoidable ingredient of every utterance warmed by a human voice. So beware of it. Laws may be passed against it, but laws can be evaded, and the more explicit the laws, the more subtle the evasions. After the National Academy of Sciences revealed that no fewer than 2800 of the drugs sold in the United States are ineffective, and the Federal Trade Commission reacted by clamping down on advertising claims,[1] the manufacturers began to make their claims less specific. In the fashion of old-time nostrums, the drugs were said to be good for *malaise, dysfunction, unhappiness, irregularity, that rundown feeling.*[2]

Advertisers are prone to dismiss charges of deviousness, pointing to outstanding failures of ad campaigns to prove that the public taste is arbiter after all. The chairman of the board of Foote, Cone and Belding, the agency that handled the Ford Motor Company's Edsel publicity, said after the Edsel's collapse,

> The plain fact . . . is that advertising is totally incapable of exercising the Svengali-like control over the buying habits of the public that the propounders of the subliminal influence concept claim. . . . The public cannot be cajoled, mesmerized or driven into buying a product it doesn't want.[3]

A true statement, certainly, but also a truism: the public will not desire to buy what it does not desire to buy. But desires can be implanted, and that surely accounts for much of the annual expenditure on advertising – thirty-seven billion dollars in 1977 in the United States alone. Keeping one's head above water in this flood calls for a subtlety of detection to match the subtlety of the deception. When a newspaper, editorializing against a ballot proposal, heads the editorial with the words *Look at Prop. X's Fine Print*,[4] the apparently innocent wording must be tested not for what it says but for what it implies. *Read the full text* would have carried the same advice, but *fine print* instils suspicion. It has become a cliché for trickery in legal contracts – insurance policies, for example, where all the ills and conditions not covered are spelled out. (In this particular instance, the text of the official Voters Pamphlet had the same size of type throughout.)

But mere awareness that the channels of communication are clogged is no substitute for a sturdy effort to clear them. Awareness is passive defense at the receiving end. If what is being communicated is more noise than message, it is the transmitting end that needs attention. And this calls for challenging the self-interest of the forces that control one-way communication, the print and broadcast media. It is a formidable task, because they – like their advertisers – are businesses run for profit, whose power grows with its concentration. Where entertainment and information once came primarily from newspapers, newsmagazines, photojournals, magazines, radio, movies, and – for children – comic books, now

> television has collapsed ALL these functions within that single box. And to a remarkable extent these functions are ALL performed by three networks, which are extensions of three highly profitable corporations whose own revenues, in turn, come from the most powerful corporate interests in American life.[5]

Though newspapers number many thousands, they too have been reduced by mergers and suspensions to the point that many large cities are served by a single daily – not to mention the consolidation of the wire services and the sheer boilerplate with which smaller papers serve their readers. The fewer the voices, the easier it is to control or to mute them. 'The possession of huge sums of money is the dominant method of access' to the media.[6] In 1978 the government of Argentina gave an American public relations firm around a million dollars for publicity to 'offset the image of oppressiveness and to attract favorable attention . . . for the World Cup games'.[7] That same year the American tobacco companies 'poured nearly $6 million into a high-powered advertising campaign' to defeat the California proposal to limit smoking in public buildings – 'the most expensive political campaign in California history',[8] in which the tobacco companies outspent the opposition ten to one – and achieved their objective with 54 per cent of the vote, close enough to leave little doubt that the outcome was determined by the paid-for propaganda. The public relations department of US Steel in 1968 had a budget for the year of four million dollars and a staff of almost two hundred executives, secretaries, and clerks.[9] Nor should we forget government itself, one of the largest subsidizers of paid advertising with its 'public service' messages.[10]

To challenge the media is only to demand what one of the founders of modern public relations believed the public was entitled to. As president of the American Telephone and Telegraph Company, Theodore N. Vail earned a reputation for following his own advice: 'It is not only the right but the obligation of all individuals, or aggregations of individuals, who come before the public, to see that the public have full and correct information.'[11] Most admen fundamentally want the same thing, and failure to live up to it makes advertising one of the most insecure of professions and advertisers among the most prone to ulcers.

> One adman asked, 'If the force of over $17 billion of advertising expenditures a year approves self-serving lies as permissible lies, how does that affect the nation's ethics, the moral standards of children and adults?'
> The obvious answer is a hard one for admen to swallow.[12]

The adman's conscience is potentially a powerful ally.

The method of the challenge can only be political, but its nature is linguistic. It consists in demanding that information passing through the one-way channels of the media be in the form of testable propositions. There are many ways to approach this complex problem, but four will suffice to frame it.

First, messages must be clear. Here the shaman comes into his own, for clear language is palatable as well as understandable. An honest message does not have to sacrifice style or humor, and if it tries to do so, it will become less intelligible. A conscientious and properly self-critical commentator can gauge the total effect of what he writes or says, and irony or paradox along the way will not mislead the receiver. All the shaman's skills come into play to accomplish this – even his attention to scapegoats, which as distractors IN PUBLIC COMMENTARY may need to be avoided.

Second, the message must identify itself with what it says, not with who says it. We have no need of professional jargon as guarantee of the importance, authority, or authenticity of the source. Once again the shamans are the best guides, or at least the editors and critics among them, who have to contend professionally with gobbledegook.

Third, the message has to be free of snares – to shun biases as much as possible, or, if it allows them, to contrive to cancel them out. Now it is the linguist's turn. All that he knows about presuppositions and entailments, concealed agents, existentials, deletions, hidden sentences of all kinds, question-begging epithets, and the running commentary of intonation and gesture – this must be brought to bear, and as much more as he can learn, from logicians and psychologists, of every form of indirection in word and structure. Propositional language calls for dragging prejudgments to the surface. When an advertiser reifies a product with a name that sounds as if it could not have been invented unless the product were one of life's specific realities, we are not to be taken in by it – *instant dispersal Daxaids; direct-from-laboratory processing; new one-action Swift carpet shampoo; Condor Sliced, the flake with the flavor*[13] – things half of whose substance is in the words that designate them. When a million small acts of improvidence are added together – consumers demanding luxury imports and higher wages to pay for them, sellers demanding higher profits, governments printing money to pay off their internal debts, reckonings postponed while interest on them mounts – the creation of a verbal monster called *inflation* will not serve to shift the responsibility to some monster impersonal agent. When a US president addresses an audience in a tobacco state and calls for 'an accurate and enlightened education program to make the smoking of tobacco even more safe than it is today',[14] he needs to be reminded that his *even* is the trick of a verbal smuggler. (Just as, to turn the spotlight on ourselves, the epithet *smuggler* makes the act seem worse than to call it *a trick of verbal smuggling*.) When clichés are bandied about they must be caught and unmasked – *The power to tax is the power to destroy* is matched for emptiness by *The power to tax is the power to build*. Some of this is common ground for linguist and shaman. Obfuscation reaches back to jargon.

Fourth, there must be no sanctuaries, no sacred precincts guarded by taboos or traditional courtesies from which the message cannot be sent because propositional probing is forbidden. This covers more than the ritual guarding of what is off limits to inquiry. There is an elaborate scheme of silences that affects the whole world of the media, more intense in some places than in others, but with pockets of things-not-talked-about everywhere. Television is a Pollyanna world:

> The high frequency of good/better/best [in advertising] contrasts with the low frequency of its antonym bad/worse/worst. In fact against nearly a hundred occurrences of *good* there was not a single instance of *bad* in the television sample. If *bad* is avoided, the pejorative counterparts of adjectives of more enthusiastic praise (ghastly, dreadful, etc as opposed to wonderful, delicious, etc) are even less likely.[15]

The quintessential television entertainment is the soap opera, in which there are no social problems, only personal ones. Marriage, divorce, the commission of violent crime and the tracking of criminals, family conflicts and rivalries, the doctor, lawyer, and priest each coping with some small, detached crisis – these are stock subjects that are safe because they do not ruffle the feelings of sponsors or governments. The same is true of sports. But poverty, political unrest, unscrupulous medical practices, canting preachers, chauvinistic generals, shadowy financiers, government agents snooping in private files, policemen moonlighting as security guards, professors neglecting classes to run after government contracts – these conditions and types are never part of the ENTERTAINMENT side of television – the figments of mass viewing that substitute for the way things are – except humorously or by indirection, or when the miscreants can be shown as individual transgressors whose faults and weaknesses are their own and not of their class or of the system. Television has no Dickens (though of course it has Dickens – poverty in nineteenth-century London is a safe subject), no Zola or Dreiser, even on a small scale. Optimism is essential to business, and business controls the pursestrings.

Still, television is as much a symptom as a cause. No one likes to dwell on the unpleasant, but where *progress* is a fetish, social unpleasantness becomes virtually taboo. Lock up the unruly Blacks, put the misfits in psychiatric wards, drive the beggars off the sidewalks, keep the cripples out of sight, make it illegal for drunks to sleep in the park, delegate the butchering of animals to slaughterhouses, make death and burial a cosmetic ritual, dress up fortune as a Santa Claus with giveaway programs – the seamy side is neither to be seen nor talked about, and society itself is a sort of euphemism on a grand scale. With the best will in the world and the most careful choice of words, it is difficult enough to draw a picture of reality as it presents itself through our foggy vision in all its variety and instability, without having to surmount the barriers erected against the free flow of messages. There should be no off-limits to language. To speak only half the truth is to speak in half-truths.

These four steps have a prerequisite: to make language serve the flow of messages as it should, we must be free to talk about language itself. We must build the fabled fire in the wooden stove and use language to expose language. Our courts, bureaus, businesses, and advertisers must be held accountable not only for what they do but for what they say and the way they say it. Language is no one's personal domain, and there should be no diffidence toward invading it, no embarrassment at pointing out an abuse of the passive or an underlying structure of presuppositions or a semantic net that has been spread to catch some poor fish. It should be as natural to comment on the linguistic probity of public figures as to comment on their financial probity – in both cases they are manipulating symbolic systems that are the property of everyone.

Four ways of achieving foursquare messages, and hoping ever to achieve them fully is doubtless a millennial hope. But one goal is within reach, for it has been attained in limited ways. Bias cannot be eliminated, human nature and the nature of language being what they are, and attempting to reduce it only tends to drive it further underground; but it can be countered. The airways have been declared public property, and the fairness doctrine is falteringly applied. We saw an instance of effective counter-propaganda when the anti-cigaret forces, with only a fraction of the broadcast time enjoyed by their opponents, successfully opposed cigaret advertising on television. The same happened to the overconfidence of voiceprint enthusiasts when they knew they were going to be challenged in court (page 112). Just knowing that a fair and cogent brief is going to be presented by the opposition is enough sometimes to discourage those who are not quite sure of their own case. There is something at least to be said for the RELATIVE power of truth. Given bias against bias, and EQUAL ACCESS to make the contest fair, the public can make informed and rational choices. Language was meant for talking WITH people more than for talking TO them; revitalize the *con*– part of conversation and there will be less to fear from the self-interest that plagues every spoken word.

The problem of equal access to public language is the problem of distributive justice everywhere. In language as in economics we now have justice of a different kind:

> Mostly our thought and regulations about economic justice have to do with what is called 'commutative justice,' making sure that different classes of people have an equal right to make contracts, to borrow and lend. It is harder for us to deal with the initial inequities in distribution . . . .[16]

Anyone is free to buy radio and television time or to place an ad in a newspaper or magazine, but to counter any sort of powerful opposition one has to outspend it. The forum is available only at so much per minute or column inch. A familiar jibe at monopolies is that if it were practical to get a corner on the atmosphere and package it for sale, everyone would pay for the privilege of breathing. It has been so long since the public lands were fenced off that we have forgotten the rape once performed on them – something as absurd to our nomadic forebears (and to an Alaskan Eskimo today – see pages 150–1) as the rape of the air. Yet public language, though we think of it as air-like and free, has been cut into sections and quarter sections and parceled out as if it were so much real estate. Not that there was ever any Eden where language is concerned – the ownership of public language has been an outgrowth of language going public; by their existence in their present form, the media imply heavy capital investment. But that does not mean that they should remain inaccessible, any more than private ownership of a beach signifies that it cannot be taken by eminent domain. If public ownership deserves to be asserted anywhere, that place is language – enough of it, at least, to prevent annihilation of a point of view through nothing more than silence.

Active control through language has become in our time the most devastating form of control, for it works at the source. Language is the extended arm, developed through millennia of evolution, by which our race has managed nature and built cooperative societies. It is material as well as instrument, a vicarious world in which anything can be arranged through verbal plans, then transferred to reality. Now the plans must include that part of reality that is language itself, to ensure that all may share as architects of the rest.

To make a beginning, language must take its place alongside diet, traffic safety, and the cost of living as something that everyone thinks about and talks about. 'Tell me how much a nation knows about its own language,' writes John Ciardi, 'and I will tell you how much that nation cares about its own identity.'[17]

Notes to chapters

Notes to Chapter 1

1. Discussed on page 46.
2. *I want it all* is possible, but more demanding.
3. Laurence Urdang in *Verbatim* 3 (1977) 4.6.
4. *Usage in Dictionaries and Dictionaries of Usage.* University, Alabama: American Dialect Society, 1975, p122.
5. 'Such condemnations, if voiced frequently and vigorously enough, usually carry great weight among individuals aspiring to recognition as members of a well-educated, highly literate élite.' *Ibid, p* 127.
6. In *James B. McMillan: Essays in Linguistics by His Friends and Colleagues.* University, Alabama: University of Alabama Press, 1977, 53–71, *p* 69.
7. Garden City, New York: Doubleday Anchor Books, 1960.

Notes to Chapter 2

1. William S. Condon and Louis W. Sander, 'Synchrony Demonstrated between Movements of the Neonate and Adult Speech', *Child Development* 45 (1974) 456–62.
2. 'La Vive Voix: Dynamique et Changement', *Journal de Psychologie* 1976, Nos 3–4, 273–304.
3. See Erving Goffman, 'Response Cries', *Language* 54 (1978) 787–815.
4. Walburga von Raffler-Engel, 'We Do Not Talk Only with Our Mouths', *Verbatim* 4 (1977) 3.1–3, *p* 2.
5. See D. Robert Ladd, Jr, 'Stylized Intonation', *Language* 54 (1978) 517–40.
6. George Esper, 'Doctor Tries to Find How Autistic Child Sees World', AP release, Los Angeles *Times*, 19 November 1978, Part I *pp* 2, 29.
7. See Gordon W. Hewes, *Language Origins: A Bibliography.* Boulder, Colorado: Department of Anthropology, University of Colorado, 1971.
8. See for example their 'Teaching Sign Language to a Chimpanzee', *Science* 165 (1969) 664–72.
9. See Francine Patterson, 'Conversation with a Gorilla', *National Geographic* 154 (1978) 438–65.
10. See *Psychology Today* 13 (1979) 6.63–91 for editorial introduction and articles by H. S. Terrace and Thomas A. and Jean Umiker Sebeok.
11. *Ibid, p* 63.

Notes to Chapter 3

1. 'Process, System, and Symbol: A New Anthropological Synthesis', *Daedalus* Summer 1977, 61–80, *p* 77.
2. Randolph Quirk, 'Taking a Deep Smell', *Journal of Linguistics* 6 (1970) 119–24.
3. Jacob Korg, 'Hopkins' Linguistic Deviations', *PMLA* 92 (1977) 977–86, p 977.
4. *discretion, ravaged, fob + foist*

Notes to Chapter 4

1. It isn't that the indirect object with *to* means exactly the same thing as the indirect object without *to*, only that the difference is so slight that it can be ignored much of the time. The *to* means what it says – there is someone or something to or toward which or whom something is directed; if there is nothing really directed, nothing received, then *to* is not used:

   He gave me a book = He gave a book to me.
   He gave me a look   *He gave a look to me.

2. Like the indirect object, the passive has a meaning, which differs from that of the active: it speaks of something 'really happening to' the thing or person involved in the action. Take the active sentence *I met George at the airport*. It can refer to either a casual encounter or a pickup, as in

   I was at the airport the other day and happened to meet George.
   I arranged to meet George at the airport to take him to his hotel.

   Only the second of the two senses is normal in the passive: *George was met at the airport*. Although the contrast is rather tenuous with certain verbs, this characteristic of the passive is nevertheless a universal tendency. See Edward L. Keenan, 'Foregrounding and Backgrounding: The Case of Passive', in Timothy Shopen et al (eds), *Language Typology and Field Work* (to appear; *p* 27 of MS).
3. Derek Bickerton, 'Discourse and Syntax: Two and Indivisible?' Symposium on Discourse and Syntax, University of California at Los Angeles, November 1977, *p* 19. (Unpublished paper.)
4. Susan Steele, 'Word Order Variation: A Typological Study', in Joseph H. Greenberg (ed), *Universals of Human Language, Vol. 4, Syntax*. Stanford, California: Stanford University Press, 1978, 585–623, *p* 590.
5. Henri Charrière, *Papillon*, translated by June P. Wilson and Walter B. Michaels. New York: Pocket Books, 1971, *p* 83.
6. The symbol ʔ indicates a glottal stop, the sound that occurs in the middle of the English interjection *oh–oh!* when it means 'don't' or 'we have made a mistake'.
7. Robert F. Longacre, 'The Paragraph as a Grammatical Unit', in Talmy Givón (ed), *Syntax and Semantics, Vol 12, Discourse and Syntax*. New York: Academic Press, 1979, 115–34, *p* 120.
8. Edwin Ardener, 'Some Outstanding Problems in the Analysis of Events', in Mary LeCron Foster and Stanley H. Brandes (eds), *Symbol as Sense: New Approaches to the Analysis of Meaning*. New York: Academic Press, 1980, 301–21, p 309.

Notes to Chapter 5

1. Dr Peter J. Steincron, Wilmington, Delaware *Morning News*, 25 February 1969, *p* 21.
2. Wallace Chafe, *Meaning and the Structure of Language*. Chicago: University of Chacago Press, 1970, *p* 31.

Notes to Chapter 6

1. This sentence was actually an EXPLANATION of a more cryptic remark in Geoffrey Lincoln's *No Moaning at the Bar*. It is from Randolph Quirk, *The Use of English*. London: Longman, 1962, *p* 23.
2. 'Who does he think he is?'
3. *An Uttermost Part*. Chicago: Moody Press, 1971, *p* 88.
4. Jean-Pierre Goudaillier, 'A Nouveau les Puristes contre le Langue', *La Linguistique* 13 (1977) 2.85–98.
5. Barney Miller Show, 8 December 1977.
6. Quoted by Walter M. Brasch, 'Journalist Attitudes about American Black English: Ignorance, Bias, or Something Else?'. Paper at meeting of American Dialect Society, San Francisco, California, December 1975, *p* 13 of MS.
7. Examples from William Labov, 'Contraction, Deletion, and Inherent Variability of the English Copula', *Language* 45 (1969) 715–62.
8. The standard can manage this, somewhat ambiguously, by maneuvering the adverb *now*, with and without an accent: *Is John WORKing NOW?* for being busy at the moment, *Is John WORKing now?* for the steady job. Plain *Is John working?* makes no distinction.
9. Geneva Gay and Roger D. Abrahams, 'Does the Pot Melt, Boil, or Brew? Black Children and White Assessment Procedures,' *Journal of School Psychology* 11 (1973) 330–40, *p* 333.
10. *Ibid, p* 331.
11. *Ibid, p* 338.
12. J. T. Chandler and J. Plakos, 'Spanish-speaking Pupils Classified as Educable Mentally Retarded', *Integrated Education* 7 (1969) 6.28–33.
13. Lorene C. Quay, 'Language, Age, and Intelligence-test Performance in Disadvantaged Black Children', *Child Development* 45 (1974) 463–68. Peggy A. Long and John J. Anthony, 'The Measurement of Mental Retardation by a Culture-specific Test', *Psychology in the Schools* 11 (1974) 310–12.
14. This is the so-called 'Pygmalion Effect'. See Robert Rosenthal, 'The Pygmalion Effect Lives', *Psychology Today* 7 (1973) 56–63. These experiments have been challenged.
15. UPI dispatch, Los Angeles *Times*, 13 September 1978, Part 1-B *p* 3.
16. William Marckwardt, 'The English Language: A Long View', in Leonard F. Dean, Walter Gibson, and Kenneth G. Wilson (eds), *The Play of Language*. London: Oxford University Press, 1971, *pp* 8–18.
17. Washington, DC *Post*, 'Outlook' section, 29 May 1977, *p* B8.
18. Geneva Smitherman, 'Writing Right but Not Doing Right', in *Conference Proceedings: Money, Power, and Language*, University of Southern Mississippi, 16 October 1976, 1–20, *p* 3.

19. Shirley Brice Heath, 'Language and Politics in the United States', *Georgetown University Round Table on Languages and Linguistics 1977*, 267–97, *p* 282.
20. *Ibid, p* 279.
21. Adebisi Afolayan, 'Acceptability of English as a Second Language in Nigeria', in Sidney Greenbaum (ed), *Acceptability in Language*. The Hague: Mouton, 1977, 13–25, *p* 14.
22. Quirk, *op cit, p* 12.
23. Jim Quinn, 'Wonderful English Teachers and Other Word Snobs', San Francisco, California *Chronicle*, 'Sunday Punch' section, 15 January 1978, *p* 7.
24. Palo Alto, California *Times*, 5 February 1979, *p* 1.
25. For example, H. Stephen Straight, 'Comprehension versus Production in Linguistic Theory', *Foundations of Language* 14 (1976) 525–40.
26. In *Harper Dictionary of Contempory Usage*, 1975, *p* xii.
27. Shirley Brice Heath, 'Social History and Sociolinguistics', *The American Sociologist* 13 (1978) 84–92, *pp* 87–90.
28. Both passages cited by Marckwardt, *op cit, p* 9.
29. 'The Death of Words', *English* 7 (1948) 56–9.
30. Actually *They all took one another's classes* and *They (both) took each other's classes*, if we preserve the shamanite distinction between more than two and just two. But that distinction – to the extent that it existed – was already lost before plurality itself began to fade. Besides, by shaman's standards *each other* should be regarded as incorrect – *either other* would be the historically correct form for two.
31. Charles A. Ferguson, 'Diglossia', *Word* 15 (1959) 325–40, *p* 330.
32. Quoted by Brasch, *op cit, p* 1.

Notes to Chapter 7

1. K. A. McElhanon, 'Idiomaticity in a Papuan (Non-Austronesian) Language', *Kivung* 8 (1975) 103–44, *p* 109.
2. Dina Dahbany-Miraglia, 'Verbal Protective Behavior among Yemenite Jews', *Working Papers in Yiddish and East European Jewish Studies*, No 13: July, 1975, YIVO Institute for Jewish Research, New York.
3. New York *Times*, 11 October 1976, *p* 31.
4. *Ibid*, 20 August 1975, *p* 79.
5. *Ibid*, 11 April 1976, VI, *p* 4.
6. 1967 edn, Vol 6, *p* 528.
7. 'Table of the Springs of Action', in Paul McReynolds (ed), *Four Early Works on Motivation*. Gainesville, Florida: Scholars' Facsimiles and Reprints, 1969, 481–512, *p* 481.
8. Charles E. Osgood, 'Conservative Words and Radical Sentences in the Semantics of International Politics', *Studies in the Linguistic Sciences* (Department of Linguistics, University of Illinois) 8 (1979).
9. Commencement address, University of California, Berkeley, 1977.
10. Samm S. Baker, *The Permissible Lie*. Cleveland and New York: World, 1968, *p* 38.
11. Victor Turner, 'Process, System, and Symbol: A New Anthropological Synthesis', *Daedalus*, Summer 1977, 61–80, *p* 65.

12. *General Systems Theory*. New York: Braziller, 1968, *p* 215.
13. Hans Fummer, in *UCLA Monthly*, Los Angeles, California, July-August 1977, *p* 2.
14. 'Louis S. B. Leakey and Robert Ardrey in a Dialogue on Man, the Killer', *Psychology Today* 6 (1972) 4.73–85, *p* 84.

Notes to Chapter 8

1. San Francisco radio KGO, 17 May 1978, 9.55 pm.
2. 'The Limits of Awareness'. Lecture at Harvard Anthropology Seminar, Cambridge, Massachusetts, 1 November 1977. See also, for the ability to 'talk about talk', Kathy Hirsh-Pasek, Lila R. Gleitman, and Henry Gleitman, 'What Did the Brain Say to the Mind? A Study of the Detection and Report of Ambiguity by Young Children', in A. Sinclair, R. J. Jarvella, and W. J. M. Levelt, *The Child's Conception of Language*. Berlin and Heidelburg: Springer Verlag, 1978, 97–132.
3. Carol Myers Scotton, 'Strategies of Neutrality: Language Choice in Uncertain Situations', *Language* 52 (1976) 919–41.
4. 'Table of the Springs of Action', in Paul McReynolds (ed), *Four Early Works on Motivation*. Gainesville, Florida: Scholars' Facsimiles and Reprints, 1969, 481–512, *p* 488.
5. San Francisco *Examiner*, 29 January 1978, *p* 1.
6. 'Terms for Low Intelligence', *American Speech* 49 (1974) 197–209.
7. Cited by Edward D. Seeber, 'Franklin's "Drinkers Dictionary" Again', *American Speech* 15 (1940) 103–5.
8. *The Marble Faun*, Chapter 1.
9. 'Humpty-Dumptian Semantics', *The Progressive*, February 1978, *pp* 6–7.
10. Biased nouns include many that do not quite reach the status of epithets – they fail to show degrees – but are nevertheless derogatory. Compare *female* with *crybaby*:

   > *She is such a female that you always have to be sympathetic with her.
   > She is such a crybaby that you always have to be sympathetic with her.

   or *shrink* with *quack*:

   > *He is such a shrink that I don't trust him to treat me.
   > He is such a quack that I don't trust him to treat me.

11. Review of Fionn MacColla, *Too Long in This Condition* (*Ro fhada mar so a tha mi*), in *Scottish Literary Journal*, Supplement 3 (1976) 47–9, *p* 49.
12. See Bolinger, 'Gradience in Entailment', *Language Sciences* 41(1976) 1–12.
13. Barney Miller Show, 5 January 1978.
14. Julia Stanley and Susan Robbins, 'Forced Inference: Uses and Abuses of the Passive', *Papers in Linguistics* 10 (1977) 299–311. See also Stanley, 'Passive Motivation', *Foundations of Language* 13 (1975) 25–39.
15. John D. May, 'At Issue', *Columbia Journalism Review*, October 1978, *pp* 21–2.
16. Donald R. Smith, 'Experiencer Deletion', *Glossa* 9 (1975) 181–201.
17. Rolf Sandell, *Linguistic Style and Persuasion*. London, New York, and San Francisco: Academic Press, 1977, *p* 130. Similarly, 'Propositional sentences

are most compelling when their propositional status remains implicit.'
Charles E. Osgood, 'Conservative Words and Radical Sentences in the
Semantics of International Politics', in G. Abcarian and J. W. Soule (eds),
Social Psychology and Political Behavior, Columbus, Ohio: Merrill, 1971,
101–29, *p* 114.

Notes to Chapter 9

1. 'On Language, Race and the Black Writer', Los Angeles *Times*, 29 April
1979, Part V *p* 1.
2. See Susan Sontag, 'Illness as Metaphor', *New York Review of Books*, 26
January 1978, *pp* 10–16.
3. New York: Norton, 1964, *pp* 237–54.
4. Barrie Thorne and Nancy Henley (eds), *Language and Sex: Difference and
Dominance*. Rowley, Mass: Newbury House, 1975, *p* 67.
5. *Ibid*, *p* 61.
6. Julia P. Stanley, 'Paradigmatic Woman: The Prostitute', in David L.
Shores and Carole P. Hines (eds), *Papers on Language Variation*.
Birmingham, Alabama: University of Alabama Press, 1977, *pp* 303–21.
Muriel Schulz, 'The Semantic Derogation of Woman', in Thorne and
Henley, *op cit*, *pp* 64–75.
7. San Francisco radio KGO, 13 March 1978, 7.30 am.
8. From an elementary school textbook, cited by Professor Ann Holmquist in
an interview with Michael Fallon, Sacramento, California *Union*, 26 March
1978, *p* A4.
9. Cited by Julia P. Stanley, 'The Sexist Tradition: Words and Meaning', *Iowa
English Bulletin* 27 (1978) 2.5–10, *p* 9.
10. Alma Graham, 'The Making of a Nonsexist Dictionary', in Thorne and
Henley, *op cit*, 57–63, *p* 58.
11. C. E. Tittle, 'Women and Educational Testing', *Phi Delta Kappan* 55 (1973)
2.118–19.
12. Cited in *The Progressive*, January 1977, *p* 11.
13. Stanley, 'The Sexist Tradition' (note 9 above), *p* 6.
14. Hyatt Hotel advertisement, San Francisco radio KCBS, 22 April 1978,
7.08 am.
15. See Maija S. Blaubergs, 'On "The Nurse Was a Doctor"', in Reza
Ordoubadian and Walburga von Raffler-Engel (eds), *Views on Language*.
Murfreesboro, Tennessee: Inter-University Publishing, 1975, 87–95.
16. *The Future of the Women's Movement*. London: Bell, 1913, *p* vii.
    Sydney J. Harris, 'Labor Department's Unisex Dictionary', San
Francisco *Examiner and Chronicle*, 1 June 1975, *p* B3.
18. M. Stanley Whitley calls *themself* 'far more stigmatized'. See his 'Person
and Number in the Use of *We*, *You*, and *They*', *American Speech* 53 (1978)
18–39, *p* 35. Among his examples is one from the Boston, Massachusetts
chief of police: *And pretty soon, the law-abiding citizen, who won't own
handguns, won't be able to defend themself.* (*p* 30).
19. *Essentials of English Grammar*. London: Allen and Unwin, 1933, *p* 193.
20. *The American Language*. New York: Knopf, 1955, *p* 460.
21. Sacramento, California *Union*, 27 March 1978, *p* C10.
22. Los Angeles *Times*, 12 May 1978, *p* 7.

23. In Danny Steinberg and Leon A. Jakobovits, *Semantics*. London: Cambridge University Press, 1971, 308–28, *pp* 316–17.
24. Hilary Abramson, 'The Games Computers Play', Sacramento, California *Union*, 14 April 1978, *p* C2.
25. *The Progressive*, February 1978, *p* 36.
26. Fallon-Holmquist interview (note 8 above).
27. Palo Alto, California *Times*, 9 November 1977, *p* 12.
28. Otto Weininger, *Sex and Character*. New York: Putnam, 1906, *p* 189.
29. *Language*. New York: Norton, 1964, *p* 253.
30. *Male/Female Language*. Methuen, New Jersey: Scarecrow Press, 1975, *p* 15.
31. Donna S. Geffner and M. F. Dorman, 'Hemispheric Specialization for Speech Perception in Four-Year-Old Children from Low and Middle Socioeconomic Classes', Haskins Laboratories *Quarterly Report*, April–September 1975, *pp* 241–5.
32. Interview with William J. Cromie, Enterprise Science News, San Francisco *Chronicle*, 'This World' magazine section, 22 January 1978, *p* 47.
33. William Austin, quoted by Sally McConnell-Ginet, 'Intonation in a Man's World', *Signs: Journal of Women in Culture and Society* 3 (1978) 3.541–49, *p* 549.
34. Pitch is perceived in two ways, first through the fundamental or singing tone of the voice (the actual musical tune or intonation that is always present except in whisper), second through the overtones produced during articulate speech and which are the basis – among other things – for distinguishing one vowel from another. The vowel in *seat*, for example, has one very high-pitched and one very low-pitched cluster of overtones; the vowel in *boot* has two clusters at low pitch relatively close to each other. The range varies from one speaker to another, but the relative position tells the ear what vowel is being uttered. For vowel pitches in boys, see Jacqueline Sachs, 'Cues to the Identification of Sex in Children's Speech', in Thorne and Henley (note 4 above), *pp* 152–71, especially *p* 156.
35. Blaubergs, *op cit*, *p* 88.
36. Palo Alto, California *Times*, 12 January 1978, *p* 10.
37. Robin Lakoff, 'Language and Woman's Place', *Language in Society* 2 (1973) 45–80.
38. McConnell-Ginet, *op cit*, *p* 554.
39. Key, *op cit*, *p* 37.
40. Johanna S. DeStefano, 'Women's Language – By and About', in Ordoubadian and von Raffler-Engel (note 15 above), 66–76, *p* 70.
41. *Ibid*.
42. Blake Green, 'Teaching a Man to Sound Female', San Francisco *Chronicle*, 16 February 1978, *p* 34.
43. McConnell-Ginet, *op cit*, *p* 542.
44. Stanley, 'The Sexist Tradition' (note 9 above), *p* 8.
45. *Op cit*, *p* 15.
46. Cited in Fallon-Holmquist interview (note 8 above).
47. Blaubergs, *op cit*, *p* 90.
48. Fallon-Holmquist (note 8 above).
49. Cited by Julia Stanley, 'Prescribed Passivity, the Language of Sexism', in Ordoubadian and von Raffler-Engel (note 15 above), 96–108, *p* 99.
50. Fallon-Holmquist (note 8 above).

Notes to Chapter 10

1. Malcolm D. MacDougall, *We Almost Made It*. New York: Crown Publishers, 1977, *p* 11.
2. Niccolò Machiavelli, *The Prince*, translated by Luigi Ricci. New American Library (Mentor Classic), 1952, *p* 93.
3. *Reader's Digest*, April 1948, *p* 74.
4. AP dispatch, Palo Alto, California *Times*, 10 October 1978, *p* 16.
5. Philip Nobile, interview with Carl Bernstein, San Francisco *Chronicle*, 'Sunday Punch' Section, 23 October 1977, *p* 7.
6. Text kindly supplied by Mr Randy Riddle, San Francisco radio KCBS.
7. Advertisement for Ex-Lax, San Francisco Station KCBS, 25 April 1978, 10.03 pm.
8. Robert N. St Clair, 'The Politics of Language', *Word* 29 (1978) 44–62, *p* 56.
9. *Encyclopaedia Britannica*, 11th Ed, s.v. *oath*, *p* 942.
10. Wayne Sage, 'Sleuths of Sound', *The UCLA Monthly*, November–December 1977, *pp* 1–2.
11. Harry Hollien, 'Status Report of "Voiceprint" Identification in the United States', in *Proceedings of the 1977 International Conference on Crime Countermeasures, Science and Engineering*, July 25–9, 1977. Oxford, England.
12. Al Martínez, 'Debate Over Truth about Lies', Los Angeles *Times*, 24 April 1978, Part I *pp* 1, 26–8.
13. Harold Gilliam, 'A Machine that Winks when a Lie is Told', San Francisco *Chronicle*, 29 March 1978, *p* 6.
14. Information kindly supplied by Dr Jacobs.
15. 'Symbols, Song, Dance and Features of Articulation: Is Religion an Extreme Form of Traditional Authority?' *Archives Européennes de Sociologie* 15 (1974) 55–81.
16. D. G. Kehl, 'Religious Doublespeak and the Idols of the Marketplace', *Public Doublespeak Newsletter* 3 (1977) 4.1–2, *p* 2.
17. Vance Packard, *The People Shapers*. Boston: Little, Brown, 1977, *p* 149.
18. John Cunningham, 'Words which Flatter to Deceive', *The Guardian*, 12 October 1977, quoting Kenneth Hudson, *A Dictionary of Diseased English*. London: Macmillan, 1977.
19. *More* and *all* appeared among the top ten but are omitted here because they are not DESCRIPTIVE adjectives.
20. Thomas C. Agoston and Walburga von Raffler-Engel, 'A Linguistic Analysis of Some Commercial Television Advertisements'. In Robert St Clair (ed), *Perspectives on Applied Sociolinguistics*. Lawrence, Kansas: Coronado Press, *p* 9 of MS.
21. Geoffrey N. Leech, *English in Advertising*. London: Longman, 1966, *p* 152.
22. By Marghanita Laski, *Atlantic Monthly*, July 1949, *pp* 92–3.
23. 'Sell Words Food Makers Use', San Francisco *Chronicle*, 15 May 1978, *p* 4. Reprinted from the Washington *Post*.
24. Agoston and von Raffler-Engel, *op cit*, *p* 11 of MS.
25. Jeffrey Schrank, *Deception Detection*. Boston: Beacon Press, 1975, *p* 4.
26. Packard, *op cit*, *p* 81.
27. San Francisco *Sunday Examiner and Chronicle*, 12 March 1978, *p* A6.
28. MacDougall, *op cit*, *p* 31.
29. *Ibid*, *p* 118.

30. 'Table of the Springs of Action', in Paul McReynolds (ed), *Four Early Works on Motivation*. Gainesville, Florida: Scholars' Facsimiles and Reprints, 1969, 481–512, *pp* 489–90.
31. St Clair, *op cit*, *p* 53.
32. San Francisco *Chronicle*, 'Sunday Punch' section, 4 June 1978, *p* 1.
33. 'How Federal Consumer Protection Died', *Co-Op News*, Palo Alto, California, 17 April 1978, *p* 3.
34. David Ignatius in *Columbia Journalism Review*, May-June 1977, *p* 26.
35. Palo Alto, California *Times*, 1 February 1978, *p* 3.
36. The Miami *Herald*, 'Tropic Magazine', 2 May 1971, *p* 42.
37. Elizabeth F. Loftus and John C. Palmer, 'Reconstruction of Automobile Destruction: An Example of the Interaction between Language and Memory', *Journal of Verbal Learning and Verbal Behaviour* 13 (1974) 585–9.
38. Leech, *op cit*, *p* 82.
39. San Francisco *Sunday Examiner and Chronicle*, 11 June 1978, *p* A18.
40. Schrank, *op cit*, *p* 6. Leech, *op cit*, *pp* 160–1 has further examples.
41. Agoston and von Raffler-Engel, *op cit*, *p* 14 of MS.
42. *Ibid*, *p* 15 of MS.
43. Leech, *op cit*, *p* 129.
44. *Ibid*, *p* 141.
45. *Ibid*, *pp* 144–5.
46. *Ibid*, *p* 150.
47. *Ibid*, *p* 154.
48. Schrank, *op cit*, *p* 16.

Notes to Chapter 11

1. *Public Doublespeak Newsletter* 3 (1977) 3.5.
2. Geoffrey Nunberg, 'Slang, Usage-conditions, and l'Arbitraire du Signe', in Donka Farkas, Wesley M. Jacobson, and Karol W. Todrys (eds), *Parasession on the Lexicon*. Chicago: Chicago Linguistic Society, 1978, 301–11, *p* 305.
3. California Spinach Talk', San Francisco, California *Chronicle*, 'Sunday Punch' section, 4 December 1977, *p* 2.
4. Cited by Mary Ann Seawell, 'Satirist Skewers " Self-indulgent" Marin Lifestyle', Palo Alto, California *Times*, 10 October 1977, *p* 13.
5. San Francisco radio KCBS, 2 July 1978, 7.25 am.
6. Kindly supplied by Geoffrey Leech.
7. D. G. Kehl, 'Religious Doublespeak and the Idols of the Marketplace', *Public Doublespeak Newsletter* 3 (1977) 4.1–2.
8. Alan Simpson, 'Liberal Education in a University', *Washington University Magazine*, February 1961, 14–18, *p* 17.
9. From a paper by Charles Goodwin titled 'The Interactive Construction of the Sentence Within the Turn at Talk in Natural Conversation', at the annual meeting of the American Anthropological Association, 1975, MS *p* 33.

10. San Francisco *Examiner and Chronicle*, 25 January 1976, *p* A12.
11. San Francisco radio KGO, 21 July 1974.
12. Cited by David C. Ferris, 'Scoring Jargon', *Verbatim* 4 (1977) 2.3–4.
13. *Reader's Digest*, September 1977, *p* 95.
14. Ferris, *op cit*.
15. Donald Zochert, 'Don't Freak Out – *Some* Slang is Here to Stay', Chicago *Daily News*, 17 September 1977, *p* 1.
16. John Dean, *Blind Ambition*. New York: Simon and Schuster, 1976, *p* 81.
17. San Francisco radio KGO, 13 June 1976, 7.40 am.
18. San Francisco radio KCBS, 27 June 1978, for *Better Homes and Gardens*.
19. *Newsweek*, 15 April 1974, *p* 7.
20. Henry Steele Commager, 'The Defeat of America', *New York Review of Books*, 5 October 1972, *p* 10.
21. Example from D. R. Ladd, private communication.
22. San Francisco radio KCBS, 6 September 1978, 10.04 pm.
23. Radio report, 27 June 1978.
24. Palo Alto, California *Times*, 27 September 1978, *p* 1.
25. Israel Shenker, 'Zieglerrata', *The New Republic*, 12 April 1974, *pp* 21–3, cited *Public Doublespeak Newsletter* 1 (1974) 3.7–8.
26. Cited *ibid p* 7.
27. Cited by Robert Kirk Mueller, *Buzzwords: A Guide to the Language of Leadership*. New York etc: Van Nostrand Reinhold Co, 1974, *p* 21.
28. Example from D. R. Ladd, private communication.
29. Cited by Ernest Gowers, *Plain Words: Their ABC*. New York: Knopf, 1962, *pp* 46–7.
30. Morrie Landsberg, 'Speak Not in Doublespeak', Sacramento, California *Bee*, 30 October 1975, *p* B4.
31. Robert Reinhold, 'A Federal Crackdown: Gobbledegook Has to Go!', San Francisco *Examiner and Chronicle*, 'This World' section, 1 January 1978, *p* 26.
32. Carrie Peyton, 'Man Changes Gobbledegook into English', Palo Alto, California *Times*, 25 November 1977, *p* 7.
33. AP dispatch, Palo Alto, California *Times*, 18 April 1978, *p* 33.
34. *Op cit, p* 4.
35. 'Plastic English', *Atlantic Monthly*, October 1972, *p* 32.
36. 'Graffiti vs Doublespeak: The Anti-Establishment Strikes Back', *English Journal*, February 1978, *pp* 20–5.
37. *A Civil Tongue*. Indianapolis and New York: Bobbs-Merrill, 1976, *p* 146.
38. *National Enquirer*, 11 July 1978, *p* 18.

Notes to Chapter 12

1. Brenda Danet, '"Baby" or "Fetus"? Language and the Construction of Reality in a Manslaughter Trial'. *Semiotica*, in press.
2. Palo Alto, California *Times*, 17 November 1978, *pp* 12–13. Permission to quote kindly granted by the author, Sydney J. Riser.
3. Peter H. Salus, 'Opposites and Polarities.' Paper at Association Internationale de Linguistique Appliquée (AILA V), Montreal, August 1978.
4. 'Universals, Relativity, and Language Processing', in Joseph H. Greenberg (ed), *Universals of Human Language, Vol 1: Method and Theory*. Stanford,

California: Stanford University Press, 1978, *pp* 225–77.
5. *Philosophy of Literary Form*. Baton Rouge, Louisiana: Louisiana State University Press, 1941, *p* 152. Cited in Harry Hoijer (ed), *Language in Culture*. Chicago: University of Chicago Press, 1954, *p* 71.
6. Robert R. Verbrugge and Nancy S. McCarrell,'Metaphoric Comprehension: Studies in Reminding and Resembling', Haskins Laboratories *Status Report on Speech Research*, SR-53, January–March 1978, Vol 1, 87–125, *p* 121.
7. See Elizabeth Closs Traugott, 'On the Expression of Spatio-Temporal Relations in Language', in Greenberg, *ibid*, *pp* 368–400.
8. British Airways Flight 8188, 5 July 1978.
9. 'The Life and Times of Judge Roy Bean.'
10. *American Scholar* 32 (1963) 532.
11. 'The Old Man and the C', *New West* 24 (April 1978) 21–5, *p* 21.
12. San Francisco radio KGO, 5 January 1978, 10.17 pm.
13. *The Dumb Waiter*, in Tom Mascher (ed), *New English Dramatists, Vol 3*. Harmondsworth, Middlesex: Penguin, 1961, 185–215, *p* 197. Reference thanks to Eugene Bell.
14. *Figure of speech* because technically this is not an instance of metaphor but of metonymy. Psychologically there is little if any difference, which justifies taking METAPHOR loosely as has been done in this chapter. Metaphor, metonymy, and synecdoche have in common the requirement that B stand for A, with which it can be connected through resemblance or some other association of the respective referents: *John is an ogre*, for a resemblance between a trait of John and a defining trait of ogres; *John is a brain* for the part-whole relationship between him and his brain and the association between the brain and thinking, and between thinking and intelligence. As in the last example, one often finds mixed figures: it would be difficult to separate metaphor from synecdoche in the sentence from a popular movie, *He's a pistol*, referring to his sexual prowess. See Linda Waugh, 'Marked and Unmarked – a Choice Between Unequals in Semiotic Structure', *Semiotica*, to appear, for metaphor as the unmarked or inclusive term.
15. Murray Edelman, 'Language, Myths and Rhetoric', *Society* 12 (1975) 5.14–21, *p* 21.
16. Charles E. Osgood, 'Conservative Words and Radical Sentences in the Semantics of International Politics', *Studies in the Linguistic Sciences* (Department of Linguistics, University of Illinois) 8 (1979).
17. Edelman, *op cit, p* 21.
18. Michael Osborn, 'The Hidden Traps of Language'. Preprint, 1978.
19. *Ibid.*
20. Margot Hornblower, San Francisco *Chronicle*, 'Sunday Punch' section, 11 September 1977, *p* 2. Reprinted from the Washington *Post*.
21. Malcolm D. MacDougall, *We Almost Made It*. New York: Crown Publishers, 1977, *p* 114.
22. Niccolò Machiavelli, *The Prince*, translated by Luigi Ricci. New American Library (Mentor Classic), 1952, Chapter 18.
23. *Publications of the Modern Language Association* 93 (1978) 361–7, *p* 362.
24. William Steif, 'A Drug Prices Guide', Palo Alto, California *Times*, 30 September 1978, *p* 8.
25. Britannica *Book of the Year*, 1963, *p* 638.
26. Jeffrey Schrank, *Deception Detection*. Boston: Beacon Press, 1975, *p* 13.

Notes to Chapter 13

1. Cited in *London Daily News*, 8 July 1869, *p* 5.
2. The physician in question, Dr Jonathan Rhoads, made the statement in 1975, and repudiated it in 1977 (as far as diseases other than lung cancer were concerned) – in a publication circulated AMONG ADVERTISERS; but the advertising agency conducting the campaign ignored the disavowal and published the statement without qualification – a prime example of literalism.
3. UPI dispatch, Palo Alto, California *Times*, 11 January 1979, *p* 4.
4. First citation under *cigarette* in the *Oxford English Dictionary*.
5. The British wording is *Cigarettes can seriously damage your health* – a less tempting metaphor, but no more threatening, since it is hedged with *can*.
6. Maurine Neuberger, *Smoke Screen: Tobacco and the Public Welfare*. Englewood Cliffs, New Jersey: Prentice-Hall, 1963, *p* 37.
7. Ron Javers, 'Now the Anti-Smokers Are On the Attack', San Francisco *Chronicle*, 19 September 1978, *p* 15.
8. R. C. Smith, 'The Magazines' Smoking Habit', *Columbia Journalism Review*, January-February 1978, *pp* 29–31.

Notes to Chapter 14

1. The Dick Cavett Show, 11–2 January 1978. A later airing that same year covered five days and included several linguists on the panel, but the liveliest part of the discussion was still on the puristic question of the speaker's 'right to his own language' (should Black English be condoned or stamped out?), and the session dedicated to political language had little about the ethics of jargon and much about the popularity of political clichés.
2. *Esquire*, April 1978, *p* 35.
3. New York: Harper and Row, 1975.
4. *Ibid*, *pp* 155–7.
5. *Ibid*, *p* 33.
6. *Ibid*, *p* 40.
7. *Ibid*, *p* 101.
8. *Ibid*, *p* 77.
9. Barzun limits his rule to 'proper names', but does not explain why. The apostrophe-*s* applies equally to common nouns.
10. *Op cit*, *p* 123.
11. *Ibid*, *p* 67.
12. *Ibid*, *p* 68.
13. See Dwight Bolinger, *That's That*. The Hague: Mouton, 1972.
14. *Op cit*, *p* 120.
15. *Ibid*, *p* 197.
16. Here are two examples that illustrate the extension of this pattern among nouns of place:

    The city that they happen to live . . . . (Ron Owens, talkmaster on San Francisco radio KGO, 10.12 pm, 31 March 1978. Owens said this twice.)
    No matter what part of the Bay Area you live . . . . (San Francisco radio

KCBS, 7.13 am, 10 August 1978.)

17. Barzun, *op cit*, *p* 49.
18. *The American Sociologist* 13 (1978) 89.
19. 14 April 1977, 10.32 am EST.
20. San Francisco radio KCBS, November 1978, 6.57 am.
21. *Reader's Digest*, January 1962, *p* 72.
22. See Dwight Bolinger, *Forms of English*. Cambridge, Mass: Harvard University Press, 1965, *pp* 309–15.

Notes to Chapter 15

1. *Britannica Book of the Year*, 1977, *p* 422.
2. T. A. Vonder Haar, 'Cures that can Kill', *The Progressive*, April 1977, 40–3, *p* 43.
3. L. L. L. Golden, *Only by Public Consent*. New York: Hawthorn Books, 1968, *p* 366.
4. Palo Alto, California *Times*, 4 November 1978, *p* 8.
5. Jeff Greenfield, 'TV Is Not the World', *Columbia Journalism Review*, May–June 1978, 29–34, *p* 32.
6. *Ibid*, *p* 34.
7. Amnesty International circular letter (nd), 1978.
8. AP dispatch, Palo Alto, California *Times*, 8 November 1978, *p* 1.
9. Golden, *op cit*, p 15.
10. *Britannica Book of the Year*, 1974, *p* 53.
11. Golden, *op cit*, p 33.
12. Samm S. Baker, *The Permissible Lie*. Cleveland and New York: World, 1968, *pp* 145–54. Comparing the figure of 17 billion with that of 37 mentioned above, we see that advertising expenditures have doubled in a decade.
13. Geoffrey N. Leech, *English in Advertising*. London: Longman, 1966, *pp* 120–1, 140, 156–7.
14. *ASH* (Action on Smoking and Health) *Newsletter*, July–August 1978, *p* 1.
15. Leech *op cit*, *p* 153.
16. Jock Brown, 'Distributive Justice', *Church at Work* (Northern California Ecumenical Council), August 1978, *p* 3.
17. 'Stumping the Boondocks for Idioms', Chicago *Tribune*, 'Book World' section (section 7), 27 August 1978, *p* 2. Reference thanks to Dr Diana Van Lancker.

Further reading

In a field as broad as linguistics – with the appended fields that are affected by language – any list of readings can only be a rather trivial sample. The titles that follow should be regarded as introductory. Most of them, with their references and bibliographies, will lead the reader in almost any direction where interest beckons.

Articles

DUNN, JUDY. 'Playing in Speech'. In Leonard Michaels and Christopher Ricks (eds), *The State of the Language*. Berkeley, Los Angeles, London: University of California Press, 1980, *pp* 202–12. Creativity in children's wordplay.

GRIMSHAW, ALLEN D. 'Mishearings, Misunderstandings and Other Nonsuccesses in Talk: A Plea for Redress of Speaker-oriented Bias', *Sociological Inquiry* (to appear, 1980). How messages and their meanings are negotiated between speakers and hearers.

LANDAU, SIDNEY T. 'The Egalitarian Spirit and Attitudes Toward Usage', *American Speech* 54 (1979) 3–11. Purism, especially in its current forms.

'Language Engineering Molds Indonesian Language', *The Linguistic Reporter*, June 1961, *pp* 1 *ff*. The guided development of an adopted national language.

LODGE, DAVID. 'Where It's At: California Language'. In Michaels and Ricks (above), *pp* 503–13. Psychobabble in social interaction.

MCCONNELL-GINET, SALLY. 'Prototypes, Pronouns, and Persons'. In M. Mathiot (ed), *Ethnolinguistics: Boas, Sapir, and Whorf Revisited*. The Hague: Mouton, 1979, *pp* 63–83.

PRICE, BRUCE D. 'Noun Overuse Phenomenon Article'. *Verbatim* 2 (1976) 4.1–3. For 'nounspeak', the overuse of nouns.

REID, DAVID. 'At Home in the Abyss: Jonestown and the Language of Enormity'. In Michaels and Ricks (above), *pp* 277–88. Psychobabble as an escape from moral reality and responsibility.

VAIZEY, MARINA. 'Art Language'. In Michaels and Ricks (above), *pp* 331–42. 'Images searching forlornly for the words that will give them their support system.' On the importance of naming in art.

Books

ALATIS, JAMES E.; and G. RICHARD TUCKER (eds). *Language in Public Life.* (Georgetown University Round Table on Languages and Linguistics 1979.) Washington, D.C.: Georgetown University Press, 1979. Language in advertising, medicine, law, etc.

BLACK, MAX (ed). *The Importance of Language.* Englewood Cliffs, New Jersey: Prentice-Hall (Spectrum Books), 1962. Essays by Aldous Huxley, C. S. Lewis, and others.

BOLINGER, DWIGHT. *Aspects of Language,* 2nd Edn. New York: Harcourt Brace Jovanovich, 1975. An introductory text.

GIVÓN, TALMY. *On Understanding Grammar.* New York: Academic Press, 1979. For the serious student of language.

HERZOG, ARTHUR. *The B. S. Factor: The Theory and Technique of Faking It in America.* New York: Simon and Schuster, 1973. Incisive account of obfuscation.

KEY, MARY. *Paralanguage and Kinesics.* Metuchen, New Jersey: Scarecrow Press, 1975. For non-verbal communication.

LAKOFF, ROBIN. *Language and Woman's Place.* New York: Harper and Row (Colophon Books), 1975. Sexism in language.

MILLER, CASEY; and KATE SWIFT. *Words and Women.* Garden City, New York: Anchor Press, 1976. Likewise on sexism.

O'BARR, WILLIAM M. and JEAN F. (eds). *Language and Politics.* The Hague: Mouton, 1976. Essays on social, legal, and political implications of language in several areas of the world.

PEDERSEN, HOLGER. *The Discovery of Language: Linguistic Science in the Nineteenth Century.* Translated by John Webster Spargo. Bloomington, Indiana: Indiana University Press (Midland Books), 1962. A classic text on the rise of linguistics as a science.

QUIRK, RANDOLPH. *The Use of English,* 2nd Edn. London: Longman, 1968. A discussion of English from all sides: speakers, structure, correctness, etc.

RANK, HUGH (ed). *Language and Public Policy.* Urbana, Illinois: National Council of Teachers of English, 1974. On social abuses of language.

ROSEN, R. D. *Psychobabble: Fast Talk and Quick Cure in the Era of Feeling.* New York: Atheneum, 1978. The counterfeit of self-revelation.

SAPIR, EDWARD. *Language.* New York: Harcourt Brace Jovanovich (Harvest Books), 1949. A classic introduction to linguistics.

SHOPEN, TIMOTHY (ed). *Languages and Their Speakers.* Cambridge, Mass: Winthrop, 1979. Insights into a variety of cultures and languages.

—*Languages and Their Status.* Cambridge, Mass: Winthrop, 1979. A companion volume to the preceding. Essays in both volumes are by scholars in each field. One can learn, for example, how Russian or Swahili 'looks'.

TRAUGOTT, ELIZABETH. *Linguistics for Students of Literature.* New York: Harcourt Brace Jovanovich, 1980. A textbook that bridges a long-standing gap between fields.

Periodicals

American Speech. University of Alabama Press, University, Alabama 35486. A quarterly about the languages of America, but mostly English. Scholarly yet readable.

The Linguistic Reporter: A Newsletter in Applied Linguistics. Center for Applied Linguistics, 1611 North Kent Street, Arlington, Virginia 22209. For references to current publications and events.

Public Doublespeak Newsletter. Committee on Public Doublespeak, National Council of Teachers of English, 1111 Kenyon Road, Urbana, Illinois 61801. Matters of jargon.

Verbatim. Essex, Connecticut 06426. A quarterly on English usage. Written in a light vein but with a fair amount of linguistic sophistication.

Among the technical journals available at better libraries are *Language, Language in Society, Lingua, Linguistic Inquiry, Journal of English Linguistics, Word, Linguistics, Language Problems and Language Planning.* The journals of anthropology (for example, *The American Anthropologist*) frequently contain articles on linguistics, as do those of psychology.

Index